Sāṁkhya-Yoga Epistemology

Contemporary Researches in Hindu Philosophy & Religion

(ISSN 0971-9628)

1. Idealistic Thought in Indian Philosophy; by Shuchita C. Divatia (ISBN 978-81-246-0021-4)
2. Karma and Reincarnation: The Vedāntic Perspective; by Muni Narayana Prasad (ISBN 978-81-246-0022-1)
3. Stonemill and Bhakti: From the Devotion of Peasant Women to the Philosophy of Swamies; by Guy Poitevin and Hema Rairkar (ISBN 978-81-246-0059-7)
4. Śaivism: Some Glimpses; by G.V. Tagare (ISBN 978-81-246-0076-4)
5. Advaita: A Conceptual Analysis; by A. Ramamurty (ISBN 978-81-246-0067-2)
6. Mind-Body Dualism: A Philosophic Investigation; by Alpana Chakraborty (ISBN 978-81-246-0071-9)
7. Hinduism and Scientific Quest; by T.R.R. Iyengar (ISBN 978-81-246-0077-1)
8. Indra and Other Vedic Deities — A Euhemeristic Study; by Uma Chakravarty (ISBN 978-81-246-0080-1)
9. Brahma-Vāda: Doctrine of Śrī Vallabhācārya; by G.V. Tagare (ISBN 978-81-246-0112-9)
10. The Science of Enlightenment: Enlightenment, Liberation and God — A Scientific Explanation; by Nitin Trasi (ISBN 978-81-246-0130-3)
11. Retrieving Sāṁkhya History: An Ascent from Dawn to Meridian; by Lallanji Gopal (ISBN 978-81-246-0143-3)
12. The Philosophical Foundations of Hinduism; by A. Ramamurty (ISBN 978-81-246-0163-1)
13. The Eternal Hinduism; by Baidyanath Saraswati (ISBN 978-81-246-0249-2)
14. Vedānta and its Philosophical Development; by A. Ramamurty (ISBN 978-81-246-0347-5)
16. A Sourcebook of Classical Hindu Thought; by Arvind Sharma (ISBN 978-81-246-0643-8)
17. A Treatise on Advaita Vedānta; by S. Bhuvaneshwari (ISBN 13: 978-81-246-0707-7)
18. Advaita Metaphysics: A Contemporary Perspective; by Tapti Maitra (ISBN: 978-81-246-0747-3)
19. The Journey of Advaita; by Priti Sinha (ISBN 978-81-246-0934-7)

Contemporary Researches in Hindu Philosophy & Religion, no. 15

Sāṁkhya-Yoga Epistemology

Mukta Biswas

DK PRINTWORLD
Publishers of Indian Traditions

Cataloging in Publication Data [DK
[Courtesy: D.K. Agencies (P) Ltd. <docinfo@dkagencies.com>]

Biswas, Mukta, 1956- author.
Sāṁkhya-yoga epistemology / by Mukta Biswas.
pages cm. — (Contemporary researches in Hindu philosophy & religion ; no. 15)
Reprint. Originally published: 2007.
Originally presented as the author's thesis (Ph. D.) — Gauhati University.
Includes bibliographical references and index.

1. Sankhya. 2. Yoga. 3. Knowledge, Theory of — India. I. Title. II. Series: Contemporary researches in Hindu philosophy & religion ; no. 15.

LCC B132.S3B57 2018 | DDC 181.41 23

ISBN 978-81-246-0371-0
First published in India in 2007
Second impression in 2018

Printed and published by:
D.K. Printworld (P) Ltd.
Regd. office : *Vedaśrī*, F-395, Sudarshan Park
(Metro Station: ESI Hospital) New Delhi - 110 015
Phones : (011) 2545 3975, 2546 6019
e-mail : indology@dkprintworld.com
Web : www.dkprintworld.com

Dedicated

to the memory of my parents

late Rabindra Kumar Bhattacharjee

and

late Asha Bhattacharjee

Preface

IN the present work I have made an endeavour to give a comprehensive and critical ideal of the Sāṁkhya-Yoga epistemology. Epistemology of the Sāṁkhya-Yoga school is a wide subject. However, a systematic approach on the subject has remained so far elusive. Though early works explicitly declare that knowledge of the objects depends upon the proper understanding of the means of knowledge, perusal of extant texts of Sāṁkhya-Yoga leaves behind an impression that this aspect has not been dealt with extensively and such an observation prompts us to take a view that the philosophers of both the schools were interested in metaphysical doctrines rather than being involved in the logical explanation of epistemology. It therefore becomes imperative to study the status of epistemology in Sāṁkhya-Yoga philosophy. Thus the present work encompasses the studies of epistemology as evidenced in the works like *Sāṁkhyakārikā* of Īśvarakṛṣṇa, *Yogasūtra* of Patañjali, *Yuktidīpikā*, *Māṭharavṛtti*, and other schools of Indian philosophy. Efforts have been made to include the various judgements of the critics of Sāṁkhya-Yoga system in order to bring out a critical analysis of the subject. However, I am aware of the possibility that the entire existing relevant documents on the subject might not have been incorporated in the present discussion despite best attempt. I am hopeful that this book will be of immense help for students and researchers to comprehend the idea of epistemology of Sāṁkhya-Yoga thought in the proper perspective.

I have no words to express my deep sense of gratitude to my teacher, Professor Dr. Rajendra Nath Sarma, M.A., Ph.D., D.Lit, Mimamsa-Vyakaraṇa Sastri, formerly Head of the deptt. of Sanskrit, Gauhati University for his ungrudging guidance and untiring help offered to me during the preparation of the work. Without his help, advice and supervision the work would have never come to completion.

My acknowledgement would remain incomplete if I do not express my deep sense of indebtedness to my husband Dr. Ranjan Kumar Biswas who has been instrumental and chief inspirator in my taking up this course of study and has made possible to see it the light of the day.

I am greatly thankful to Mr. Susheel K. Mittal of D.K. Printworld for kindly accepting the work for publication and evincing keen interest towards the completion of the work.

July 11, 2006 **Mukta Biswas**
Gauhati University

Contents

Key to Transliteration

VOWELS

अ *a*	आ *ā*	इ *i*	ई *ī*	उ *u*	ऊ *ū*
(b<u>u</u>t)	(p<u>a</u>lm)	(<u>i</u>t)	(b<u>ee</u>t)	(p<u>u</u>t)	(p<u>oo</u>l)
ऋ *ṛ*	ए *e*	ऐ *ai*	ओ *o*	औ *au*	
(<u>rhy</u>thm)	(pla<u>y</u>)	(<u>ai</u>r)	(t<u>oe</u>)	(l<u>ou</u>d)	

CONSONANTS

Guttural	क *ka*	ख* *kha*	ग *ga*	घ *gha*	ङ *ṅa*
	(s<u>k</u>ate)	(bloc<u>kh</u>ead)	(<u>g</u>ate)	(<u>gh</u>ost)	(si<u>n</u>g)
Palatal	च *ca*	छ* *cha*	ज *ja*	झ *jha*	ञ *ña*
	(<u>ch</u>unk)	(cat<u>ch h</u>im)	(<u>j</u>ohn)	(hedg<u>eh</u>og)	(bu<u>n</u>ch)
Cerebral	ट *ṭa*	ठ* *ṭha*	ड *ḍa*	ढ* *ḍha*	ण* *ṇa*
	(s<u>t</u>art)	(an<u>th</u>ill)	(<u>d</u>art)	(go<u>dh</u>ead)	(u<u>n</u>der)
Dental	त *ta*	थ *tha*	द *da*	ध* *dha*	न *na*
	(pa<u>th</u>)	(<u>th</u>under)	(<u>th</u>at)	(brea<u>the</u>)	(<u>n</u>umb)
Labial	प *pa*	फ* *pha*	ब *ba*	भ *bha*	म *ma*
	(s<u>p</u>in)	(<u>ph</u>ilosop<u>hy</u>)	(<u>b</u>in)	(a<u>bh</u>or)	(<u>m</u>uch)
Semi-vowel	य *ya*	र *ra*	ल *la*	व *va*	
	(<u>y</u>oung)	(d<u>r</u>ama)	(<u>l</u>uck)	(<u>v</u>ile)	
Sibilants	श *śa*	ष *ṣa*	स *sa*	ह *ha*	
	(<u>sh</u>ove)	(bu<u>sh</u>el)	(<u>s</u>o)	(<u>h</u>um)	
Others	क्ष *kṣa*	त्र *tra*	ज्ञ *jña*	ळ* *ḷ*	ॠ* *ṝ*
	(*<u>kṣa</u>triya*)	(*<u>tr</u>iśūla*)	(*<u>jñā</u>nī*)	(*p<u>la</u>y*)	

अं (ं) *ṁ anusvāra* (nasalisation of preceding vowel) like *sa<u>ṁ</u>skṛti*

अः *visarga* = *ḥ* (aspiration of preceding vowel) like (*prāta<u>ḥ</u>*)

ऽ *Avagraha* consonant #'consonant (like: *ime 'vasthitā*)

Anusvāra at the end of a line is presented by *m* (म्) and not *ṁ*

*No exact English equivalents for these letters.

Abbreviations

AK	:	*Amarakoṣa*
AS	:	*Aṣṭasāhasari*
ASa	:	*Arthaśāstra*
BC	:	*Buddhacarita*
BHC	:	*Bhāttacintāmoni*
BP	:	*Bhāsāpariccheda*
BPu	:	*Bhāgavata Purāṇa*
BS	:	*Brahmasūtra*
Cit	:	*Citsukhi's Tattvapradīpikā*
COS	:	*Critique on Śabda*
CU	:	*Chāndogya Upaniṣad*
DV	:	*Devībhāgavata*
GB	:	*Gauḍapadabhāṣya*
GG	:	*Gītagovindam*
HIE	:	*History of Indian Epistemology*
HIP	:	*History of Indian Philosophy*
IP	:	Indian Philosophy
IPh	:	*Indian Philosophy — A modern approach*
IPS	:	*Indian Philosophical Studies*
ITE	:	Indian Theories of Error
ITK	:	*Indian Theory of Knowledge*

JM	:	Jayamaṅgalā
JOR	:	*Journal of Oriental Research*
JTP	:	*Jaina Theory of Perception*
K	:	Kārikā
Ka	:	*Kārikāvalī*
Kir	:	*Kiraṇa on Yogasūtra*
KS	:	*Kumārasambhava*
KU	:	*Kaṭha Upaniṣad*
KV	:	*Kiraṇāvali*
MB	:	*Mahābhāṣya*
Mb	:	*Mīmāṁsābhāṣya*
MBh	:	*Mahābhārata*
MD	:	*Mīmāṁsādarśana*
Manu	:	*Manusmṛti*
MM	:	*Mānameyodaya*
MP	:	*Matsya Purāṇa*
MS	:	*Mīmāṁsāsūtra*
MU	:	*Maitrāyaṇī Upaniṣad*
MV	:	*Māṭharavṛtti*
NB	:	*Nyāyabindu*
NBh	:	*Nyāyabhāṣya*
NBT	:	*Nyāyabinduṭīkā*
NC	:	*Naiṣadhacaritam*
ND	:	*Nyāyadarśana*
NK	:	*Nyāyakandalī*
NKC	:	*Nyāyakumudacandra*
NKM	:	*Nyāyakusumāñjali*

NL	:	*Nyāyalīlāvatī*
NM	:	*Nyāyamañjarī*
NMV	:	*Nyāyamuktāvalī*
NP	:	*Nyāyapariśuddhi*
NR	:	*Nyāyaratnākara*
NRM	:	*Nyāyaratnamālā*
NS	:	*Nyāyasūtra*
NSV	:	*Nyāyasūtravṛtti*
NTK	:	*Nyāya Theory of Knowledge*
NV	:	*Nyāyavārttika*
NVTT	:	*Nyāyavārttikatātparyaṭīkā*
NVV	:	*Nyāyavārttikavṛtti*
ODSST	:	*Origin and Development of Sāṁkhya System of Thought*
ONP	:	Order of naming Pramāṇas
PB	:	*Praśastapādabhāṣya*
PDS	:	*Padārthadharma Saṁgraha*
PKM	:	*Prameyakamalamārttaṇda*
PLM	:	*Paramalaghumañjuṣā*
PNT	:	*Pramāṇanyāyatattvāloka*
PP	:	*Prakaraṇa Pañcikā*
Pra.P.	:	*Pramāṇa Prakaraṇa*
PR	:	*Pramāṇa Ratna*
PS	:	*Pravacanasāra*
PaSū	:	*Pāṇinī Sūtra*
PSa	:	*Pramāṇasamuccaya*
PU	:	*Praśna Upaniṣad*
PV	:	*Pramāṇavārttika*

PVT	:	*Pramāṇavārttikaṭīkā*
Ṛg Bhā	:	*Ṛgveda Bhāṣya*
ŚB	:	*Śābarabhāṣya*
SāB	:	*Śāṅkarabhāṣya*
SBG	:	*Śrīmadbhagavad-Gītā*
SC	:	*Sāṁkhyacandrikā*
SD	:	*Śāstradīpikā*
SDS	:	*Sarvadarśana Saṁgraha*
SIK	:	*Siddhāntakaumudī*
SK	:	*Sāṁkhyakārikā*
SKD	:	*Śabdakalpadruma*
SKV	:	*Śrutyāntakalpavallī*
SM	:	*Siddhāntamuktāvalī*
SP	:	*Saptapadārthī*
SPb	:	*Sāṁkhya Pravacanabhāṣya*
SPR	:	*Studies in the Pramāṇa Ratna*
SS	:	*Sāṁkhya-Sūtra*
SSM	:	*Ṣaḍdarśanasamuccaya*
SSV	:	*Sāṁkhyasūtravṛtti*
ST	:	*Sārobodhiniṭīkā*
STK	:	*Sāṁkhyatattvakaumudī*
SU	:	*Śvetāśvatara Upaniṣad*
SV	:	*Ślokavārttika*
SVM	:	*Syādvādamañjarī*
SVR	:	*Syādvādaratnākara*
SYDP	:	*Sāṁkhya Yoga definition of Pramāṇa*
TAS	:	*Tattvārthādhigama-Sūtra*

TB	:	*Tarkabhāṣā*
TCM	:	*Tattvacintāmaṇi*
TK	:	*Tarkakaumudī*
TKD	:	*Tattvakaumudī*
TM	:	*Tarkāmṛta*
TP	:	*Tarkapāda*
TPJ	:	*The Philosophy of Jainism*
TPSED	:	*The Practical Sanskrit-English Dictionary*
TR	:	*Tārkikarakṣā*
TS	:	*Tarkasaṁgraha*
Ts	:	Traditional statement
TSa	:	*Tattvasaṁgraha*
Tsp	:	*Tattvasaṁgrahapañcikā*
TV	:	*Tattvavaiśāradī*
TVa	:	*Tantravārttika*
UIP	:	*Upamāna in Indian Philosophy*
V	:	Verse
VB	:	*Vaiśeṣika Bhāṣya*
VaB	:	*Vātsyāyana Bhāṣya*
VP	:	*Vedānta Paribhāṣā*
VS	:	*Vaiśeṣika-Sūtra*
YB	:	*Yogabhāṣya*
YD	:	*Yuktidīpikā*
YMD	:	*Yatindramatadīpikā*
YP	:	Yoga Philosophy
YS	:	*Yogasūtra*
YV	:	*Yogavārttika*

1

Introduction

The Nature of Philosophy

Philosophy literally means "love of wisdom," "philos" means "love" and sophia means "wisdom." It enquires into the nature of the universe in which we live, the nature of the human soul and its destiny, and the nature of God or the absolute, and their relation to one another. It enquires into the nature of matter, time, space, causality, evolution, life and mind and their relation to one another. It is the art of thinking of all things logically, systematically and persistently. Philosophy has three parts: (i) Epistemology, (ii) Ontology, and (iii) Axiology. Epistemology is the theory of knowledge. Ontology is the theory of reality. Axiology is the theory of values. In Indian literature, philosophy has been denominated as *darśana*. The term *darśana* is derived from the root *dṛś* which means "vision" and also the "instrument of vision." It stands for the direct, immediate and intuitive vision of reality, the actual perception of truth and also includes the means which lead to this realization.[1] India has made an immense contribution in the world of thought particularly in the field of philosophy and religion. For over a period of four thousand years, Indian ascetics developed their systems of philosophy. Indian philosophy is intensely spiritual and has always emphasized

---

1. *dṛśyate yathārthatattvamanena iti darśanam,* — *SKD.*

the need for practical realization of truth. It signifies a natural and a necessary urge in human beings to know themselves and the world in which they live and move and have their being.

A man cannot live without philosophy. The philosophical thinking began with the *Ṛgveda* itself, prominently revealed in the hymns like the Devīsūkta, Puruṣasūkta, and the *sūkta*s ascribed to Dīrghatamas. The Puruṣasūkta and the Devīsūkta show the germs of monistic idealism and the *sūkta*s of Dīrghatamas contain the germs of the dualistic realism. Thus as a result of this nucleus, there arose six philosophical systems in India, based on either monistic idealism or dualistic realism. These six schools accept the authority of the Vedas and the Upaniṣads as the base. They believe in the common tenets of Indian philosophy like *karma*, rebirth, *dharma* and liberation. The six systems are as follows:

Nyāya was founded by Gotama. It is purely a system of logic, concerned with the means of acquiring right knowledge which it classifies under sixteen topics.

Vaiśeṣika founded by Kaṇāda is the revelation of knowledge leading to the realization of the self. It classifies all knowledge of the objective world under seven realities and discusses how the various combinations of these seven basic realities bring all things into being.

Sāṁkhya founded by Kapila is pure philosophy and tries to harmonise the teaching of the Vedas through reason. It is a systematic account of the process of cosmic evolution. It shows that all derived things in this world are produced from two realities, *Prakṛti* and *Puruṣa* which are considered as the ultimate realities.

Yoga founded by Patañjali, gives an integrated approach in teaching the aspirant to train his body and mind to achieve the goal of existence which is trance or *samādhi*.

Mīmāṁsā or Pūrva-Mīmāṁsā founded by Jaiminī lays down the nature of *dharma* and emphasises the ritual and ethical aspects of religion rather than the philosophical component.

Vedānta or *Uttara-Mīmāṁsā* founded by Bādarāyaṇa is the culmination of Indian philosophical wisdom based on the teachings of the Upaniṣads. The central theme is the relation between God and the world and that between the individual and the cosmic world.

Two Broad Divisions of Indian Philosophy

The schools of Indian philosophy are divided into two broad classes — *āstika* (orthodox) and *nāstika* (heterodox). In Indian philosophy the terms *āstika* and *nāstika* are used in different senses by different thinkers. In common usage *āstika* means one who believes in the existence of God or the Absolute and *nāstika* means one who does not believe in the existence of God or the Absolute. In the view of the philosophers, the *āstika* is one who believes in the validity of the Vedas and the *nāstika* is one who does not believe in the validity of the Vedas. Similar interpretation of the terms *āstika* and *nāstika* have been recorded in the *Śabdakalpadruma* as well.[2] The term *nāstika* is used in various senses: (i) one who disregards the Vedas,[3] (ii) who denies the existence of the other world (*nāsti paralokaḥ*) — this is the view of grammarians like Patañjali, Kaiyaṭa,

2. *veda prāmāṇyavādī (āstikaḥ) vedāprāmāṇyavādī (nāstikaḥ),*
— *SKD*, p. 96 and p. 519.

3. *yavamanyate te mule hetuśāstrāśrayād dvijaḥ* ।
sa sādhubhirbahiṣkāryyonāstiko vedanindakaḥ ॥ — *Manu*, 2, 11.

Nāgeśa Bhaṭṭa, Bhaṭṭojī Dīkṣita and others,[4] (iii) who does not believe in the transmigration of *jīva*, or (iv) who denies the existence of Īśvara.

Thus *āstika* means orthodox school and *nāstika* means heterodox school. Nyāya, Vaiśeṣika, Sāṁkhya, Yoga, Mīmāṁsā and Vedānta are the six orthodox schools whereas Cārvāka, Bauddha and Jaina are the three heterodox systems.

The Jainas are regarded as *nāstikas* because they do not regard the Vedas with the same reverence and esteem as the orthodox and also because they deny the existence of Īśvara.[5]

But the Bauddhas and the Jainas may be treated as *āstika* since they believe in the existence of the other world (*paralokaḥ*). The Jainas do not say that the world of our perception is the only reality. They accept different places of existence like heaven, hell, etc. lying beyond the perceptible world. Further they do not say that our life ends in death. In their opinion, there is a distinct reality called self which in its unliberated stage undergoes birth and rebirth and in its liberated stage exists for an unending time in the supersensuous uppermost region called Siddhaśīla.[6] It is remarkable that Haribhadra Sūri in his *Ṣaḍdarśanasamuccaya* includes the Jainas in the group of the *āstikas*.[7]

---

4. *Aṣṭādhyāyī*, 4.4.60 — *asti iti asya matiḥ āstikah.* *nāsti iti asya matiḥ nāstikaḥ* — *MB.*

   paralokaḥ asti iti matir yasya ṣa āstikaḥ, tadviparītaḥ nāstikaḥ - pradīpa, paralokaḥ asti iti yasya matir asti sa āstikaḥ, tadviparītaḥ nāstikaḥ - kāśikā, asti paralokaḥ ityevaṁ matir yasya sa āstikaḥ, nāsti iti matir yasya sa nāstikaḥ. — *SIK*

5. *SVM*, Ka. 6.

6. *bhavād bhavāntara — prāptimantaḥ saṁsāriṇaḥ.* — *SDS*, p. 3.

7. *evaṁ āstika vādānāṁ kṛtaṁ saṁkṣepa-kīrtanaṁ.* — *SDS*, p. 77.

Buddha though generally described as a *nāstika* is, in reality, never so, rather he is a real *āstika*, since he believes in the other world and since his teachings are essentially in conformity with those of the Upaniṣads — the speculative aspect of the Vedas. There are some old thinkers also who have looked upon Buddha not as a *nāstika* but as an *āstika*. Śaṅkara, Jayadeva and others describing Buddha as an incarnation of God suggest that, in their view, Buddha is not a *nāstika*.[8]

Different Opinions Regarding the Number of Systems

The earliest reference to the number of systems is found in the *Śivamahimnastotra* of Puṣpadanta where it is said that there are only four schools of philosophy, namely Sāṁkhya, Yoga, Pāśupata and Vaiṣṇava. According to the author of the *Arthaśāstra*, Sāṁkhya, Yoga and Lokāyata are the three philosophical systems. The *Sarvadarśanasaṁgraha* attributed to Mādhavācārya, classifies Lokāyata, Ārhata, Bauddha, Rāmānuja, Madhva, Nakulīśa, Pāśupata, Śaiva, Raśesvara, Vaiśeṣika, Nyāya, Sāṁkhya, Yoga and Vedānta as different philosophical systems. In the *Hayaśīrṣa Pañcarātra*, a Brāhmaṇic work, supposed to have been introduced in Bengal by Raja Ballal Sen (about 1158-70 CE) as well as in the *Guru Gitā* of *Viśvasāra Tantra*, the six systems of Gotama, Kaṇāda, Kapila, Patañjali, Vyāsa and Jaimini. Madhusūdan Sarasvati in his *Prasthānabheda* divides *darśana* into *āstika* and *nāstika*. Under the former he includes Nyāya, Vaiśeṣika, Karma-mīmāṁsā, Śaṅkara-mīmāṁsā, Pañcarātra and Pāśupata, while under the latter the four schools of Buddhism, Digambara school of Jaina and the school of Cārvāka.

The author of *Nyāyakoṣa* is of the opinion that there are only six *darśanas*, namely: two Yogas, two Mimāṁsās and two

8. *keśava dhṛta buddha śarīra jaya jagadīśa hare.* — GG.

Tarkas. This also is undoubtedly regarding the *āstika darśanas* alone.

Though both Sāṁkhya and Yoga systems have found a place of honour separately in the group of the *āstika darśanas* in Indian philosophy, the two systems will be taken together in the present discussion, because from general, metaphysical and epistomological standpoints and on conceptions of the ideal of life both the systems hold a similar view.

The Significance of Sāṁkhya Philosophy and the Origin of the Word Sāṁkhya

Tradition unanimously ascribes the authorship of the Sāṁkhya system to the sage Kapila.[9] Sāṁkhya philosophy is also known as Kāpila Darśana named after the author. Of all the philosophical systems, Sāṁkhya has been considered to be the most ancient. The *Mahābhārata* also mentions that Sāṁkhya and Yoga are very ancient.[10] Therefore the importance of this *śāstra* is recognized by all the systems. In the Śānti Parva of the *Mahābhārata*, there is reference given by Bhiṣma to Yudhiṣṭhira that Sāṁkhya is the highest and most profound of all knowledge. "There is no knowledge like that of Sāṁkhya, no power like that of Yoga. You should have no doubt as to Sāṁkhya being the highest knowledge."[11] Weber holds that the Sāṁkhya is the oldest of the existing systems of Indian thought.

---

9. *sāṁkhyasya vaktā kapilaḥ paramarṣiḥ purātanaḥ* ।
hiranyagarbho yogasya vaktā nānya purātanaḥ ॥ — *SU*, V. 2, *MBh* Mokṣadharma.

10. *sanātane dve*. — *MBh*., XII.137.11.

11. *nāsti sāṁkhyasamaṁ jñānaṁ nāsti yogasamaṁ balaṁ* ।
atra bah samsaya mā bhut jñānaṁ sāṁkhyaṁ param mataṁ ॥
— *MBh*. Śānti Parva, 316.2.

The word *sāṁkhya* occurs for the first time in the *Śvetāśvatara Upaniṣad* wherein it is stated that the Supreme reality is to be achieved by Sāṁkhya and Yoga.[12] Again Sāṁkhya reflections are found even in the *Ṛgveda* and the other Upaniṣads, e.g. in the *Chāndogya,*[13] *Praśna,*[14] *Kaṭha,*[15] *Gītā*[16] and in the Smṛtis and the Purāṇas.

The word *sāṁkhya* is derived from the word *saṁkhyā* which is again etymologically derived from the root *khyā* (*jñāna*) preceded by the suffix *saṁ*. Generally *sāṁkhya* means number, i.e. counting of one, two, three, four, etc. The śāstra where there is the counting of *tattva*s is called Sāṁkhya. This is the common derivation of the word *sāṁkhya*.[17] Again the word *sāṁkhya* is used in the sense of thinking and counting.[18] Thinking may be with reference to correct knowledge of self. Counting refers to the twenty-five principles, three qualities, three sources of valid knowledge and dualism of *Puruṣa* and *Prakṛti*. In the *Mahābhārata,* the term *sāṁkhya* has been used in the sense of spiritual discipline.[19] *Vyāsa-Smṛti* defines *sāṁkhya* to be the knowledge of the true nature of the self. According to *Śāṅkarabhāṣya*, the discriminative knowledge of *paramārtha* is Sāṁkhya.[20] Śrīdhara Svāmin explains that by which *vastutattva*

12. *tatkāraṇaṁ sāṁkhyayogādhigamyaṁ..........,* — *SU*, VI.13.
13. *CU*, VI.2.
14. *PU*, VI.2.
15. *KU*, 1.3, 10-13.
16. *eṣa te'bhihita sāṁkhye,* — *SBG*, II.39.
sāṁkhayogau pṛthag valaḥ, — *ibid*, V.4.
yat sāṁkhyai prāpyate sthānaṁ — *ibid*, V.5.
17. *sāṁkhyaṁ saṁkhātmakatvañca kapilādibhirucyate* — *MP*, 3/26.
18. *carcā sāṁkhyā vicāranā* — *AK*, 1. V.3.
19. *droṇa api śāstrānyutsṛjya paramaṁ sāṁkhyamasthitaḥ* — *MBh,* VII.
20. *sāṁkhye paramārthavastuvivekaviṣaye* — *SaB*.

is rightly manifested is called Sāṁkhya; where there is the manifestation of the self is Sāṁkhya.[21] *Sāṁkhya* and *sāṁkhyāna* are two synonymous words formed with different suffixes having the same meaning, i.e. *buddhi* or *viveka*. Thus the application of the word *sāṁkhyāna* is found in the *Śrīmadbhagavadgitā*[22] and in the *Bhāgavata Purāṇa*[23]. Again sometimes *prakhyā* is used in lieu of *sāṁkhya* to convey the same sense, i.e. *buddhi* or *jñāna* in the *Vyāsabhāṣya* of *Yogasūtra*.[24] Somewhere again, the word *prasaṁkhyāna* or *parisaṁkhyānā* in the same sense has been used. Patañjali uses the term *prasaṁkhyāna* in his *Yogasūtra* in the sense of Supreme knowledge.[25] Kālidāsa in the *Kumārsambhavam*, canto III, uses the word *prasaṁkhyāna* in the sense of highest knowledge.[26]

In the *Śrīmadbhagavadgītā*, the word *sāṁkhya* is used in the sense of *jñāna*. That is why in the *Śrīmadbhagavadgītā*, the alternative name of *jñānayoga* is *Sāṁkhya*.[27] The *Śrīmadbhagavadgītā* uses *sāṁkhya kṛtānta*, i.e. Siddhānta Śāstra to indicate this system.[28]

---

21. *samyak khyāyate prakāsyate vastutattvamanayā iti sāṁkhya, samyak jñānam, tasyāṁ prakāsmanātmatattvaṁ sāṁkhyam* — Śrīdhara Svāmins.

22. *procyante guṇasāṁkhyāne* — *SBG*, XVIII.19.

23. *namo bhāgavate mahāpuruṣāya sarvaguṇa sāṁkhyāyana.* — *BPu*, 5.17.17.

24. *cittaṁ hi prakhyāpravṛtti sthitiśīlatvāt triguṇaṁ, tatparaṁ prasaṁkhyānaṁ ityā cākṣate dhyāyinaḥ* — *VB* of *YS*, I.2.

25. *prasaṁkhyāneapykusīdasya sarvathā vivekakhyāte dharmameghaḥ samādhiḥ* — *YS*, IV.29.

26. *hare prasaṁkhyānaparo babhūva* — *KS*, III.40.

27. *jñānayogena sāṁkhyānām.* — *SBG*, III.3.
yat sāṁkhyai prāpyate sthānam. — *Ibid.*, V.5.

28. *sāṁkhye kṛtānte proktāni* — *Ibid.*, XVIII.13.

Charitra Singha Gani, a Jaina in his gloss on Haribhadra Sūri's *Ṣaḍdarśanasamuccaya* gives a very interesting account of the origin of the word *sāṁkhya*. He admits the connection of Kapila with the Sāṁkhya, but adds that the school has been so named after the founder of the school of Saṅkha or Śaṅkha.[29] From all these explanations the system of Kapila comes to be known as Sāṁkhya since it is more or less endowed with the attributes of knowledge, contemplation, investigation, etc. The word *sāṁkhya* appears to convey a systematic, precise, exhaustive and metaphysical inquiry into the nature of the spirit and universe.

Sāṁkhya Literature

Works dealing with the Sāṁkhya are really not many and most of the texts before us are either summaries or commentaries. The Sāṁkhya system is unfortunate for not having a *sūtrakāra* or *bhāṣyakāra* just like all the other systems have. Kapila does take his place as the founder of the system with the other founders like Jaiminī, Bādarāyaṇa, Gotama Kaṇāda and Patañjali, but no work of his has come down to us as works of all the others have. Though the *Tattvasamāsa* and the *Sāṁkhyapravacana* have been attributed to Kapila it is difficult to accept that these are Kapila's works, as their late nature is too obvious. The *Ṣaṣṭitantra*, therefore, appears to be the only known work that goes to the pre-*kārikā* period, for Īśvarakṛṣṇa himself suggests that his *kārikā*s are based on the *Ṣaṣṭitantra*.

Ṣaṣṭitantra: This work is known to us through references and quotations in Jayamaṅgalā. Prof. M. Hiriyanna has critically

29. *sāṁkhya iti puruṣanimittayaṁ saṁjñā, saṁkhyasyaime sāṁkhyāḥ tālavya va śakāraḥ sāṁkhya nāma ādipurusaḥ* ॥ — *SDS.*

studied the references to the *Ṣaṣṭitantra* in the Jayamaṅgalā[30] in his article "Ṣaṣṭitantra and Vārṣagaṇya" and has come to some interesting conclusion about this important work of the Sāṁkhya. These references clearly indicate that Pañcaśikha, the sage, was the author of the *Ṣaṣṭitantra*. Secondly, the work had sixty parts and thirdly, it dealt with sixty topics. It was perhaps for the fact that it had sixty parts and it dealt with sixty topics, it was called *Ṣaṣṭitantra*. The *Ṣaṣṭitantra* is also referred to in the *Vyāsabhāṣya* on *Yogasūtra*.[31] Īśvarakṛṣṇa also in his *Sāṁkhyakārikā*[32] tells us that Pañcaśikha did elaborate the doctrine. It is true that *Ahirbudhnya Saṁhitā* metions sixty topics in chapter twelve but it is extremely doubtful whether these are the sixty topics dealt with either by the *Ṣaṣṭitantra* or Pañcaśikha. Some of the important topics from the list of the *Ahirbudhnya Saṁhitā* like *Brahman, kāla, niyati*, etc. are not to be found in the *Sāṁkhyakārikā* which must be taken to closely follow the entire *Ṣaṣṭitantra* in the matter of the topics.

There is a view, according to which Vārṣagaṇya is the author of the *Ṣaṣṭitantra*, for an author of reputation like Vācaspati quotes the verse from *Ṣaṣṭitantra* and considers Vārṣagaṇya[33] as its author. It ia also suggested that Kapila's

30. (i) *trividhamanumānamākhyātaṁ iti ṣaṣṭitantre vyakhāyataṁ, pūrvavat, śeṣavat sāmānyatodṛṣṭamiti* — p. 7.

(ii) *ete ṣaṣṭiḥ padārthāḥ, tadarthaṁ śāstraṁ ṣaṣṭitantramuccyate* — p. 56.

(iii) *atra ṣaṣṭitantre bahaborthā teatra noktā ityāha* — p. 89.

(iv) *pañcaśikhena muninā bahudhā kṛtaṁ tantraṁ, ṣaṣṭitantrākhyāṁ ṣaṣṭikhaṇḍaṁ kṛtamiti, tatraiba hi ṣaṣṭīrarthā vyākhyātāḥ* — p. 68, cf. *JOR*, pp. 107-12.

31. *atraiva ṣaṣṭitantraśāstrasyānuśiṣṭi* —*TV*, IV.13.

32. *etat pavitramagnaṁ munirāsurayeanukampyayā pradadau āsurirapi pañcaśikhāya tena ca bahudhā kṛtaṁ tantram* — *SK*, *K*. 70.

33. Bhāmati on *BS*, II. J. 3.

work was named as Saṣṭitantra and Śaṅkara in his commentary on the *Brahamasūtra* suggests that Kapila's work, a *smṛti* was named as tantra.[34]

The Sāṁkhyakārikā: Tradition is fairly unanimous and authoritative regarding the text of this manual of the Sāṁkhya. This work is the earliest available and the most popular text of the Sāṁkhya, and one that gives a fairly systematic treatment of the doctrine. The work consists of seventy stanzas and is on that account sometimes designated as the *Sāṁkhyasaptati*. It contains a brief but exceedingly lucid exposition of the theoretical teaching of the system and has been described as the pearl of the whole scholastic literature of India. This book with a commentary, whose identity is not quite certain, was translated into Chinese language under the name of the "Golden Seventy Discourse" most popularly known as *Hiraṇyasaptati* or *Suvarṇasaptati* by one *Paramārtha*, a brāhmaṇa of Ujjayinī who went to China in CE 546 on the invitation of its then Emperor and spent the rest of his life there. There is divergent opinion regarding the actual date of the work, *Sāṁkhyakārikā*. Some authorities assign it to the first or the first half of the second century, while others contend that it belonged to the third century and some place it in the fifth century. But roughly speaking we may take Īśvarakṛṣṇa the author of *Sāṁkhyakārikā* to have been a contemporary of Kālidāsa. The popularity of this manual can be seen from the number of commentaries and sub-commentaries written upon it. Most important commentaries on *Sāṁkhyakārikā* are *Yuktidīpikā*, *Māṭharavṛtti* of Māṭhara, *Sāṁkhyattvakaumudī* of Vācaspati Miśra, and Jayamaṅgalā of Śaṅkarācārya. Another important commentary on *Sāṁkhyakārikā* is Gauḍapāda's *bhāṣya*.

---

34. *smṛtisca tantrākhyā paramarṣiprahitā*. — *BS*, II.I.1.

The Tattvasamāsa : This is a work containing a brief statement of the Sāṁkhya system and probably belongs to the fourteenth century. It is often ascribed to Kapila but this cannot be seriously taken. Vijñānabhikṣu ascribes the *Sāṁkhyasūtra* and the *Tattvasamāsa* to one and the same author. The different order of categories and the numerous names not elsewhere used led Max Müller to think that the work was primitive and original, in fact, the first real text of the Sāṁkhya. Max Müller further points out that the work belongs to a period anterior to the *Sāṁkhyakārikā*, for wherever these two works agree, the *Tattvasamāsa* appears to be the older. Mādhava in his *Sarvadarśanasaṁgraha* written in CE 1380 does not cite the *Tattvasamāsa* but uses the *kārikā* for his account of the Sāṁkhya. The work, therefore, may be presumed to belong to the period after Mādhava, i.e. the fourteenth century.

The Sāṁkhyasūtra: This work appears to have been written by some unknown author after the ninth century. Tradition ascribes it to Kapila, which indeed, need not be taken seriously. Svapneśvara in his *Kaumudīprabhā* appears to consider Pañcaśikha as the author of the sūtras.[35]

The work has six chapters, of which the first three give an exposition of the Sāṁkhya principle, the fourth some illustrative tales, the fifth, refutation of rival views and the sixth a recapitulation.

The *Sāṁkhyasūtra* has the following commentaries:

1. The *Aniruddhavṛtti* by Aniruddha.
2. The *Sāṁkhyavṛttisāra* by Mahādeva Sarasvatī.

   This work, though an abridgement of Aniruddha's work, has also original remarks.

---

35. Cf. *SK* of Īśvarakṛṣṇa by T.G. Mainkar.

3. *Sāṁkhya-pravacana-bhāṣya* — the most important commentary on the *Sāṁkhyasūtra* is Vijñānabhikṣu's *Sāṁkhya-pravacana-bhāṣya*. It is assigned to the sixteenth century. In it, the author endeavours to minimise the distinction between the Sāṁkhya and the theistic Vedānta, which he regards as the genuine Vedānta, while the Advaita Vedānta is its modern falsification.
4. The *Laghu-Sāṁkhya-Sūtravṛtti* is written by Nāgojī Bhaṭṭa. This is an abstract of Vijñānabhikṣu's work.
5. *The Sāṁkhyataraṅga* is written by Viśveśvaradatta Miśra. The popular name of this author appears to have been Kāṣṭhajihva.

The Sāṁkhyasāra: This is a work of Vijñānabhikṣu who wrote in the sixteenth century. Vijñānabhikṣu reflects the theistic spirit of his age and further symbolizes the compromise between the Sāṁkhya and the Vedānta. It is again this text that contains very clear exposition of some of the Sāṁkhya concepts, as for instance, of the *guṇa*s as well as some original views on problems that have been left vague by the earlier thinkers.

The Sāṁkhya-tattva-pradīpa: This is a work of Kavirāja Yati, disciple of Vaikuṇṭha. This work is similar in nature to that of Vijñānabhikṣu but of much inferior value.

The Sāṁkhya-tattva-kaumudī: It is a philosophical work of Vācaspati Miśra. The *Sāṁkhya-tattva-kaumudī* is an excellent exposition of *Sāṁkhyakārikā*. The commentary is very lucid and expressive, and like the *Yuktidīpikā*, it is not bound to raise any hair-splitting argument in elucidating the text of Īśvarakṛṣṇa.

The Yuktidīpikā: The *Yuktidīpikā* is the earliest available commentary on the *Sāṁkhyakārikā* of Īśvarakṛṣṇa. It is the most extensive and the most comprehensive in import. It expounds the system of Sāṁkhya in all possible details and justifies it with all possible arguments. It tries its best to save the theories of Sāṁkhya from the intellectual onslaught at the hands of the other systems. The unique feature of the *Yuktidīpikā* which raises it to the height of importance, is the reference to the views of pre-Īśvarakṛṣṇa Sāṁkhya teachers, the works of whom are lost to us. It easily fills the gaps in the literacy continuity of Sāṁkhya. It is rightly termed as the "illuminator of reasoning" (to justify the system of Īśvarakṛṣṇa). This makes the study of the *Yuktidīpikā* essential for the complete understanding of Sāṁkhya.

Tattvacandra: It is a commentary based chiefly on the work of Vācaspati Miśra written by Nārāyaṇatīrtha. It is a sub-commentary as it is written on the basis of *Sāṁkhya-tattva-kaumudī* of Vācaspati Miśra which is an important commentary on *Sāṁkhyakārikā* by Īśvarakṛṣṇa. Some authorities say that it is a treatise on Gauḍapāda's work.

Sāṁkhyacandrikā: It is a commentary on the *Sāṁkhyakārikā* of Īśvarakṛṣṇa written by Nārāyaṇatīrtha.

Sāṁkhyataruvasantaḥ: The latest commentary is the *Sāṁkhya-taruvasantaḥ* by Muḍumba Narasiṁhasvāmin, who tries to relate the Vedānta and the Sāṁkhya.

Two latest works of philosophical value are Sīmānanda's *Sāṁkhyatattvavivecana* and Bhāvagaṇeśa's *Sāṁkhyatattva-yathārthyadīpana*.

List of most available works on Sāṁkhya system:

Title	*Author*
Sāṁkhyasūtraṁ or *Sāṁkhyapravacana sūtra*	Kapila
Tattvasamāsa	Kapila
Sāṁkhyapravacanabhāṣya	Vijñānabhikṣu
Tattvakaumudivyākhyā	Yati
Sāṁkhyakārikā	Īśvarakṛṣṇa
Sāṁkhyatattvakaumudī	Vācaspati Miśra
Sāṁkhyasāra	Vijñānabhikṣu
Sāṁkhyacandrikā	Nārāyaṇatīrtha
Rājāvārttika	Bhojarāja
Ṣaṣṭitantra	Pañcaśikha
Māṭharavṛtti	Māṭharācārya
Yuktidīpikā	Author unknown
Sāṁkhyasūtravṛtti	Aniruddha
Sāṁkhyatattvavivecana	Sīmānanda
Sāṁkhyatattvayathārthyadīpana	Bhāvagaṇeśa
Sāṁkhyakaumudī	Rāmakṛṣṇa
Jayamaṅgalā	Śaṅkaracārya

Sāṁkhya Teachers

The *Smṛtis*, the *Mahābhārata*, the *Sāṁkhyakārikā* and the commentary literature refer now and then to many Sāṁkhya thinkers. They are as follows: (1) Kapila, (2) Āsuri, (3) Pañcaśikha, (4) Vindhyavāsa, (5) Vārṣagaṇya, (6) Jaigīṣavya, (7) Voḍhu, (8) Devala, (9) Sanaka, (10) Sananda, (11) Sanātana, (12) Sanatkumāra, (13) Bhṛgu, (14) Śukra, (15) Kāśyapa, (16) Parāśara, (17) Garga, (18) Gautama, (19) Nārada, (20) Ārṣṭīṣeṇa,

(21) Agastya, (22) Pulastya, (23) Hārīta, (24) Ulūka, (25) Vālmīki, (26) Śuka.

It is obvious that this list has a limited historical value, for many of the personalities mentioned here appear to be mythical names and nothing more. Tradition is not unanimous regarding the authorship of works ascribed to many in this list, as for instance, Kapila, Pañcaśikha and others.

A BRIEF ACCOUNT OF THE IMPORTANT SĀṀKHYA TEACHERS

Kapila: Kapila, the great sage, is regarded as the propounder of the Sāṁkhya thought. In the Sāṁkhya tradition, he is held to be the first among the wise (Ādividvān) and he appears at the beginning of each cycle of creation. He is the foremost of the *siddhas*.[36] His *siddhi* or perfection is regarded as an instance of what is called *janmasiddhi,* i.e. he was endowed with perfection from the very moment of his birth. It is stated that out of compassion, he imparted the knowledge of Sāṁkhya to Āsuri, his first disciple. Kapila through his supernatural power appeared before Āsuri to impart to him the knowledge of Sāṁkhya. This shows that Kapila had no physical body and thus, he cannot be regarded as a historical person. The *Mahābhārata* also mentions him to be the propounder of Sāṁkhya.[37] But he is somewhere stated as the incarnation of fire,[38] somewhere as the light residing in the orb of the sun and elsewhere as one of the mind-born sons (*mānas-putra*) of the god Brahmā. The *Bhāgavata Purāṇa*[39] mentions him to be

36. *siddhānāṁ kapilo muniḥ — SBG,* X 26.

37. *sāṁkhyasya vaktā kapilaḥ paramarṣiḥ purātanaḥ hiraṇyagarbho yogasya vaktā nānyaḥ purātanaḥ — MBh* Mokṣadharma.

38. *agni sa kapila nāmo — SPB,* VI.70.

39. *pañcamaḥ kapilo nāmo — BP,* 1.3.10.

the fifth incarnation of Viṣṇu. All these facts clearly point to his mythological origin and he may not be taken as a historical personage.

Āsuri: If this Sāṁkhya Āsuri be the same as the Āsuri of the *Śatapatha Brāhmaṇa* then in all probability he lived before 600 BC. Everywhere consistently Āsuri is mentioned as the successor of Kapila. Garbe is not inclined to accept Āsuri as a historical personality and holds him to be different from the Āsuri of the *Śatapatha Brāhmaṇa*. Kaviraj Gopinath, however, regards Āsuri to have been a real Sāṁkhya teacher. The *Mahābharata* describes Pañcaśikha a student of Āsuri.

Pañcaśikha: In the gradation of the Sāṁkhya teachers Pañcaśikha comes next to Āsuri from whom he is said to have obtained the knowledge of Sāṁkhya. Like Kapila and Āsuri he is also portrayed mythologically in the Purāṇas. He is an authority on the Sāṁkhya philosophy. His views are preserved and he is supposed to have flourished sometime between 100 and 300 CE. The Śāntiparva of *Mahābhārata*[40] speaks of a Pañcaśikha belonging to the family of Parāśara and we have a Gandharba Pañcaśikha moving about the Buddha, in the Buddhist tradition. It is extremely doubtful whether all these Pañcaśikhas are identical. Aśvaghoṣa also in his *Buddhacarita* in one place mentions Āsuri and Pañcaśikha as celestial beings.

Vindhyavāsa: Vindhyavāsa is one of the celebrated exponents of Sāṁkhya whose views are referred to here and there in the Sanskrit literature.[41] He is somewhere mentioned as Vindhanivāsa and elsewhere as Vindhyavāsa. The Chinese

---

40. *MBh.* (Śānti. 320.23).

41. (a) *antarābhavadehastu niṣiddha vindhyavāsinā. — SV.*

(b) *puruṣaobikṛtatmaiva svanirvāsamacetanaṁ manaḥ karoti sānidhyādupādheḥ sphaṭika yathā. — SS.*

tradition appears to regard Vindhyavāsa as the author of the *Sāṁkhyakārikā*, while Belvalkar regards him to be the commentator of the same. Vindhyavāsa, according to the Chinese account, rewrote a work by Vārṣagaṇya, and lived before Vasubandhu. Paramārtha suggests that Vindhyavāsa was so called because he lived in Vindhya mountain. He studied the Sāṁkhya under Vārṣagaṇya and composed the *Sāṁkhyaśāstra*. He had discussion with Buddhamitra, the teacher of Vasubandhu on various philosophical matters and was awarded by king Vikramāditya three lakh of gold coins for his work. Returning to his grotto, Vindhyavāsa died and became a stone. Keith is of the view that there might have been many Vindhyavyāsas.

Vārṣagaṇya: Vārṣagaṇya is a distinguished teacher of Sāṁkhya and Yoga but unfortunately none of his systematic works has come down to us. All that we can know from him are a few references to his views in the literature.[42] Vācaspati quotes about this great personality as "Bhagavāna Vārṣagaṇya." The *Mahābhārata*[43] mentions him as a teacher of Sāṁkhya. The name of him also appears in the *Mahābhāṣya*.[44] Keith suggests the possibility of the *purusādhiṣṭhitaṁ pradhānaṁ pravartate* to be found in both Gauḍapāda and Māṭhara as coming from Vārṣagaṇya. Commentator Balarāma expressly states Vārṣagaṇya to be the author of the *Ṣaṣṭitantra*.

Jaigīṣavya: The Kūrma Pūrāṇa suggests that Jaigīṣavya and Pañcaśikha studied together, perhaps under the same teacher.

---

42. *mūrtivyavadhijātibhedābhāvannāsti mūlapṛthaktvaṁ vārṣagaṇyaḥ*,
— *Vyāsabhāṣya*, II.53.

pañcaparva avidyā ityāha sma bhagavān vārṣagaṇya, *STK* on K. 47.

43. *MBh*. XII.318-59.

44. *MB*, I.1.51.

Yogasūtra shows him as a teacher of the Yoga[45] doctrine. Vācaspati refers to him as an author of *Dhāraṇaśāstra*.[46] Aśvaghoṣa said that Jaigīṣavya won liberation through[47] Sāṁkhya. Beyond this no information is available about Jaigīṣavya.

Voḍhu: He is mentioned in the epic as a teacher of Sāṁkhya along with Sana, Sanaka, Sanātana, Sanatkumāra, and Sanatasujāta. Weber reads Voḍhu as a degraded form of Buddha, but without any justification whatsoever. The name of Voḍhu appears in the list of the Sāṁkhya teachers to whom oblation of water is daily offered after Kapila and Āsuri but before Pañcaśikha while he is placed even before Āsuri in an Atharva Pariśiṣṭa.

Devala: The Aparārka, a commentary on the *Yājñavalkya-Smṛti*, contains quotations from Devala. According to Kane, Devala would probably belong to some time between the fourth and the sixth centuries CE, since he is regarded as a contemporary of Bṛhaspati and Kātyāyana. Udayavir Shastri would place him much earlier before second century BC arguing that the *Mahābhārata* frequently mentions Devala and the epic was completed by the second century BC.

The Rest: As has been observed earlier, many of the names mentioned in the list of the Sāṁkhya teachers are purely mythical and legitimate doubts can be entertained about their historicity. Thus the verse and a part quoted by Gauḍapāda contains the names of the seven sons of Brahmā: Sanaka, Sanandana, Sanātana, Āsuri, Kapila, Voḍhu and Pañcaśikha.

---

45. *YS*, II.54 cf. *SK* of Īśvarakṛṣṇa, ed. by T.G Mainkar.
46. *NS*, III.2.43.
47. *BC*, 12.67.

kapilaścāsuriścaiva vodhu pañcaśikhastathā
saptaite mānasaḥ putrā brahmanaḥ parameṣṭhinaḥ

The *Mahābhārata*[48] gives a similar list but with different names. Sana, Sanatsujāta, Sanaka, Sanandana, Sanatkumāra, Kapila and Sanātana. The others namely Sanatkumāra, Bhṛgu, Śukra, Kāśyapa, Parāśara, Garga, Gautama, Nārada. Ārṣṭiṣeṇa, Agastya, Pulastya, Hārīta appear as writers of Smṛti works but their actual contribution to the Sāṁkhya doctrine or the part they played in the elaboration or propagation of the doctrine is extremely doubtful and is a matter of conjecture only.

Sāṁkhya System

Sāṁkhya is undoubtedly one of the oldest systems of Indian philosophy. Tradition regards Kapila as the founder of this system. But *Sāṁkhyapravacanasūtra* which is attributed to him is generally regarded by scholars as a work of fourteenth century. Īśvarakṛṣṇa's *Sāṁkhyakārikā* seems to be the earliest available and the most popular work of this system. Besides this we have Gauḍapāda's *Sāṁkhyakārikābhāṣya*, Vācaspati Miśra's *Tattvakaumudī* and Vijñānabhikṣu's *Sāṁkhya-pravacana-bhāṣya.*

The word *sāṁkhya* is derived from the word *saṁkhyā* which means right knowledge as well as number. The *Gītā* uses this word in the sense of knowledge, so does *Mahābhārata* at other places also. *Sāṁkhya* means the philosophy of right knowledge. Right knowledge is the knowledge of the separation of the *Puruṣa* from the *Prakṛti*. Yoga, as the counterpart of Sāṁkhya, means action or practice and tells us how the theoretical metaphysical teachings of Sāṁkhya might be realized in actual

48. *MBh*, Śāntiparva, 340, 67-79.

practice. Thus Sāṁkhya-Yoga forms one complete system, the former being the theoretical while the latter being the practical aspect of the same teaching. Sāṁkhya is also the philosophy of numbers, because it deals with twenty-five categories.

Sāṁkhya maintains a clear-cut dualism between *Puruṣa* and *Prakṛti* and further maintains the plurality of the *Puruṣa*s, and is silent on God. Sāṁkhya believes in *satkāryavāda*. All material effects are the modification of *Prakṛti*. They pre-exist in the eternal bosom of *Prakṛti* and simply came out of it at the time of creation and return to it at the time of dissolution. There is neither new production nor utter destruction. Production means development or manifestation, destruction means envelop-ment or dissolution. Production is evolution, destruction is involution.

The theory that causation means a real transformation of the material cause leads to the concept of *Prakṛti* as the root cause of the world of objects. All worldly effects are latent in this uncaused cause, because infinite regress has to be avoided. As the uncaused root cause it is called *Prakṛti*, as the first principle of this universe, it is called *pradhāna*, as the unmanifested state of all effects it is known as *avyakta*, as the extremely subtle and imperceptible thing which is only inferred from its products it is called *anumāna*, as the unintelligent and unconscious principle, it is called *jaḍa*, and as the ever active unlimited power, it is called *śakti*. The products are caused, dependent, relative, many and temporary as they are subject to birth and death or to production and destruction, but *Prakṛti* is uncaused, independent, absolute, one and eternal, being beyond production and destruction.

Prakṛti is said to be the unity of the three *guṇa*s held in equilibrium. The three *guṇa*s are *sattva, rajas* and *tamas*. They are the constituents of *Prakṛti* and through it of the worldly objects. Being subtle and imperceptible their existence is inferred from their effects — pleasure, pain and indifference respectively. They themselves possess qualities like lightness, activity, heaviness, etc. They are extremely fine and everchanging elements. They make up *Prakṛti* which is nothing apart from them. They are not the qualities which *Prakṛti*, the substance, possesses, on the other hand they themselves constitute *Prakṛti*. They are the factors or the constituents or the elements of *Prakṛti*.

The other of the two co-present co-eternal realities of Sāṁkhya is the *Puruṣa*, the principal of pure consciousness. *Puruṣa* is the soul, the self, the spirit, the subject, the knower. It is neither body nor senses nor brain nor mind (*manas*) nor ego (*ahaṁkāra*) nor intellect (*buddhi*). It is not a substance which possesses the quality of consciousness. Consciousness is its essence. It is itself pure and transcendental consciousness. It is the ultimate knower which is the foundation of all knowledge. It is the pure subject and as such can never become an object of knowledge. It is the silent witness, the neutral seer.[49] It is beyond time and space, beyond change and activity. It is uncaused, eternal and all-pervading.

Prakṛti is regarded as essentially dynamic. If motion were not inherent in *Prakṛti* it could not be given to it by any outside agency and if motion once ceased in *Prakṛti*, it could not reappear. Hence *Prakṛti* is always changing.[50] Even in dissolution there is homogeneous change in *Prakṛti* when all the three *guṇas* are in the state of equilibrium. It is only when heterogeneous change takes place and *rajas* vibrates and makes

49. *tasmācca viparyāsāt siddhaṁ sākṣittvamasya puruṣasya, kaivalyam mādhyasthaṁ draṣṭṛttvamakartṛbhāvaśca.* — SK, K, 19.

50. *saṁghātaparāthatvād triguṇadiviparyāyadadhisthānāt puruṣa asti bhoktṛbhāvāt kaivalyārthaṁ pravṛtteśca.* — SK, K, 17.

sattva and *tamas* vibrate then the equilibrium is disturbed and evolution takes place. *Sattva*, the principle of manifestation and *rajas*, the principle of activity were formerly held in check by *tamas*, the principle of non-manifestation and non-activity. But when *rajas*, the principle of activity vibrates and makes the other two vibrate, the process of creation begins. And creation is not the new creation of the worldly objects, but only their manifestation. It is only making explicit of that which was formerly implicit. There is no continuous progress in one direction, but alternating periods of evolution, and dissolution in a cyclic order. Evolution is again said to be teleological and not mechanical or blind. Evolution takes place for serving the purpose of the *Puruṣa*, *Prakṛti*, the *guṇa*s, the senses, the mind, the ego, the intellect, the subtle body — all are constantly serving the end of the *Puruṣa*. This end is either worldly experience or liberation. *Puruṣa* needs *Prakṛti* for enjoyment as well as for liberation, for *saṁsāra* as well as for *kaivalya*. Evolution supplies objects to be enjoyed to the *Puruṣa* and also works for his liberation by enabling him to discriminate between himself and *Prakṛti*.

The first product of the evolution is called *mahat*, the Great. It is the germ of this vast world of objects including intellect, ego and mind. It is cosmic in its nature but it has a psychological aspect also in which it is called *buddhi* or intellect. *Buddhi* or intellect, being the evolute of *Prakṛti* is material. It is made of finest matter and is thus capable of reflecting clearly the consciousness of the *Puruṣa*. On account of the reflection of the *Puruṣa* in it, it becomes apparently conscious and intelligent. The senses, the mind and the ego function for *buddhi* or intellect which functions directly for the *Puruṣa*. It arises when *sattva* predominates. Its original attributes are virtue, (*dharma*), knowledge (*jñāna*), detachment (*vairāgya*) and power (*aiśvarya*);

when it gets vitiated by *tamas*, these attributes are replaced by their opposites.

Mahat produces *ahaṁkāra*. It is the principle of individuation. Its function is to generate self-sense (*abhimāna*). It produces the notion of the "I" and the "mine." It is the individual ego-sense. *Puruṣa* wrongly identifies himself with this ego and knows himself as the agent of actions. *Ahaṁkāra* is of three kinds: (a) *vaikārika* or *sāttvika*, (b) *bhūtādi* or *tāmasa*, and (c) *taijasa* or *rājasa*.

Manas or mind which arises from the *sāttvika ahaṁkāra* is the subtle and central sense-organ. It can come into contact with the several sense-organs at the same time. The *sāttvika ahaṁkāra* produces besides *manas* the five sensory and the five motor-organs. The five sensory organs (*jñānendriya*) are the functions of sight, smell, taste, touch and sound. The five motor-organs (*karmendriya*) are the functions of speech, prehension, movement, excretion and reproduction. From *tamas* arises the five subtle essences which are called *tanmātras*. These are the essences of sight, smell, taste, touch and sound. From the essence of sound arises the element of ether (*ākāśa*) together with the quality of sound. From the essence of touch combined with the essence of sound, arises the element of air together with the qualities of sound and touch. From the subtle essence of colour or sight combined with those of sound and touch, arises the element of fire or light together with the qualities of sound, touch and colour. From the essence of taste combined with those of sound, touch and colour arises the element of water together with the qualities of sound, touch, colour and taste. And lastly, from the essence of smell combined with those of sound, touch, colour and taste arises the element of earth together with the qualities of sound, touch, colour, taste and smell.

Evolution is the play of these twenty-four principles which, together with the *Puruṣa* who is a mere spectator and outside the play of evolution, are the twenty-five categories of Sāṁkhya. Out of these twenty-five principles, the *Puruṣa* is neither a cause nor an effect, *Prakṛti* is only the cause and not the effect. *Mahat*, *ahaṁkāra* and the five subtle essences are both causes and effects, while the five sensory and the five motor-organs and the five gross elements and *manas* are the effects only.[51]

A chart of the twenty-five principles of classical Sāṁkhya:

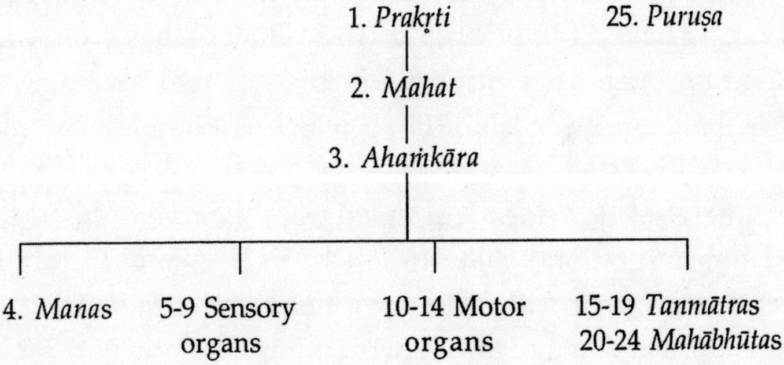

The 25th is the *Puruṣa*, untouched by this evolution.

The earthly life is full of three kinds of pain. The first kind, called *ādhyātmika*, is due to intra-organic psychophysical causes and includes all mental and bodily sufferings. The second, *ādhibhautika* is due to extra-organic natural causes like men, beasts, birds, thorns, etc. The third *ādhidaivika*, is due to supernatural causes like the planets, elemental agencies,

51. *mūlaprakṛtiravikṛtirmahadādyāha prakṛtivikṛtaya sapta ṣoḍaśakastu vikāro na prakṛtirṇa vikṛtiḥ puruṣa.* — *SK, K,* 3.

ghosts, demon, etc. Wherever there are *guṇa*s there are pains. Even the so-called pleasures lead to pain. Even the life in heaven is subject to the *guṇa*s. The end of man is to get rid of these three kinds of pain and sufferings. Liberation means complete cessation of all sufferings which is the *summum bonum*, the highest end of life (*apavarga* or *puruṣārtha*).

Sāṁkhya believes that bondage and liberation alike are only phenomenal. The bondage of the *Puruṣa* is a fiction. It is only the ego, the product of *Prakṛti*, which is bound. And consequently it is only the ego which is liberated. *Puruṣa*, in its complete isolation, is untouched by bondage and liberation. If *Puruṣa* were really bound, it could not have obtained liberation even after hundred births, for real bondage can never be destroyed. It is *Prakṛti* which is bound and *Prakṛti* which is liberated. Īśvarakṛṣṇa says: *Puruṣa* is neither bound nor liberated nor does it transmigrate. Bondage, liberation and transmigration belong to *Prakṛti* in its manifold forms.[52] *Prakṛti* binds itself with its seven forms.[53] Just as a dancing girl retires from the stage after entertaining the audience, *Prakṛti* also retreats after exhibiting herself to the *Puruṣa*.[54]

The original Sāṁkhya was monistic and theistic. But the classical Sāṁkhya, perhaps under the influence of materialism, Jainism and early Buddhism became atheistic. It is orthodox because it believes in the authority of the Vedas. It does not establish the non-existence of God. It only shows that *Prakṛti* and *Puruṣa* are sufficient to explain this universe and therefore

52. *tasmānna badhyate nāpi muccyate nāpi saṁsarati kaścit, saṁsarati badhyate muccyate ca nānāśrayā prakṛtiḥ.* — *SK, K*, 62.

53. *rupai saptavīreva tu badhnātyātmānamatmanā prakṛti, saiva ca puruṣārthaṁ prati vimocayatyekarūpeṇa.* — *SK, K*, 63.

54. *raṅgasya darśayitvā nivartate nartakī yathā nṛtyāt, puruṣasya tathātmānaṁ prakāśya vinivartate prakṛtiḥ.* — *SK, K*, 59.

there is no reason for postulating a hypothesis of God. But some commentators have tried to repudiate the existence of God, while the later Sāṁkhya writers like Vijñānabhikṣu have tried to revive the necessity for admitting God.

The Important Tenets of the Sāṁkhya System

The important tenets of the Sāṁkhya system are as follows:

(1) *Padārtha*s — twenty-five in number (*mahat*, etc.).

(2) *Pramāṇa*s — three in number (perception, inference and verbal testimony).

(3) The theory of causation — *satkāryavāda* (i.e., the effect pre-exists in the cause).

(4) The theory of *guṇa*s — three in number (*sattva, rajas* and *tamas).*

(5) Establishment of the multiplicity of the self (*puruṣabahutva*).

(6) The theory of change (*pariṇāmavāda*).

(7) The theory of liberation or *mokṣa* (*kaivalya*).

The Significance of Yoga Philosophy

The Yoga system was propounded by Patañjali which came into existence almost at the same time as the Sāṁkhya. Yoga is generally understood to mean certain practices by which it is believed that one can attain supernormal powers through concentration. It is as such often associated with hypnotism, clairvoyance, clairaudience and similar other occult phenomena. Better informed persons know that it accepts the Sāṁkhya system of philosophy, but believes in God (Īśvara) and adopts a body of practices for the attainment of its ultimate goal — emancipation. But the difference between Yoga and the Sāṁkhya of Kapila has never been satisfactorily explained. Yoga is counted as one of the six orthodox systems of philosophy, but if its philosophy is identical with that of the Kapila Sāṁkhya, it would be meaningless to call it a system of philosophy merely for the sake of its code of disciplinary practices. Thus we find that though the influence of Yoga on Hindu thought and life has been very great, the position of Yoga as a system of philosophy has always been misunderstood. It is probably for this reason and for the stress that it laid on its disciplinary course of practices that it sometimes wandered from its true ideal and became associated with magic, medicine and occultism.

It is true that Yoga owes much to the Sāṁkhya philosophy but Yoga did not borrow its materials from Kapila Sāṁkhya, but being itself a modification from the original Sāṁkhya text it has as much right to pass by the name of Sāṁkhya as Kapila Sāṁkhya. Conformably to this we find that both the Kapila *Sāṁkhyasūtra* and the *Pātañjala Yogasūtra* call themselves *Sāṁkhyapravacanasūtra*. It will also appear that though the Yoga and the Kapila Sāṁkhya are fundamentally the same in their general metaphysical positions, they hold quite different views on many points of philosophical, ethical and practical interest. It has been a long-felt need that the Yoga philosophy should be studied in all its metaphysical, ontological, psychological, theological, physical and practical bearings in such a manner that its different parts could be understood in their mutual relations.

Origin of the Word Yoga

The word 'Yoga' is used in various senses. It means spiritual unification, i.e. the union of the soul with absolute, concentration of the mind and complete suppression of the mental modes. In the *Amarakośa*[55] and the *Mahābhārata*[56] the word *Yoga* is used in the sense of means. The word *yoga* occurs in the *Ṛgveda* in various senses such as yoking or harnessing, achieving the unachieved connection and the like. The word *yoga*, however, became gradually rarer and rarer in its original meaning, as it began more often to be used in the sense of yoking the senses. With the growth of religious and philosophic ideas in the *Ṛgveda* we find that religious austerities were getting a prominent place among thinking people. In the light of the growth of these ideas of asceticism and self control, it is easy to understand that when the force of the flying passions was felt to be as uncontrollable as that of a spirited steed, the word *yoga* which was originally applied to the control of steeds was applied to the control of the senses. That the senses were regarded as uncontrollable horses is evident from such passages of *Kaṭha*[57] and *Maitrāyaṇī*.[58]

The root *yujir* in the sense of connection as given in Pāṇini's list of roots is a root form derived later from the noun form *yoga* (yoking), or that *yoga* also was originally formed from *yujir yoge*, but as *yoga* had taken a technical meaning in Pāṇini's time he invented a new fanciful root *yuja* in the sense of concentration. In Pāṇini we find that the word *yoga* had already attained its technical meaning, for he distinguishes between the root *yuj* in the sense of concentration (*samādhi*)[59] and *yujir* in the sense of joining or connecting.[60] But the root

55. *yoga saṁnahana upāya dhyāna saṁgati yuktiṣu.* — *AK*, 3.3.22.

56. *eko hi yoga asya bhaved badhāya.* — *MB*, XII.

57. *indriyāṇi hayānāhurviṣayansteṣu gocarān ātmendriyamanyuktaṁ bhoktetyāhurmanīṣinaḥ.* — *KU*, I.III.4.

58. *MU*, II.6.

59. *yuj samādhau.* — *Pa Su*, 7.1.71.

60. *yujir yoge.* — *Ibid.*

yuj is not used as verb, it only occurs in the derivative forms as *yoga, yogin*. Pāṇini has himself used the word many times in his grammar, but the sense in which it has been used in those places is that of connecting or joining. The fact that there is no verbal use of the root *yuj* in the sense of concentration,[61] goes a great way to show that the root in *yuj samādhau* was only an imaginary analysis of a root form which had no use as a verb and was only found in the noun and adjective forms of *yuga, yugya* and *yogin*. The *Gītā* defines *yoga* as that state than which there is nothing higher or worth realizing and firmly rooted in which a person is never shaken even by the greatest pain and misery. The *Gītā* also says that evenness of mind is *yoga*.[62] *Yoga* is also defined in the *Gītā* as skill of preserving the equanimity or equality of the mind.[63] Again *yoga* is defined in the *Gītā* as the equality of the mind which is separation of the mind from union with sorrow, i.e., cessation of suffering.[64] The term *yoga* according to Patañjali's definition, is the final annihilation of all the mental states.[65] In Patañjali's Yoga philosophy, *yoga* means an internal discipline by which the mind is progressively stilled and taken up into the stage of *samādhi*. Bhoja states that in Patañjali's Yoga philosophy the term *yoga* does not mean union but separation. According to Yājñavalkya the conjunction of the individual and the supreme soul is called *yoga*.[66]

---

61. *yujyate brahmacāri yogaṁ*. — *MB*, III.2.87.
62. *samattvaṁ yoga ucyate*. — *SBG*, II.48.
63. *yoga karmasu kauśalaṁ*. — *SBG*, II.50.
64. *taṁvidyāt duḥkhasaṁyogaviyogaṁ yogasaṁgītaṁ, sa niścayena yoktavya yoganirvinna cetasā*. — *SBG*, vi.23.
65. *yogascittavṛttinirodhaḥ*. — *YS*, 1.2.
66. *saṁyoga yoga ity ukto jivātmaparamātmanor iti*. — *SDS*, XV.

The origin of the yoga is untraceable and lost in antiquity. Yoga postures depicted on seals, stones and statues discovered among the relics of the Indus Valley civilization indicate that it was prevalent in India even before the advent of the Aryans. There are references to the *yoga*s in the Upaniṣads as well.[67] The Buddhists and the Jainas opine that *yoga* was in vogue among the philosophers of the sixth century BC.

Patañjali, the author of the *Yogasūtras* is said to be the same Patañjali who wrote the famous *Mahābhāṣya* on Pāṇini's *Aṣṭādhyāyī*. Vācaspati and Vijñānabhikṣu, the two great commentators on the *Vyāsabhāṣya* (the earliest commentary on Patañjali's *Yogasūtra*) agree in holding that Patañjali was not the founder of the Yoga but an editor. An analytical study of the *sūtra*s also brings the conviction that the *sūtra* does not constitute an original attempt but is a masterly and systematic compilation supplemented by befitting contribution.[68] According to *Yājñavalkya-Smṛti*, Hiraṇyagarbha is the founder of the Yoga system and Mādhava points out that this does not contradict Patañjali's authorship of the *Yogasūtra* since Patañjali calls his work *anuśāsana* where the preposition *anu* implies that his statement follows a primary revelation and is not itself the first formulation of the system.[69]

Now the vexed question of the probable date of the famous Patañjali, the author of the *Yogasūtra* is to be discussed. Weber tries to connect him with Kāpyapātañcala of *Bṛhadāraṇyaka*. In Kātyāyana's *Vārttika*, we get the name Patañjali, which is explained by later commentators as he for whom the hands

---

67. *tṛrunnataṁ sthāpya samaṁ śarīram hṛdindriyānimanasā sanniveśya brahmaḍupena pratareta vidvān śrotānsi sarvāṇibhayāvahāni,*

— *SU*, II.8.

68. *HIP*, vol. I, p. 229.

69. *SDS*, XV.

are folded as a mark of reverence (*patanaḥ ānjalayaḥ yasmai*) but it is difficult to come to any conclusion merely from the similarity of names. There is, however, another theory which identifies the writer of the great commentary on Pāṇini, called the *Mahābhāṣya*, with the Patañjali of the *Yogasūtra*. This theory has been accepted by many Western scholars, probably on the strength of some native commentators who seem to have identified the two Patañjalis. Of these, one is the writer of *Patañjalicarita* (Rāmabhadra Dīkṣita) who could not have flourished earlier then the eighteenth century.[70] The other one is cited in Śivarāma's commentary on Vāsavadattā which Aufrecht assigns to the eighteenth century.[71] The other two are King Bhoja of Dhāra and Cakrapāṇidatta, the commentator of Caraka, who belonged to the eleventh century AD. Cakrapāṇi says that he adores the Ahipati (mythical serpent chief) who removed the defects of mind, speech and body by *Pātañjala Mahābhāṣya* and the revision of Caraka. Bhoja says — "victory be to the luminous words of that illustrious sovereign Raṇaraṅgamalla who, by composing his grammar, by writing his comment on Patañjali and by producing a treatise on medicine called Rājamṛgāṅka has, like the lord of serpents, removed defilement from speech, mind and body." These remarks are, however, based upon an old tradition that Patañjali, the grammarian, was the incarnation of Śeṣa (the mythical serpent) who fell upon the palms of Pāṇini (*Pata* = falling and *añjali* = folded hands). The adoration hymn of Vyāsa, which is considered to be an interpolation even by orthodox scholars, is also based upon the same tradition.

---

70. *pātañjala mahābhāṣya carakapratisaṁskṛtaiḥ manovākkyādoṣānāṁ hantre hipataye namaḥ.* — cf. *YP*, p. 54.

71. Cf. *YP*, p. 54.

Yoga Literature

The *Yogasūtra* of Patañjali is the oldest textbook of the Yoga school. It has four parts, of which the first treats the nature and aim of *samādhi* or meditative absorption (*samādhi pāda*), the second explains the means of attaining this end (*sādhanapāda*), the third gives an account of the supernormal powers that can be attained through the Yoga practices (*vibhūtipāda*) and the fourth sets forth the nature of liberation (*kaivalyapāda*). Vyāsa's commentary on the *Yogasūtra* gives the standard exposition of the yoga principles. Vacaspati wrote a glossary on *Vyāsabhāṣya* called *Tattvavaiśāradī*. Bhoja's *Rājamārttaṇḍa* is a work of considerable value. Vijñānabhikṣu's *Yogavārttika*, a running commentary on *Yogabhāṣya* and *Yogasārasaṁgraha* are useful manuals. Some of the later Upaniṣads such as Maitrī, Śāṇḍilya, Yogatattva, Dhyānabindu, Haṁsa, Varāha and Nādabindu attach great importance to the principles of the Yoga. The other works on the Yoga system such as those of Nāgojī Bhaṭṭa (Nāgeśa Bhaṭṭa), Nārāyaṇabhikṣu and Mahādeva modify Patañjali's views so as to suit their preconceptions.

List of most available works on Yoga systems:

Title	*Author*
Yogasūtra	Patañjali
Vyasabhāṣya (commentary on Yogasūtra)	Vyāsa
Tattvavaiśāradī (commentary on Vyāsabhāṣya)	Vacaspati Miśra
Rājamārttaṇḍa	Bhoja
Yogavārttika (commentary on Vyāsabhāṣya)	Vijñānabhikṣu

The Yoga System

Patañjali is the traditional founder of the Yoga system. The Yoga system of Patañjali should not be confused with magic and Tantra and self-hypnotization. It is a great system of spiritual discipline. The word *yoga* literally means "union," i.e. spiritual union of the individual soul with the universal soul and is used in this sense in the Vedānta. According to Patañjali, Yoga does not mean union but spiritual effort to attain perfection through the control of the body, senses and mind, and through right discrimination between *Puruṣa* and *Prakṛti*.

Yoga is intimately allied to Sāṁkhya. The *Gītā* calls them one. Yoga means spiritual action and Sāṁkhya means knowledge. Sāṁkhya is theory, Yoga is practice. For all practical purposes Sāṁkhya and Yoga may be treated as the theoretical and practical sides of the same system. The metaphysical and epistemological views of both the schools are the same. Yoga accepts the three *pramāṇas* — perception, inference and testimony of Sāṁkhya and also the twenty-five metaphysical principles. Yoga believes in God as the highest self distinct from other selves. Hence, it is sometimes called "*seśvara* Sāṁkhya" or "theistic Sāṁkhya" as distinct from classical Sāṁkhya which is *nirīśvara* or atheistic.

Pātañjala Yoga is also known as Rāja-Yoga. Patañjali defines Yoga as the cessation of the modifications of *citta*.[72] This cessation is through meditation or concentration which is also called *yoga*. *Citta* means the three internal organs of Sāṁkhya — *buddhi* or intellect, *ahaṁkāra* or ego and *manas* or mind. *Citta* is the same as *antaḥkaraṇa*. It is *mahat* or *buddhi* which includes *ahaṁkāra* and *manas*. *Citta* is the first evolute of

72. *yogaścittavṛttinirodha*. — *YS*, 1.2.

Prakṛti and has the predominance of *sattva*. It is itself unconscious but being finest and nearest to *Puruṣa*, it has the power to reflect the *Puruṣa* and, therefore, appears as if it is conscious. When it gets related to any object, it assumes the form of that object. This form is called *vṛtti* or modification. The light of consciousness which comes from the *Puruṣa* and illuminates this "form" is called *jñāna*. *Puruṣa* is essentially pure consciousness and is free from the limitations of *Prakṛti*. But it wrongly identifies itself with its reflection in the *citta* and appears to be undergoing change and modification. *Citta*, therefore, is the physical medium for the manifestation of the spirit. Just as in a red-hot iron ball, formless fire appears spheral and cold iron appears hot, similarly on account of its reflection in the *citta*, *Puruṣa* appears as moving when seen reflected in the moving waves, and waves appear as luminous. Similarly *Puruṣa* appears as undergoing modifications and *citta* appears as conscious due to *Puruṣa*'s reflection in it. When the *Puruṣa* realizes that it is completely isolated and is only a passive spectator, beyond the play of *Prakṛti*, it ceases to identify itself with its reflection in the *citta* with the result that the light is withdrawn and the modifications of the *citta* fall to the ground. This cessation of the modification of the *citta* through meditation is called *yoga*.

The modifications of the *citta* are of five kinds, (1) right cognition (*pramāṇa*), (2) wrong cognition (*viparyaya*), (3) verbal cognition or imagination (*vikalpa*), (4) absence of cognition or sleep (*nidrā*), and (5) memory (*smṛti*). Right cognition is of three kinds: (a) perception (*pratyakṣa*), when the *citta*, through the sense-organs, comes into contract with the external object and assumes its form or comes into contact with the internal mental state; (b) inference (*anumāna*), when the *citta* cognizes the generic nature of things; and (c) verbal testimony (*śabda*) is the mental operation concerning the object derived from the word. *Viparyaya* is positively wrong knowledge like that of a rope snake. *Vikalpa* is mere verbal cognition like that of a hare's horn. *Nidrā* is called absence of cognition, yet it is a mental modification because after sleep a person says, "I slept sound and knew nothing" and, therefore, there must be some mental modification to support this absence of knowledge. *Smṛti* is the recollection of past experience through the impressions left behind.

Puruṣa is eternally pure and transcendental consciousness. It is the *citta* with the reflection of the *Puruṣa* in it or the *Puruṣa* as reflected in the *citta* which is phenomenal ego or *jīva*, which is subject to birth and death, and transmigration and to all painful or pleasurable experiences; and which imagines itself as the agent and the enjoyer. There are five kinds of sufferings (*kleśa*) to which it is subjected. These are: (1) ignorance (*avidyā*), (2) egoism (*asmitā*), (3) attachment (*rāga*), (4) aversion (*dveṣa*), and (5) clinging to life and instinctive fear of death (*abhiniveśa*). The bondage of the self is due to its wrong identification with the mental modification and liberation, and therefore, means the end of this wrong identification through proper discrimination between *Puruṣa* and *Prakṛti* and the consequent cessation of the mental modifications.

There are five levels of mental life (*cittabhūmi*). The differences in the levels are due to the predominance of the different *guṇas*. The lowest level is called *kṣipta* or restless, because the mind here is restless due to the excess of *rajas*. The second is called *mūḍha*. The mind here has the predominance of *tamas* and tends towards ignorance, sleep and lethargy. The third is called *vikṣipta* or distracted. Here *sattva* predominates, but *rajas* also asserts itself at times. The fourth is called *ekāgra* or concentrated. The mind here is entirely dominated by *sattva*, and *rajas* and *tamas* are subdued. The mind becomes concentrated on the object of meditation. The fifth and the highest level is called *niruddha* or restricted. Here the mental modifications are arrested, though their latent impressions remain.

Yoga advocates control over the body, the senses and the mind. According to the Sāṁkhya, the discriminative knowledge that the self is distinct from the body, mind, senses and *buddhi* leads to the realization of the true nature of the self. While the Yoga allows for the Sāṁkhya theory of liberation through discrimination, the main emphasis is on the other means of achieving freedom, the suppression of mental activities. The suppression of mental activities does not mean the state of deep sleep. By Yoga or concentration, the superficial layers are excluded and we get at the inner spirit.

The self remains hidden behind the veils of flesh and restless mind all of which offer hindrances to the method of Yoga. From deep concentration or *samādhi* arises discriminative knowledge that the self is distinct from the *citta*. The hindrances of the flesh and the restless mind can be overcome and the complete suppression of the mental states and processes is achieved by the eight-fold method of Yoga, known as *yogāṅga*, consisting of *yama* (abstention), *niyama* (observance), *āsana* (posture), *prāṇāyāma* (regulation of breath), *pratyāhāra* (withdrawal of senses), *dhāraṇā* (attention), *dhyāna* (meditation), and *samādhi* (concentration).

Yoga accepts the existence of God. Patañjali defines God as a special kind of *Puruṣa* who is always free from pains, actions, effects and impressions.[73] He is eternally free and was never bound nor has any possibility of being bound. He is above the law of *karma*. He is omniscient, omnipresent and

---

73. *kleśakarmavipākāśayair parāmṛṣṭa puruṣaviśeṣa īśvara.* — *YS*, I.24.

omnipotent. But God of Yoga is not the creator, preserver or destroyer of this world. He is only a special *Puruṣa*. He does not reward or punish the soul. Innumerable *Puruṣas* and *Prakṛti*, all eternals and absolutes, are there to limit him. He cannot grant liberation. He can only remove the obstacles in the upward progress of the aspirants. Directly he has nothing to do with bondage and the liberation of the *Puruṣas*. The end of human life is not the union with God, but only the separation of *Puruṣa* from *Prakṛti*.

The Yoga system is founded on the metaphysics of Sāṁkhya and gives us a practical path of purification and self-control in order to realise the true nature of man.

The Important Tenets of the Yoga System

The important tenets of the Yoga system are as follows:

(1) *Padārtha* — twenty-six in number (*citta* etc.).

(2) *Pramāṇas* — three in number (*pratyakṣa, anumāna* and *āgama*).

(3) The modification of *citta* — five in number (*pramāṇa, viparyaya, vikalpa, nidrā* and *smṛti*).

(4) *Kleśa* (sufferings) — five in number (*avidyā, asmitā, rāga, dveṣa* and *aviniveśa*).

(5) *Cittabhūmi* — five levels (*kṣipta, mūḍha, vikṣipta, ekāgra* and *niruddha*).

(6) *Aṣṭāṅga Yoga* — Eight in number (*yama, niyama, āsana, prāṇāyāma, pratyāhāra, dhāraṇā, dhyāna* and *samādhi*).

(7) The theory of *guṇas* — three in number.

(8) The theory of liberation or *mokṣa*.

(9) The existence of God.

The Relation of Sāṁkhya System with Yoga

The Sāṁkhya and Yoga are described as allied systems. The *Mahābhārata* mentions the Sāṁkhya and the Yoga as two eternal system of thoughts.[74] The Yoga adopts the Sāṁkhya metaphysics and engrafts the concept of God upon it. It is called the theistic Sāṁkhya (*sveśvara* Sāṁkhya) while the Sāṁkhya system is called atheistic Sāṁkhya (*nirīśvara* Sāṁkhya). In the early works the Yoga principles appear along with the Sāṁkhya ideas.[75] The Sāṁkhya and the Yoga are so much interrelated in the Sanskrit literature that whenever any occasion arises for explaining or referring to the tenets and doctrines of the Sāṁkhya, those of the Yoga also are not generally overlooked. The Sāṁkhya believes in the reality of twenty-five principles, *prakṛti, mahat, ahaṁkāra, manas*, ten external sense-organs, five *tanmātras*, five gross elements and *Puruṣa*. The Yoga assumes the reality of twenty-five principles and adds the principle of God to them. It recognizes the reality of twenty-six principles. It adopts the Sāṁkhya ontology with slight variations. It agrees with the Sāṁkhya in holding that bondage is due to non-discrimination between the self and *Prakṛti* and that liberation can be achieved only by knowledge and hence both the systems aim at attaining the discriminative knowledge. But it lays stress on the practice of Yoga which is an indispensable means to the realization of absolute freedom. This is the special feature of the Yoga system. The Sāṁkhya lays emphasis upon knowledge which is regarded as the only means for attaining the supreme reality, whereas the Yoga gives its wholehearted support to meditation by which the

---

74. *sāṁkhyañca yogañca sanātane dve.* — *MBh*, xiii.30.

75. Vyāsa's commentary on the *Yogasūtra* is also called *sāṁkhya-pravacanabhāṣya* which brings out the intimate relation between the *Sāṁkhya* and *Yoga.* — cf. *IP*, p. 342.

mind is progressively stilled and thus gradually becomes fit for achieving the supreme stage. The former is specially busy with the theoretical investigation whereas the latter deals with the practical side. Both Sāṁkhya and Yoga admit three *pramāṇas* (sources of valid knowledge) and these are *pratyakṣa, anumāna* and *śabda*.

Both Sāṁkhya and the Yoga trace bondage to illusion (*avidyā*). According to the Sāṁkhya, *avidyā* consists in the non-apprehension of the difference between *Puruṣa* and *Prakṛti*. The Yoga on the other hand, regards the illusion as consisting in mis-apprehensions, i.e. in apprehending *buddhi* as the *Puruṣa*. The Sāṁkhya holds the *sadasat* theory of illusion while the Yoga holds the *anyathākhyāti* theory of illusion.

The Sāṁkhya and the Yoga give a silghtly different account of the evolution of *Prakṛti*. According to Sāṁkhya, *Prakṛti* produces *mahat* which, again, gives rise to *ahaṁkāra*, from *ahaṁkāra* arises the five sense-organs, five motor-organs, the mind and the five *tanmātras*. From the *tanmātras* arise the five *mahābhūtas*. But the Yoga holds that *Prakṛti* produces *mahat*. From *mahat* develops, on the one side *ahaṁkāra* or *asmitā*, the mind, the five sense-organs and the five motor-organs, and on the other the five *tanmātras*, which develop into five *mahābhūtas*. According to the Yoga, there are two parallel lines of evolution of *mahat* into the subjective series consisting of *ahaṁkāras*, mind and the ten external sense-organs and the objective series consisting of the five *tanmātras* and the five *mahābhūtas*.

The Sāṁkhya thinks that the future purposes (*anāgata puruṣārtha*) of the *Puruṣas* move *Prakṛti* to action. There is therefore an unconscious teleology in the activities of *Prakṛti*. But the Yoga holds that God consciously realizes the purposes of the *Puruṣa* in the evolution of *Prakṛti*. There is, therefore, conscious teleology in the evolution. *Puruṣas* do not move *Prakṛti*. God is the prime mover. He consciously adopts the evolution of *Prakṛti* to the purposes of the *Puruṣa*'s experience and liberation.

The two systems of Sāṁkhya and Yoga though differing slightly here and there in minor points are akin in the fundamental principles. Thus in their essential metaphysical foundation both Sāṁkhya and Yoga are the same. The practice of Yoga is essential for the realisation of Sāṁkhya philosophy. Kauṭilya in his *Arthaśāstra* mentions both Sāṁkhya and Yoga and describes them to be the *āṇvikṣikīs*, i.e. the system which try to establish merits and demerits of something by means of reasoning.[76]

Reference of Sāṁkhya and Yoga in the Upaniṣads

SĀṀKHYA IN THE UPANIṢADS

It is impossible to find in the Upaniṣads any real evidence of the Sāṁkhya system. But the presence of Sāṁkhya ideas in germinal form in the Upaniṣads is an undisputed fact. There are, however, elements here and there which mark the growth of ideas which later were thrown into systematic form in the Sāṁkhya. We have in the Upaniṣads scattered hints which were later amalgamated into one system. Just like the Vedānta of Śaṅkara or the Vedānta of Bādarāyaṇa, the Sāṁkhya is a system built on the Upaniṣads. The Sāṁkhya philosophy advocates the existence of dual prinicples of *Puruṣa* and *Prakṛti* and this dualistic tendency is not totally absent in the Upaniṣads. A much more developed account of Sāṁkhya type is to be found in *Śvetāśvatara Upaniṣad*, which is no doubt older than the *Praśna*, but later than the *Kaṭhopaniṣad*. The Upaniṣads

76. *sāṁkhyam yogo lokāyatam cetyānvīkṣakī* — Kauṭilya under *Vidyā-samuddeśa*. — *ASa*.

are definitely deistic; Rudra who bears the epithet but not the name, Śiva, being the object of devotion and belief, but at the same time being regarded as the absolute and supreme spirit, rather than as derived from that spirit. On the other hand, the Upaniṣads contain a series of numbers which are best to be explained as referring to enumerations accepted by the Sāṁkhya school. Thus the individual self is compared to a wheel with three tyres, sixteen ends, fifty spokes, twenty counter-spokes and six sets of eight.[77] These are interpreted as the three *guṇas*, the set of sixteen consisting of the ten organs, mind and the five elements, the fifty psychic states of the classical Sāṁkhya, the ten senses and their objects, and the six sets of the five elements, mind, individuation and intellect; the eight elements of the body, the eight perfections, the eight psychic states which form in the Sāṁkhya an alternative to the fifty, eight gods and eight virtues. But there is other and much more convincing evidence of the existence of Sāṁkhya views. The individual self, the *vijñānātman* or *Puruṣa,* is described as the power of God enveloped in his own *guṇas*, which shows plainly that, while the absolute is still the source of all, nevertheless a new element has been introduced in the conception of the *guṇas* through which the absolute becomes the individual soul.[78]

YOGA IN THE UPANIṢADS

Yoga, however, as a system of thought or discipline, apart from the general metaphysical position which it holds in common with Sāṁkhya cannot be traced before the *Svetāśvatara*

77. *tamekanemim tṛbṛtaṁ ṣoḍaśāntaṁ śatārdhāraṁ viṁśatipratyarābhiḥ aṣṭakai ṣaḍbhiviśvarupaika-pāśaṁ trimārgabhedaṁ dvinimittaikamohaṁ* — *SU*, I.4.

78. *ajāmekāṁ lohitaśuklakṛṣṇāṁ bahvīḥ prajāḥ sṛjamānāṁ sarūpāḥ aja hyeka juṣamāṇo anuśete jahātyenāṁ bhuktabhogāṁ aja anya.* — *SU*, IV.5.

Upaniṣad in a marked way. In the *Praśna Upaniṣad*, it is said that the vital principle (*prāṇa*) derives its existence from the self and that it is from it that the other functions of upward, downward and balancing activities of the body derive their power. In other places we find that the different vital powers all owe their existence and capacity to the main vital priniciple (*prāṇa*) to which they all ultimately return. These dependent vital activities called *apāna, samāna, udāna* and *vyāna* as performing the different motor functions of the body are also spoken of in the same strain in *Bṛhadāraṇyaka* and *Chāndogya*. From this it is clear that in the Upaniṣads the idea of a single vital principle (*prāṇa*) which derives its existence from the self and which superintends the other functions had already gained ground.

Another passage in the *Kaṭha* reminds us of the process of concentration in Yoga by which a man passes from a grosser stage to subtler and subtler stages until he reaches the supreme essence, the *Puruṣa*.[79] In another place of the *Kaṭha*, we find that Yoga is spoken of as restraint of the senses through which the final realization could be achieved. Thus we find that when the five instruments of knowledge stand still together with the mind, and when the intellect does not move, that is called the highest stage. This, the firm holding back of the senses, is what is called Yoga.[80] In the *Maitrāyaṇa*, however, Yoga is described as the method of fixing our thoughts on the object of meditation and most of the characteristics of this science have been mentioned there in this connection.

---

79. *yacchetvāṁmanasī prājñastad yacchetjñānātmani jñānamātmani mahati niyacchetad yacchecānta ātmani.* — *Ku*, I.3.13.

80. *yadā pañcābatisthanthe jñānāni manasā saha buddhiśca na viceṣṭate tāmāhuḥ paramaṁ gatiṁ.* — *Ku* II.3.10.

Thus at the end of this review we find that the Upaniṣads contain in them the germs of Sāṁkhya and Yoga thoughts.

Some Appreciation of Sāṁkhya and Yoga System

1. *tatkāraṇaṁ sāṁkhyayogādhigamyam* — *SU*
2. *nāsti sāṁkhya samaṁ jñānaṁ nahi yogasamaṁ balaṁ*
   — *Mbh,* 316.2
3. *sāṁkhyaṁ yoga lokāyataṁ cety ānvīkṣīki* — *AS*
4. *advaitaṁ sāṁkhyamityāhuryogastatraikacittata* — *GP*
5. *sāṁkhya-yoga parairdhīraiḥ pṛthaktvaikatvadarśibhiḥ abhijātaprabhāvajñāirṣibhi stattvadarṣibhiḥ* — *Vāyu Purāṇa*
6. *dvividhaṁ niḥśreyasaṁ sāṁkhyayogāviti* — *Devalavacanam*
7. *sāṁkhyaṁ yogaṁ samabhyāset puruṣaṁ vā pañcaviṁśakaṁ*
   — *Nirukta*
8. *yat sāṁkhyai prāpyate tad yogairapi gamyate*
   ekaṁ sāṁkhyaṁ ca yogaṁ ca ya paśyati sa paśyati ||
   — *Gītā,* V.5

The Nature of Knowledge

The issues like nature of knowledge, means of acquiring knowledge and criteria to determine truth of knowledge etc. comprise the subject-matter of the epistemological queries that lead to the formulation of a theory of knowledge. Knowledge is the basis of all practical activities. The function of knowledge is to illuminate things other than itself.[81] Knowledge inherently refers to an object that is known and it always belongs to a subject that knows. There can be no knowledge existing independently by itself without implying a knower and a thing known. Knowledge is a self-transcending property of the self.

---

81. *pratītiḥ vāstvāntaraprakāśasvabhāva* — *NR* on *SV, Nirālambanavāda,* 44.

In Indian philosophy different systems have adopted divergent attitudes towards the theory of knowledge. Cārvākas attempt to analyse knowledge and its means in their own way and hold the view that the problem of knowledge is not beyond solution. Knowledge, according to Nyāya, is the manifestation of objects. Knowledge is revelatory of reality (*arthaprakāśa*). Knowledge is the apprehension of objects. Gautama refers to knowledge through the term *buddhi* and states that the term *upalabdhi* and *jñāna* are its synonyms.[82] *Padārtha* is an object of valid knowledge (*pramītiviṣaya*), according to Vaiśeṣika. Kaṇāda enlists *buddhi* amongst the qualities. Praśastapāda adds one more word to the list of synonyms of *buddhi* as stated by Gautama and calls it *pratyaya*.[83] Annambhaṭṭa clearly mentions that *buddhi* is knowledge itself and not an instrument of knowledge.[84] According to the Jainas, the nature of knowledge is self-revealing as well as object-revealing.[85] Regarding the nature of knowledge Advaita Vedāntins hold that knowledge is the very stuff of the self. There is no difference between self and knowledge. The self is knowledge and as such Śaṅkara rejects the distinction between substance and attribute. Substance and its quality are identical in the same way as fire and its heat are identical. Thus there is no difference between self and knowledge. According to the Naiyāyikas knowledge is an accidental quality of the self and there is a complete difference between the self and its knowledge.

According to the Sāṁkhya-Yoga, knowledge is a mode of *buddhi*. According to them *Puruṣa* is immutable and conscious.

---

82. *buddhi upalabdhirjñānamityanarthāntaraṁ* — *NS*, 1.1.5.

83. *buddhirūpalabdhijñānaṁ pratyaya iti paryāyāḥ* — *VP*, p. 136 as quoted in *ITK*, p. 26.

84. *TS*, p. 21.

85. *svaparābhāsi* — *NVV*, I.2 cf. *JTP*, p. 22.

Pain, pleasure, etc. belong to *buddhi*, which is an evolute of *Prakṛti*. Knowledge is a mode of *buddhi* which transforms itself into the shape of the object that it cognizes. Though the *Puruṣa* is inactive due to the indiscrimination and intelligence of *buddhi*, activising of *Puruṣa* takes place and the phenomenon of cognition arises as a result.

It is relevent to make an enquiry as to how knowledge itself is known. According to the Jainas, the Buddhists, Vijñānavādins, the Prabhākara Mimāṁsakas, the Advaita Vedāntins and the Sāṁkhya-Yoga thinkers, knowledge is known by itself. Knowledge is of the nature of light or illumination according to them. Knowledge as the nature of light does not require anything to manifest it.

Knowledge is, by nature, self-revealing (*svayaṁprakāśa*) in the sense that it does not require anything else to reveal it or to know it. According to this view, knowledge is never an object of knowledge, nor known by another knowledge. If knowledge is known as an object, then each individual knowledge may require another knowledge to know it, and so on *ad infinitum* (without limit).

According to *Nyāya-Vaiśeṣika* and Bhāṭṭa Mīmāṁsakas, knowledge is known not by itself but by another knowledge known as *anuvyavasāya*. According to them knowledge is like the eyes which illumine everything but itself remain in curtain; Kumārila Bhaṭṭa admits the independent existence of external object. Every act of knowledge implies a certain relationship between the knower and the known, which involves some activity on the part of the knower. Knowledge reveals the object but cannot reveal itself. According to Kumārila, knowledge is not self-revealing because it is by nature non-perceptible and is known by means of an inference known as *jñātaliṅgakānumāna*.

Vācaspati's view on knowledge is that the self is by nature inactive. All activity belongs to *Prakṛti*. Yet the self due to its proximity is reflected in *buddhi* and through non-discrimination identifies itself with the modes of *buddhi* and thinks itself to be the knower. When an object comes into contact with the sense-organ, it produces certain modifications in the sense-organ. These modifications are analysed by the mind and are presented to *buddhi* which becomes modified or transformed into the form of the object. *Buddhi*, being unconscious in nature, cannot by itself know the object. But as *buddhi* possesses an excess of *sattva* in it, it reflects the consciousness of the self and appears as if conscious. With the reflection of consciousness of the self in *buddhi*, the unconscious modification of *buddhi* into the form of the object becomes illumined into a conscious state of perception. This is called knowledge. Just as a mirror, due to reflection of light in it, appears to have the light within it, in the same manner, *buddhi* due to a natural excess of *sattva* in it, reflects the consciousness of the self or *Puruṣa* and illuminates or cognizes the object.

According to Vijñānabhikṣu, however, when an object comes into contact with the sense-organ the *buddhi* becomes modified into the form of the object. Due to the preponderence of *sattva* in *buddhi*, it reflects the self and appears to be conscious, as a mirror reflects the light and becomes illuminating. Next, *buddhi*, which is modified into the form of the object is reflected back in the self, and the modification becomes manifested. Without this mutual reflection, the apparent experiences of pleasure and pain in the self, which is pure consciousness and free from pleasure and pain, cannot be explained.

In Indian philosophy, divergent views are held regarding the nature of the object conceived through knowledge, viz.

(a) the view of absolute permanence (*kevala nityavāda*), (b) the view of absolute change (*kevala anityavāda*), (c) the view of permanence which yet undergoes transformation (*pariṇāminityavāda*), and (d) the view of both change and permanence (*nitya-anitya ubhayavāda*). The Advaita Vedāntins accept the first view, i.e. the view of absolute permanence, because, according to them, change is mere appearence (*ābhāsamātra*). The Buddhists believe in the second view of absolute change for they are momentarists. The Sāṁkhya and Yoga schools accept the third view since they hold that everything apart from conscious elements is a transformation of a permanent substance. According to the Nyāya-Vaiśeṣikas, certain entities are absolutely permanent and certain others absolutely changing thus contributing to the last view.

Knowledge which is revelation of reality may do its function either in a true manner or in a manner which is false. When reality is revealed valid knowledge is called *pramā* and when this revelation is faulty it is treated as *apramā*. Thus knowledge requires some factors or marks, the presence of which raises it to the status of *pramā*. These factors or marks are variously interpreted by different schools of Indian philosophy as: practical value, novelty, certainty and definiteness. According to Sāṁkhya-Yoga, marks of validity of knowledge are certainty, correspondence to object and novelty. The presence of these factors or marks may be technically called *prāmāṇya*. Here, the question naturally arises as to how these factors or marks arise in a certain piece of knowledge. The first part refers to the conditions of their origin, while the second to that of their ascertainment. If they originate or are ascertained through totality of knowledge producing conditions themselves, *prāmāṇya* or validity is technically called *svataḥ* (intrinsic) and if they originate or are ascertained through some conditions additional to those giving rise to valid knowledge, the validity (*prāmāṇya*) is said to be *parataḥ* (extrinsic) because in this case the validity is caused by some other factor than the conditions giving rise to knowledge. Similarly, the same question arises about the factors leading to invalid knowledge as to whether invalidity originates and is ascertained by the same factors generating knowledge or by others additional to them. The schools of Indian philosophy have put forward divergent opinions on the issue. These are summarized by Mādhavācārya as follows: the Sāṁkhyas hold both validity and invalidity intrinsic to knowledge itself, the Naiyāyikas consider them both extrinsic, the Buddhists hold invalidity intrinsic but validity extrinsic, the Mīmāṁsakas consider validity intrinsic, but invalidity extrinsic.[86] According to Sāṁkhya, validity and invalidity are intrinsic and need no reference to external grounds for their verification. The Sāṁkhyas believe in the theory of causation which is known as *satkāryavāda*, namely, that the effect exists in the material cause even before it is produced. So, they say that validity and invalidity, which are present in all knowledge, are intrinsic and manifested by merits and demerits of the cause, since what is absolutely non-existent cannot consistently be produced. If it is said to be consistent, the result would be that even sky flower could be produced. But a specific effect can be produced only from its specific cause. A cloth can be produced only from threads. From this the conclusion is drawn that the effect exists in the material cause even before its production or appearence. The function of the causal conditions on this account is not without any

86. *pramāṇattvapramāṇattve svataḥ sāṁkhyā samāsṛtaḥ* ।
naiyāyikāste parataḥ saugatāścaramaṁ svaṭaḥ ॥
prathamaṁ parataḥ prāhuḥ prāmāṇyaṁ vedavādinah ।
pramāṇattvaṁ svataḥ prāhuḥ parataścāpramāṇatāṁ ॥ — *SDS*, p. 279.

utility, because that is for the sake of manifestation. Therefore, just like the manifestation of the cloth by the function of the causal conditions, there is only the manifestation of the validity and invalidity by merits and demertits. Hence both the validity and invalidity are intrinsic.[87]

The Buddhists believe that validity is extrinsic but argue that the invalidity is intrinsic.[88] Because according to them any verbalized knowldge is *ipso facto* false, being infected by concepts (*vikalpas*). Here it may be mentioned that, according to the Buddhists, knowledge of an object which arises for the first time alone is valid and all other knowledge regarding the object which arises later on are invalid. The latter is not valid because it apprehends what has already been apprehended.

According to the Naiyāyikas, the validity of empirical knowledge is extrinsic. It has to be verified by inference from conditions, that is to say, from other knowledge. They speak that validity is extrinsic in the case of production and apprehension. If validity requires the causes of the knowledge for its production, there would be validity even in the case of invalid knowledge, since there are causes of the knowledge. If they are not present, the production of the knowledge would be inconsistent. Invalidity does not require the causes of the knowledge, because by the same reasoning already given, the result would be invalid even in the case of valid knowledge. So, the production of validity is due to merits of the sense-organs and the production of invalidity is due to

---

87. *tasmāt kāraka-vyāpārād ghaṭādyabhivyaktivād guṇadoṣābhyāṁ prāmāṇyāprāmāṇyayor abhivyaktir eva ityubhayam api svataḥ*
— *MM*, p. 180.

88. *kiñcaprāmāṇyam apyevaṁ svata, eva prasajyate* ।
na hi svato satas tasya kutaścid api sambhavaḥ ॥ — *TS*, p. (II) 911.

their demerits or defects.[89] Hence, it proves that both are extrinsic in case of production. Similarly in the case of apprehension validity and invalidity are also extrinsic. If the validity or invalidity of knowledge were grasped by the same sources of valid knowledge which grasp the knowledge, the doubt regarding the knowledge which has arisen in us as valid or invalid, would not be removed. The recognition of validity is as follows: this knowledge (which has arisen in us) is valid because it produces a successful activity; what does not produce a successful activity is not valid as in the case of illusion in a mirage. So, the apprehension of validity is only subsequent to successful activity. Thus the inference must be understood in the case of the apprehension of invalidity. Therefore, it is proved that both validity and invalidity are extrinsic in respect of both kinds, namely production and apprehension of knowledge.

According to Mīmāṁsakas, knowledge is intrinsically valid but extrinsically invalid. A definite knowledge as opposed to doubt, produces activity. But the error of knowledge is not due to knowledge itself but due to either the defect of cause or knowledge like "this is not silver." So the erroneous knowledge is due to extrinsic conditions. According to the Prabhākaras, as knowledge naturally illuminates itself and its object as well, validity is grasped by knowledge itself. The Bhāṭṭas argue that knowledge is beyond the cognizance of the senses. Knowness is produced by knowledge perceptible and knowledge is inferred by knowness. Knowledge is grasped by an *anuvyavasāya*, as Murāri Miśra says. However, according

89. *jñānaṁ hi prāmāṇyaprāmānyayoḥ sā dhāraṇyān na svataḥ kiñcid avadhārayituṁ kṣamate, ato guṇavatā doṣavatā ca kāran enotpannau yau jñānasya guṇa-doṣau tadvaśena yathārthatva-rūpam prāmāṇyaṁ ayathārthatva rūpaṁ cāprāmāṇyaṁ nirṇetavyaṁ, ato dvayaṁ api parata iti.* — *NR*, p. 41, cf. *SPR*.

to all of them intrinsic validity belongs to all sources of right knowledge. For example, Kumārila says that for a causal efficacy by itself non-existent cannot be produced by another.[90]

Epistemology of the Sāṁkhya-Yoga school

Epistemology of the Sāṁkhya-Yoga school is a wide subject. Sāṁkhya-Yoga epistemology pre-supposes the epistemology of other systems of thought, viz. Nyāya, Vaiśeṣika and Bauddha etc. Only by a logical analysis of other rival epistemologies the true character of Sāṁkhya-Yoga epistemology can be ascertained. Many problems of importance have not been discussed in the earlier works of the Sāṁkhya-Yoga school. Hence it deserves special consideration.

What is Epistemology

The concept of knowledge has long arrested the attention of thinkers all over the world. Some thinkers hold knowledge to be an act, some others regard it as a relation, according to some it is self-subsistent, and for some others it is a quality. To quote Dr. Jwala Prasad, man finds himself in the possession of certain conviction which, roughly speaking, he calls knowledge. Further he finds that all his convictions are not of the same value and that he has to distinguish them as true and false. The awareness of this distinction naturally leads him to enquire into the origin and validity of all knowledge.[91] Such a study which late Dr. Ward describes as a systematic reflection concerning knowledge and which takes knowledge itself as the object of science is epistemology.[92]

---

90. *svataḥ sarva-pramāṇānāṁ prāmāṇyaṁ iti gamyatāṁ* ।
na hi svato sati śaktiḥ kartuṁ anyena śakyate ॥ — *SV*, p. 45.

91. *HIE*, p. 3.

92. *Ibid.*

The theory of valid knowledge or *pramāṇa* goes by the name of epistemology in philosophy. The term "epistemology" has been derived from *episteme* meaning knowledge and *logos* meaning science or theory. Epistemology, therefore, is the theory or science of knowledge. Epistemology is a science which enquires into the nature, origin, range and conditions of knowledge. It is specially concerned with the conditions of the validity of knowledge.

Epistemology is a term used in English, American and more rarely in French and in some trends of German bourgeois philosophy. The introduction of this term is attributed to the Scottish philosopher J.F. Ferrier (Institute of Metaphysics, 1854) who divided philosophy into ontology and epistemology. The word "epistemology" denotes the theory of valid knowledge, an important province of philosophical theory, the doctrine on man's ability to cognise reality, on the sources, forms and methods of cognition, the truth and the ways of attaining it. To study and generalize the origin and development of knowldege, the transition from non-knowledge to knowledge is dealt in epistemology. Knowledge in general is analysable into ideas — ideas about things of the external world, about men and about one's own self. It is to be noticed that not all ideas are of the same value and validity. Some ideas are true and some others are false. The awareness of such a distinction between true and false knowledge, what is also referred to as valid and invalid, presupposes an enquiry into the origin and validity of all knowledge. The study whose concern is a systematic reflection about knowldge, a reflection which is solely centred around knowledge itself is epistemology.

Place of Epistemology in Philosophy

In the modern age epistemology or the theory of knowledge has acquired special importance in Western philosophy particularly in the philosophies of Kant, Locke and Hume. According to Kant without a prior critical examination of the elements, sources and limits of knowledge, one should not engage in metaphysical discussion. As contrasted with his own critical philosophy Kant regarded all previous philosophy as dogmatic. Earlier, however, the American neo-realists have tried to oppose the general modern trend, initiated by Kant, that the theory of knowledge should precede the theory of reality. They are led to this position by a kind of reaction against the use of epistemology made by most modern idealists for establishing realistic theories of reality.

But in Indian philosophy epistemology is considered as an essential part of philosophy. In the course of the development of the Indian systems interest in epistemology increased and it began to claim a large share in the philosophical discussions of almost every school. From the very beginning of the different systems of philosophy until recent times discussions on the problems of knowledge (including those of doubt and error) have formed an essential part of philosophy. The reason can be found in the fact that all schools of Indian philosophy, without exception, regarded ignorance as the root cause of human suffering, so that they were all bent upon discovering the means and processes of true knowledge by means of which reality could be known and life could be so lived as to overcome misery or minimize suffering. Vātsyāyana commenting upon the first *sūtra* of Gautama, says that the study of the sources of knowledge (*pramāṇa*) is necessary, because through it we can know the reality and thereby guide our actions to attain desirable ends and avoid sufferings.

Epistemology and Ontology or Metaphysics

Epistemology is the theory of knowledge. It means the "science of knowledge." It enquires into the origin, nature, validity and extent of knowledge. It is concerned with the conditions of the validity of knowledge. It cannot enquire into the validity of knowledge without enquiring into the nature of the reality comprehended by knowledge. The nature of the reality is investigated by metaphysics. So, epistemology is closely connected with metaphysics.

What, then, is the relation of epistemology to ontology or metaphysics. Epistemology enquires into the general conditions of the validity of knowledge. Epistemology is the theory of knowing, while ontology is the theory of being or reality. Epistemology is the fundamental basis and ground work of ontology or metaphysics. Ontology must be preceded by epistemology, since we cannot investigate the ultimate nature of the reality without prior criticism of the organ of knowledge. Epistemology, thus, is the fundamental basis and ground work of ontology. As a matter of fact, epistemology and ontology are so intimately related to each other that one cannot stand without the other. The question of the nature and validity of our knowledge and the question of the ultimate nature of what we know are in reality two sides of the same enquiry — two aspects of the same study.

Formerly, without previous enquiry into the possibility of knowledge, philosophers dogmatically assumed an ultimate reality and sought to deduce everything of the universe from it. But this is sheer dogmatism.

Epistemology and Logic

The theory of knowledge goes by the name of "Epistemology." It is an enquiry into the nature, origin, range and conditions of knowledge. It seeks to answer the following questions: what is the nature of knowledge? What is the range, extent or limit of knowledge? What are the conditions of the validity of knowledge? Epistemology enquires into the general conditions of the validity of knowledge. It does not enquire into the details of the various processes of proof. Logic is the special enquiry into the estimation of evidence. Epistemology is a general enquiry into the conditions of valid knowledge. Epistemology is a more general study than logic. It is closely connected with metaphysics. Logic enquires into the various kinds of proof and the conditions of valid knowledge. It investigates the nature and validity of the various kinds of inference, deduction and induction. Logic avoids metaphysical discussion. But reasoning is not fully possible without some metaphysical discussion. Epistemology is more metaphysical than logic. Epistemology thus becomes closely linked up with metaphysics or ontology and both of them again with ethics. Knowledge and moral perfection are regarded as necessary to each other in almost all the systems of Indian thought. Sometimes knowledge is regarded as the means to a good life, while sometimes moral purity is regarded as indispensable for perfect knowledge so that morality and knowledge are regarded as the two inseparable aspects of perfection.

Knowledge is the revelation of the objective world to a subject. The function of knowledge is to convert scattered concepts into a theoretically systematised universal form, retaining in them that which may be preserved, passed on to others and developed successively as a stable basis for human activity. Knowledge is termed as understanding (*buddhi*), apprehension (*upalabdhi*),[93] concepts, judgement, awareness and cognition or cognizance which are synonymous with each

93. *buddhir upalabdhir jñānaṁ pratyaya iti paryāyah.* — *PB*, p. 410.

other. Just as the light of a lamp shows physical things, so knowledge illuminates all the objects that come before it. All knowledge is not necessarily correct. The correct or true knowledge is called *yathārtha* and the false is called *ayathārtha*.

Yathārtha or valid knowledge (i) is a true and definite knowledge of some new fact, (ii) is the apprehension which agrees with the real character of the object apprehended,[94] (iii) is the certain and unerring presentation of the object, and (iv) is the knowledge of an object as endowed with qualities which really exist in the object.[95] When one apprehends a jar with the quality of jarness, one's knowledge is valid.

If any knowledge lacks in definiteness or certitude or does not convey any new information or does not represent things as they really are, it is invalid.

Different schools of Indian philosophy sprang up out of an urge for the enquiry of reality. These schools are busy not only in deducing conclusions but also in determining the methods of arriving at them. Because of this, the Indian epistemology comes to involve four basic factors: the knower, the known object, the instrument of knowledge and valid knowledge constituting the reality:

(i) The *pramātā* — the knower of the valid knowledge

(ii) The *prameya* — the knowable, the object to be known

(iii) The *pramāṇa* — the chief instrument of valid Knowledge

(iv) The *pramā* — the valid knowledge of the object.[96]

---

94. *yatra yadasti tatra tasyānubhavaḥ pramā.* — *TCM*, vol. I, p. 401.

95. *tadvati tatprakārokānubhavo vā.* — *Ibid.*, p. 401.

96. *pramāṇaṁ pramātā prameyaṁ pramitṛti caturvargenaiva vyavahāraḥ parisamāpyate.* — *NVTT*, p. 3.

2

Valid and Invalid Knowledge

ALL the philosophical schools in ancient India sprang up out of an urge for enquiry into the real state of things (*tattvajijñāsā*). Because of such an approach, Indian epistemology involves four basic factors. They are: *pramā* (*pramiti*), *prameya*, *pramāṇa* and *pramātā*.

(i) The *pramā* or *pramiti* — the valid knowledge (of the object).

(ii) The *prameya* — the knowable, the object known, the object of valid knowledge.

(iii) The *pramāṇa* — the chief instrument or organ of knowing the source of valid knowledge.

(iv) *pramātā* — the knower or the cognizer of valid knowledge.

In Indian epistemology, two words are used to mean knowledge. They are *jñāna* and *pramā*. *Jñāna* means all kinds of knowledge, true or false. When reality reveals true knowledge it is called *pramā* or valid knowledge and when this revelation is false it is called *apramā*. The word *pramā* is used only in the sense of true knowledge or *yathārtha-jñāna* which is distinct from false knowledge. In other words, while this word *jñāna* is used to denote knowledge from the psychological standpoint that helps in cognition of an object, the word *pramā* means true knowledge in the logical sense which is able to recognize an object with its real nature and character.

Knowledge in its strict sense means a true belief that carries with it an assurance of its truth.[1] Hence, knowledge is always true. It is a tantology to speak of valid knowledge and a contradiction to speak of non-valid or invalid knowledge. The latter is no knowledge at all, since it does not stand for any belief which is true and which gives us an assurance of its truth. When we speak of *pramā* as valid knowledge, we do not forget the strict sense of the word "knowledge." But the word "knowledge" has been used in a narrow as well as a wide sense. Hence, in view of the fact that they make a distinction between true and false *jñāna* and that *pramā* implies something more than knowledge in its strict sense, we propose to use the phrase valid knowledge for *pramā*.

The term *pramā* is derived from the root *mā* with a prefix *pra* and *tāp* which means valid knowledge. All philosophers attempted in their own way to analyse valid knowledge (*pramā*) and the means of attaining it. Different systems of Indian philosophy have forwarded divergent opinions with regard to the nature of *pramā*.

Definitions of Valid Knowledge

BAUDDHA DEFINITION OF VALID KNOWLEDGE

According to the Bauddhas, the truth of knowledge consists in its practical value. They define *pramā* as the knowledge that is capable of successful volition in revealing an object[2] or as the knowledge which makes us reach the object revealed by

1. Russel, *Problems of Philosophy*, p. 217, of *NTK*, p. 54.
2. *pramāṇamavisaṁvādijñānaṁ; avisaṁvādanaśabdanirukti*, — *PV*, 1.2.

it.[3] Kamalaśīla, however, further clarifies that the valid knowledge refers to a possible successful action, though not to the actual achievement of the object.[4] In all these cases, it is common that the validity of knowledge depends upon the success in the practical activity.

THE NYĀYA VIEW

According to the Naiyāyikas, the validity of knowledge consists in the objectivity or the faithfulness of the knowledge towards the object. The *pramā* is generally defined by the Naiyāyikas as the knowledge which informs the existence of something in a place where it actually exists, or in other words *pramā* is the knowledge which predicates something of a property really possessed by it.[5] It is a definite and an assured (*asaṁdigdha*) cognition of an object, which is also true and presentational in character. Hence, it is *pramā* that excludes all kinds of non-valid knowledge, such as memory, doubt, error, hypothetical argument, etc. Memory is excluded because it is not presentational (*anubhava*). Doubt and the rest are excluded either because they are not true or because they are not definite and assured cognitions. It appears from this that *pramā* has three main characteristics, namely, assuredness, truth and presentativeness.

As to the first characteristic it can be said that *pramā*, or valid knowledge is a definite categorical assertion as distinguished from all indefinite, problematic and hypothetical knowledge. In *pramā*, there is a feeling of assurance or

---

3. *prāpakaṁ jñānaṁ pramāṇaṁ* — *NBT*, p. 4.
4. *avisaṁvādittvaṁ cābhimatārthakriyāsamārthārthaprāpaṇa śaktikattvaṁ* I *na tu prāpaṇmeva pratigandhatisambhavāt* II — *Tsp*, p. 15.
5. *tadvati tatprakārakānubhava yathārtha saiba prametyucyate* — *TS*, p. 34.

conviction in what is known. That is, valid knowledge is always connected with a firm belief. All assurances or firm beliefs, however, are not *pramā*. In illusion we firmly believe in what is false. *Pramā* implies something more than a subjective certainty.

The second characteristic of *pramā* is that it is true or unerring (*yathārtha*) knowledge. Knowledge is true when it is not contradicted by its object (*arthāvyabhicāri*). This means that knowledge is true when it reveals its object with that nature and attribute which abide in it despite all changes of time, place and other conditions.[6] What is once true of an object is always true of it, devoid of space and time. To know a thing truly is to know it as characterized by what is characteristic of it (*tadvati tatprakāraka*). Hence, according to Nyāya, the truth of knowledge consists in its correspondence to facts.

THE VEDĀNTA VIEW

According to the Advaita school of Uttara-Mīmāṁsā, the validity of knowledge consists in non-contradictoriness. The followers of this school define *pramā* as the uncontradicted knowledge of an object.[7] They do not accept novelty as an essential factor for valid knowledge nor do they oppose the view of considering novelty as a mark of valid knowledge. That is why Dharmarājadhvaryu gives two alternative definitions, viz. valid knowledge is that knowledge which apprehends an object that is not already known and which is not contradicted. He defines *pramā* with and without novelty as a mark of *pramā*. Viśiṣṭādvaita School of Uttara-Mīmāṁsā holds that the validity of knowledge consists in both the faithfulness to the object and prompting to the fruitful activity.

---

6. *NVTT*, pp. 5-21.
7. *pramāttvamanadhigatāvādhitaviṣayajñānattvaṁ* — *VP*, p. 19.

The valid knowledge is defined therein as that which apprehends an object as it really exists and which prompts fruitful activity.[8] The Dvaita,[9] the Dvaitādvaita[10] and the Śuddhādvaita,[11] school of Uttara-Mīmāṁsā also accept conformity of knowledge to the object as a mark of valid knowledge.

THE BHĀṬṬA THEORY OF VALID KNOWLEDGE

The Bhāṭṭa Mīmāṁsakas define valid knowledge as the knowledge of an unknown real object.[12] Kumārila defines valid knowledge as: valid knowledge is a firm or assured cognition of objects which does not stand in need of confirmation by other cognitions.[13] According to Umbeka the word *dṛḍha* excludes doubt from valid knowledge and the word *na visaṁvādamṛcchati* (which is not contradicted by other congnitions) excludes error or illusion. Pārthasārathi Miśra defines valid knowledge as the knowledge which represents the real nature of an object which was not attained earlier and which was not contradicted by subdued knowledge.[14] Parthasarathi mentions[15] three distinctive features of valid knowledge, viz. (1) its object is not remembered as having

---

8. *yathāvasthitavyavahārānuguṇaṁ jñānaṁ prameti* — *NP*, p. 36 cf. *UIP*.
9. *yathārthajñānaṁ pramā* — *Pra.P*, p. 9.
10. *yathārthajñānaṁ pramā, tadvati tatprakārakattvaṁ yathāthattvaṁ* — *SKV*, p. 91 cf. *UIP*, p. 8.
11. *niścaya yathārthānuvaba, ayameva prameti vyavahṛyate yāthārthyaṁ cārthānativartittvaṁ* — *Pra. P.*, p. 18 cf. *UIP*.
12. *pramā cājñāta-tattvārtha-jñānaṁ* — *MM*, p. 2.
13. *tasmātdṛḍhaṁ yadutpannaṁ nāpi saṁvādamrcchati,*
jñānāntareṇa vijñānaṁ tat pramānaṁ prattyatāṁ. — *SV*, 2.80.
14. *kāraṇadoṣavādhakajñānarahitamagṛhitagrāhī jñānaṁ pramāṇamiti* — *SD*, p. 123.
15. *NRM*, p. 35.

been previously known, (2) it conforms to the real nature of its object and (3) there is a feeling of conviction regarding its conformity or agreement with the real object. Thus, novelty, non-contradictoriness and truth are the three essential marks of valid knowledge. The Bhāṭṭa like most of other schools admits two kinds of valid knowledge, that is immediate (*aparokṣa*) and mediate (*parokṣa*). Valid knowledge is one which produces some new information about something, not contradicted by any other knowledge and not yielded by defective conditions such as defective sense-organs in the case of perceptual knowledge, fallacious premise in the case of inference, etc. The Bhaṭṭa considers knowledge in its relation to our practical needs. There is no use in knowing what are already known. Knowledge cannot be separated from the practical value it has for us. The objects of our environment are always changing and we have to make fresh adjustment to the changing circumstances and for this purpose knowledge must reveal the changing aspects of things.

THE PRĀBHĀKARA VIEW

According to the Prābhākaras all knowledge is valid. Experience is valid knowledge, and knowledge other than memory is experience.[16] The Prābhākaras say that a knowledge illuminates three things, namely, the object, its knowledge and the self or knower, just as a lamp lights the things around it, itself and its wick. In every knowledge, in other words, threefold (*tripuṭa*) features, namely, the object, the form of knowledge and the knower are experienced. It is called triple perception (*tripuṭi pratyakṣa*). Everywhere in substance, genus and quality there is validity and perceptibility for the elements

---

16. (a) *anubhūti pramāṇaṁ sā smṛterarṇyā......* — *PP*, 5.1, p. 104.
    (b) *smṛti-vyāvṛttaṁ pramātvaṁ*, — *VP*, p. 5.

of self and the form of knowledge.[17] Śālikanātha, a commentator of Prābhākaras, gives the definition of valid knowledge as follows: valid knowledge is experience, and it is something different from memory which is the name of that cognition which arises solely from the impression left by some previous experience.[18] In a continuous perception the later cognitions arising from sense-object intercourse, like the first cognition, are different from memory and hence they are valid. Recognition too is valid, because it is not produced solely from impression. It is an experience aided by impression. Memory is not valid inasmuch as it depends on a former experience. It does not determine an object independently.

THE VAIŚEṢIKA VIEW

The Vaiśeṣikas consider certainty (lack of doubt), non-contradictoriness and definiteness as the marks of valid knowledge. Praśastapāda in his *bhāṣya* on the *Vaiśeṣikasūtra* nowhere defines valid knowledge, but he distinguishes between *vidyā* and *avidyā*, the former includes perception, inference, *ārṣa* and memory, and the latter includes doubt, illusion, indefinite cognition and dream. Śrīdhara commenting on the *bhāṣya* defines *vidyā* as firm, uncontradicted and definite cognition.[19] Thus, the definition introduces definiteness as a mark of valid knowledge. It is clear that *vidyā* is valid knowledge and *avidyā* is invalid knowledge and that memory is valid knowledge. This definition mentions an additional mark of valid knowledge, viz. *adhyabasāya*.

---

17. *sākṣāt-pratītiḥ pratyakṣaṁ meya-mātṛ pramāsu sā* ।
meyeṣvindriya-yogatthā dravya-jātiguṇeṣu sā ॥ — *PP*, 5.4, p. 104.

18. *anubhūtiḥ pramāṇaṁ sā smṛterarṇyā smṛtiḥ punaḥ* ।
pūrvavijñāna-saṁskāramātrajaṁ jñānamucyate ॥ — *PP*, p. 127.

19. *niḥsandigdhāvādhitādhyavasāyātmikā pratitirvidyā tadviparitā cāvidyeti.* — *NK*, p. 414.

THE JAINA VIEW

According to the Jaina logicians definiteness is the essential mark of valid knowledge. Vādidevasūri defines valid means of knowledge as a definite knowledge which reveals itself and the other objects.[20] The characteristics of definiteness here, however, does not differ essentially from the view of the Naiyāyikas because definiteness is further stated by Jaina logicians themselves to be the determination of an object in the form in which it really exists.[21] Siddhasena considers non-contradictoriness in place of definiteness as a mark of *pramā*.[22] The definition of *pramāṇa* offered by Aklaṅka[23] reveals that he considers non-contradictoriness and novelty as the marks of valid knowledge.

THE SĀṀKHYA-YOGA VIEW

In Sāṁkhya-Yoga philosophy the term *pramā* carries different meanings than in other philosophies. *Pramā* in Sāṁkhya-Yoga philosophy is explained briefly with examples in the following way: when an object is viewed by eyes (or conceived by means of other sense-organs) the sense-organs assume the form of the object. The mind reacts due to the changes brought by sense-organs. The mind transmits the form of the object to the *ahaṁkāra* (ego) with the help of the sense-organs. The ego modifies the form of the object in its own way and transmits the same to the intellect. The intellect gets modified, determines the form of the object in its own light and eventually undertakes the process to know the object. An example will clarify the

---

20. *svaparavyavasāyi jñānaṁ pramāṇaṁ*, — *PNT*, 1.2.
21. *vastutathābhāvagrāhakattvaṁ niścayātmakattvena*, — *PKM*, p. 27.
22. *pramāṇaṁ svaparābhāsi vādhāvivarjitaṁ*, — *NVV*, 1.2 cf. *JTP*, p. 22.
23. *pramāṇaṁvisaṁvādi jñānamanadhigatārthā dhigamalakṣaṇattvāt*, — *AS*, p. 175.

topic: say a jar is in view and the eye comes in contact with the jar, as a result of which there are certain *indriyavṛttis* which are presented to the mind. The mind analyses and synthesises those *vṛttis* and presents them to the intellect. Then through the functioning of the mind and the external organs the intellect assumes the form of the jar. Finally the consciousness of the self is reflected on this objectified form of the *buddhi* and the object is immediately revealed. Then one will be able to perceive the jar. According to Vācaspati Miśra, the intellect which is endowed with the qualities of *sattva* gets reflected by *Puruṣa*. According to Sāṁkhya philosophy, *Puruṣa* is immutable and imprudent. When the intellect conceives the reflection of *Puruṣa* and the form of the object is revealed, then this revelation is called *pramā*, and the means which remain unrevealed is called *pramāṇa*.

The Sāṁkhya-Yoga holds that the validity of knowledge consists in certainty (undoubtedness), correspondence to the object and novelty. Vācaspati Miśra defines *pramā* as the *cittavṛtti* (modification of *citta*) which apprehends an object that is undoubted, real and unknown.[24] Thus, all the philosophical thinkers unanimously hold validity or truth as the characterstics of *pramā* but differ in respect of the mark of validity or truth. Prof. D.M. Datta seems to be perfectly right in his observation that "*pramā* is generally defined as a cognition having the twofold characteristics of truth and novelty (*abādhitattva* and *anadhigatattva*) and that as regards the first characteristic i.e., truth, all schools of Indian philosophy are unanimous."[25] The above discussion of the nature of *pramā* futher reveals that according to some schools like the Sāṁkhya-

24. *taccāsandigdhāviparītānadhigataviṣayā cittavṛttiḥ*
— *STK* under *SK.* K. 5.

25. The six ways of knowing, cf. — *ITK*, p. 39.

Yoga and the Pūrva-Mīmāṁsā, novelty also is an essential part of differentia of valid knowledge. Some philosophers like the Vaiśeṣikas and the Jainas do not consider novelty as a mark of valid knowledge since they include remembrance (*smṛti*) into the case of valid knowledge. Some schools like the Advaita are indifferent to the controversy. Dharmarājadhvarindra defines *pramā* in two ways, viz. with and without validity as the mark of valid knowledge. The Mīmāṁsakas and the Sāṁkhya-Yoga have accepted novelty as a mark of *pramā* to exclude remembrance from the domain of valid knowledge. The Jainas accept remembrance among the forms of valid mediate knowledge. The Advaita Vedānta is indifferent to the problem. The Naiyāyikas consider the presentative knowledge (*anubhūti*) as a mark of *pramā* and exclude remembrance (*smṛti*) which is not the presentation of an object but reproduction of previous experience solely caused by the impression (*saṁskāra*) of the past experience.

The recognition of novelty as an essential factor of valid knowledge further enquires about the inclusion of persistent knowledge of the same object (*dhārāvāhika jñāna*) into the valid knowledge, because the persistent knowledge is considered as a form of valid knowledge by all schools of Indian philosophy.

The Sources of Valid Knowledge

When reality reveals true knowledge it is called *pramā* or valid knowledge and when this revelation is false it is called *apramā* or invalid knowledge. When one comes across various convictions regarding an object one feels to verify their validity through various methods which may be roughly termed as *pramāṇa*.[26] The special source of *pramā* or valid knowledge is

26. *kaḥ punarayaṁ nyāya? pramāṇairarthaparīkṣaṇaṁ* — *NBh* under *NS*, 1.1.

called *pramāṇa*. *Pramāṇa* derivatively means the instrument of valid knowledge (*pramāyāḥ karaṇam*). Hence, generally speaking we may say that *pramāṇa* is the means or source of right knowledge. It is that which gives us valid knowledge and only valid knowledge of objects. So it has been said: there cannot be any right understanding of things except by means of *pramāṇa*. A subject arrives at the valid knowledge of objects by means of *pramāṇa*, for the existence and nature of objects are to be ascertained only by such cognitions as are based on *pramāṇa*.[27] Again *pramāṇa* is the cause of valid cognition of objects inasmuch as it gives us a knowledge of objects as they really are and exist in themselves.[28] *Pramāṇa* has a real correspondence with objects in the sense that "the nature and attributes of objects, as revealed by *pramāṇa*, uncontradictorily true of them, despite all variations in time, place and other conditions."[29]

The term *pramāṇa* is derived from the root *mā* with a prefix *pra* and suffix *lyut*. *Pramāṇa* is defined as the *karaṇa* or the extraordinary cause of a *pramā* or right knowledge. Now the question is what is *karaṇa* and how is it constituted? In order to answer the first part of this question we should follow the distinction between *karaṇa* and *kāraṇa*, means and cause. A cause has been defined as the invariable and unconditional antecedent of an effect. Conversely, an effect is the invariable and unconditional consequence. There are three kinds of causes, namely, the constituent (*samavāyī*), the non-constituent (*asamavāyī*) and the efficient (*nimitta*). The constituent cause is the substratum in which the effect inheres, e.g., the threads of the cloth. The non-constituent cause is the mediate cause of

27. *NBh*, 1.1.1, 4.2.29.
28. *Ibid.*
29. *NVTT*, 1.1.1, 4.2.29.

an effect. It determines the effect only insofar as it stands as an inherent attribute of the constituent cause. In relation to the effect, "cloth," the contact of threads is the non-constituent cause. So also the colour of the threads is the mediate cause of the colour of cloth. The efficient cause is different from both the constituent and non-constituent causes. It is not merely the passive substratum in which the effect inheres, nor any inherent attribute of the substratum that indirectly determines the effect. Rather it is the agency that acts on both the constituent and non-constituent causes and makes them produce the effect. In relation to the cloth, the loom and such other agents constitute the efficient cause. It is the efficient cause that is to be regarded as *karaṇa* or means. Now reverting to the definition of *pramāṇa*, it is said that *pramāṇa* is the unique operative cause (*kāraṇa*) of right knowledge.

Though all accept *pramāṇa* as the *karaṇa* or the extraordinary means of *pramā* yet there is difference of opinions about the characterisics of *karaṇa* or *pramāṇa*. Thus, the philosophers have different views regarding the nature of *pramāṇa*.

THE BAUDDHA VIEW OF PRAMĀṆA

It has been generally admitted by all the schools of Indian philosophy that *pramā* is the true knowledge and *pramāṇa* is the source of such knowledge. But there is much difference of opinion among them as to the nature of the truth which each of them claims for its *pramāṇa*. The Buddhists generally take the truth of knowledge to consist in its capacity to produce successful activity. *Pramā* or true knowledge is harmonious in the sense that there is no conflict between the cognition of an object and the practical activity to obtain it. In short, *pramā* is practically useful knowledge and *pramāṇa* is the source of that knowledge.[30] The Buddhists define *pramāṇa* as uncontradicted experience.[31]

THE JAINA VIEW OF PRAMĀṆA

The Jainas also take *pramāṇa* in a general sense so as to make it applicable to both immediate presentational knowledge (*pratyakṣa*) and mediate knowledge (*parokṣa*) so far as they are true. Under mediate knowledge they include sense-perception, inference, memory and recognition. In this general sense *pramāṇa* is knowledge that reveals both itself and its object in a way that is not liable to contradiction. The Jainas define *pramāṇa* as knowledge which reveals itself and its object and which must be determinate.[32]

THE VAIŚEṢIKA VIEW OF PRAMĀṆA

Kaṇāda who occupies the first place in the traceable history of the epistemological tradition states that the general definition of *pramāṇa* should be based on the principle that the cause of cognition should be free from defects.[33] The Vaiśeṣika system defines *pramāṇa* as the unique operative cause (*kāraṇa*) of both true presentational knowledge and memory.[34] It would take memory as a distinct *pramāṇa* or method of knowledge like perception and inference.

THE NYĀYA VIEW OF PRAMĀṆA

According to the Naiyāyikas *pramāṇa* is the unique operative cause (*kāraṇa*) of right knowledge. *Pramāṇa* is the complex of

30. *NBT*, Ch.1.
31. *pramāṇaṁ avisaṁvādijñānaṁ* — *PVT*, 1.3 of *JTP*, p. 22.
32. *svaparavyavasāyijñānaṁ pramāṇaṁ* — *PNT*, 1.2.
33. *aduṣṭaṁ vidyā* — *VS*, 9.2.12.
34. *smṛtyānubhavasādhāraṇaṁ pramākaraṇaṁ pramāṇaṁ* — *TK*, cf. *NTK*, p. 59.

specific conditions, other than the subject and the object, which do not normally fail to produce valid knowledge.[35] The Naiyāyikas explain the term *karaṇa* in the sense that is most conducive to the production of the effect. There is, however, difference of opinion regarding the nature of *karaṇa* between the old and the new Naiyāyikas. According to the old Naiyāyikas the *karaṇa* is a cause which is peculiar and operative.[36]

The modern Naiyāyikas, on the other hand, define *karaṇa* as the cause which is invariably and immediately followed by the product. Thus, *karaṇa*, according to the ancient Naiyāyikas, is the nature of the substance while, according to the modern Naiyāyikas it is the nature of operation (*vyāpāra*) itself. For example, in the case of cutting the wood with an axe, the *karaṇa*, according to the ancient Naiyāyikas, is the axe itself, while according to the modern Naiyāyikas, it is the operation of the axe. Among the Naiyāyikas, Jayanta Bhaṭṭa does not accept the popular view of his school and defines *pramāṇa* as the totality of causal conditions. The *pramā*, according to Jayanta, is the totality of all the sentient and non-sentient factors which lead to the knowledge of an object which is in turn different from illusion.[37]

THE BHĀṬṬA VIEW OF PRAMĀṆA

In the Bhāṭṭa Mīmāṁsā, *pramā* or true knowledge is defined as primary and original knowledge (*anadhigata*). Hence, *pramāṇa* is that which gives us new knowledge, i.e. a true cognition of objects of which we have no knowledge in the

35. Cf. *NM*, p. 15.
36. *vyāpāravadasādhāraṇaṁkāraṇaṁ karaṇaṁ* — *TS*, p. 87.
37. *avyabhicārinīmasandigdhaṁ arthopalabdhi vidadhati bodha bodhasvabhā* — *NM*, 1.12.

past. Every case of knowledge should be original in character. Real knowledge is a synthetic process adding new contents to the old stock of knowledge. *Pramāṇa* is the means of acquiring knowledge and so must lead to the acquistion of such knowledge as is not yet attained but is still to be acquired. The method of knowledge, therefore, must be concerned in knowing what has not been previously known. It follows from this that memory (*smṛti*) cannot be *pramā* or true knowledge, insofar as it is not a new experience. It has no new contents but refers only to the already acquired contents of knowledge.[38] According to the Bhāṭṭas, *pramāṇa* is that which gives us new knowledge, i.e. a true knowledge of the past.[39]

THE PRĀBHĀKARA VIEW OF PRAMĀṆA

The Prābhākara Mīmāṁsakas define *pramā* or valid knowledge as immediate experience (*anubhūti*). It is different from memory which is the impression of past experiences. All immediate experience have intrinsic validity. There cannot be any question as to the validity of immediate experience, because that is self-evident. Memory, however, is mediate knowledge, being conditioned by past experience. Hence, the truth of knowledge (*prāmāṇya*) is guaranteed by its having the character of immediacy.[40] Śālikanātha states that *pramāṇa* is an experience which is different from memory.[41]

THE ADVAITA VIEW OF PRAMĀṆA

The Advaita Vedānta defines *pramāṇa* as the operative cause (*kāraṇa*) of *pramā* or true knowledge. It defines *pramā* in two ways. First *pramā* means knowledge that has both the

38. *yathārthamagṛhītagrāhijñānaṁ pramāṇamiti* — SD, p. 45.
39. *anadhigatārthābhūtārthaniścayātmakaṁ pramāṇaṁ* — SD, p. 123.
40. *pramāṇamanubhūtiḥ sā smṛteranyā* — PP, p. 42.
41. *anubhūtipramāṇaṁ sā smṛteranyā smṛti punaḥ* — PP, p. 127.

characteristics of novelty and uncontradictoriness. This means that true knowledge is uncontradicted and original, i.e. it gives us new information. Secondly, *pramā* is taken to mean simply uncontradicted knowledge of objects. The result is that *pramā* is made to exclude or include memory accordingly as we accept the one or the other way of defining *pramā* or true knowledge.[42]

THE SĀṀKHYA-YOGA VIEW OF PRAMĀṆA

The Sāṁkhya-Yoga concept of *pramāṇa* is different from all these. Patañjali holds that *pramāṇa* is the function of *citta*.[43] Patañjali, however, shows the superiority of yogic practices and consequently the yogic perception acquired through them over the ordinary means of knowledge. He says that the *buddhi* through the discipline of Yoga gets truth-bearing knowledge (*ṛtambharā*) having no trace of wrong or perverted knowledge.[44] This knowledge comprehends the particularity (*viśeṣa*) residing in the *Puruṣa* or in the subtle elements, which is not known through any of the worldly means of knowledge.[45] Īśvarakṛṣṇa does not define *pramāṇa* explicitly in his *Sāṁkhya-kārikā* though he uses the term *pramāṇa*. He defines *buddhi* as ascertainment of an object.[46] Īśvarakṛṣṇa defines perception as ascertainment of an object brought about by sense-object contact.[47] If the two statements are correlated, it can be deduced that *pramāṇa*, according to Īśvarakṛṣṇa is ascertainment of an object which is nothing but a characteristic function of *buddhi* not different

---

42. *VP*, ch. I.
43. *pramāṇaviparyayavikalpanidrāsmṛtayoḥ* — *YS*, I.6.
44. *ṛtambharā tatra prajñā* — *YS*, I.48.
45. *sa viśeṣa bhavati bhūtasūkṣmagata vā puruṣagata vā* — *YB*, I.49.
46. *adhyavasāyo buddhiḥ* — *SK*, K. 23.
47. *prativiṣayādhyavasāya dṛṣṭam* — *SK*, K. 5.

from *buddhi* itself. Nor does Vyāsa explicitly define *pramāṇa*. He, however, remarks that *pramāṇa* apprehends a real object (*bhūtārtha viṣaya*) in opposition to erroneous knowledge which is later on contradicted by the former.[48] The *Yuktidīpikā* states that since the *citta* is one, the *pramāṇa* is also one only.[49] It is through limiting adjuncts that it is said to be threefold.[50] Vācaspati Miśra also accepts the usually accepted meaning of *pramāṇa* as the means of valid knowledge. He defines *pramāṇa* as modification of *buddhi* (*buddhivṛtti*) the object of which is not doubtful, contradictory and the like.[51] Vācaspati further gives an alternate definition of *pramā* as apprehension of *Puruṣa* which forms the results of *pramāṇa*.[52] This corresponds to the statement of Vyāsa regarding the result of *pramāṇa*. The commentators of the *Sāṁkhyatattvakaumudī* have exercised their minds to reconcile the two definitions of *pramāṇa* offered by Vācaspati. Balarāma Udāsīna holds that the earlier definition speaks of Bauddha or *āmukhya* (subordinate) *pramā* and the latter explains the nature of *mukhya* (principal) *pramā*. The first is located in *buddhi* through the instrumentality of sense-object contact while the latter arises in *Puruṣa* through the instrumentality of the operation of *buddhi*.[53] The earlier, states Śivanārāyaṇa Śāstrī, is of the form "This is pot" and the latter is of the form "I know the pot." From this Śivanārāyaṇa Śāstrī further deduces that in the Sāṁkhya system some objects like

48. *bhutārthaviṣayattvāpramāṇasya, tatra pramāṇena vādhanapramānasya dṛṣṭaṁ* — *YB*, 1.8.

49. *tadekameva buddherekattvabhyupagmāt* — *YD*, 4.

50. *upādhivasāttubhinuamāśriyate pratyakṣamanumāṇamityādi* — *YD*, 4.

51. *taccāsandigdhāviparītānadhigataviṣayā cittavṛttiḥ* — *STK* under *SK*, K. 5.

52. *bodhaśca pauruṣeyaphalaṁ pramā* — *STK* under *SK*, K. 5.

53. *evomindriyasannikarṣajanyāṁamukhyāṁ bauddhapramāṇa mākhyāya cittavṛtti phalabhūtāṁ mukhyaṁ pauruṣeyapramamākhyāti*

— *VT* on *STK*, K. 5.

the senses are the means only since they are the means of the *pramā* in the form of the operation of the *buddhi* while the operation of *buddhi* is both the *pramā* and *pramāṇa*. It is the means of the apprehension of *Puruṣa* and is *pramā* in the form of the knowledge of an object. The apprehension of the *Puruṣa* is in the *pramā* only. The *Puruṣa* reflected into *buddhi* is the cogniser only because it is the locus of the *pramā*.[54] The conciousness (*Puruṣa*) conditioned by *buddhivṛtti* is the witness only.

Śrīkṛṣṇa Vallabhācārya adds when both the function of *buddhi* and the apprehention of *Puruṣa* are said to be *pramā*, the *pramāṇa* will be both function of *buddhi* and the function of the sense-organ.[55] *Puruṣa* is never the direct cogniser but it is the witness of *pramā*.

The *Sāṁkhya-sūtra* defines *pramāṇa* as that which is most conducive to the *pramā* which is again defined as the determination of an object which is not previously cognized by either of the two.[56] Vijñānabhikṣu further explains that the expression *asannikṛṣṭa* (not previously cognized) excludes memory, the term *artha* excludes mistake or illusion (*bhrama*) and the term *paricchitti* excludes doubt from the domain of *pramā*.[57] The complete definition comes to mean that the *pramā* is the novel knowledge of a real object. The part of the definition "not cognized by either of the two" is subject to manifold interpretation. Aniruddha interprets it as not

---

54. *viṣayākāradhāriṇā buddhitattvena cetanāśakteḥ cetenasya puruṣasya yaḥ anugraha svopagṛhītānāṁ viṣayānāṁ svaprativiṁbite cetane samarpaṇaṁ tat phalaṁ iti bodha iti pramā* — *ST* on *STK*, 5.

55. *Kir* on *YS*, 1.7.

56. *dvayorekatarasya vāpyasannikṛṣṭārthaparicchittiḥ pramā tat sādhakatamaṁ yat tat trividhaṁ pramāṇaṁ* — *SS*, 1.87.

57. *smṛtivyavartanāyānadhigateti bhramavyavartanāya vastviti saṁsayavyavartanāya tvavadhāranamiti* — *SPB*, 1.87.

cognized either through the presence of the two, viz. the sense and the object, a case of direct means of knowledge or through the presence of one, viz. a word (*śabda*) in the case of inference and verbal testimony.[58] Thus, the *pramāṇa* according to Aniruddha comes to mean the cognition of an uncognized object.[59]

Vijñānabhikṣu defines *pramāṇa* as the *vṛtti* of *buddhi* and the *pramā* as the reflection of the *buddhi* having the form of the object into *Puruṣa*.[60] Vijñānabhikṣu further suggests that *buddhivṛtti* may also be taken as *pramā*. He clarifies thus: when the result of knowledge is considered to be located in the *buddhi*, the *pramāṇa* will be the sense-object contact, etc. and when the result of knowledge is considered to be located in *Puruṣa*, the *pramāṇa* will be the function of *buddhi*.[61] As a matter of fact, *Puruṣa* is the witness of knowledge and not a real cogniser.[62] He also makes it clear that the use of *pramāṇa* with reference to the senses, etc. is always indirect.[63] The statement of Vijñānabhikṣu requires futher clarification: The *karaṇa* can be defined in two ways: (1) the cause which is peculiar and operative, and (2) the cause which is invariable and immediately followed by the product. The former definition applies to the material object as *karaṇa* while the latter definition

58. *dvayoriti indriyārthayorvidyamānayoḥ pratyakṣe, ekatarasya vāpīti vidyamānasya liṅgasya śabdasya vānumāne śabda ca* — *SSV*, 1.87.

59. *etenānavagatārthagantṛ pramāṇamityuktaṁ* — *SSV*, 1.87.

60. ..... *pramānaṁ vṛttireva naḥ, pramārthākāra vṛttināṁ cetane prativimbanaṁ* — *SPB*, 1.87.

61. *yadi pramārūpaṁ phalaṁ puruṣaniṣṭhamātramucyate tadā buddhivṛttireva pramānaṁ, yadi ca buddhiniṣṭhamātra mucyate-tadendriyasannikarṣādireva pramāṇaṁ* — *SPB*, 1.87.

62. *puruṣastu pramāsākṣyeva na pramāteti* — *SPB*, 1.87.

63. *cakṣurādiṣu tu pramāṇavyavahāraḥ paraṁparaiva sarvatheti bhāvaḥ* — *SPB*, 1.87.

implies the intermediate operation as *karaṇa*. Vijñānabhikṣu favours the second meaning of *karaṇa* because the acceptance of first will imply the *buddhi* as a *karaṇa* of *pramā* and it would contradict the earlier authorities like Patañjali and Īśvarakṛṣṇa who consider function of the *buddhi* as *karaṇa* of *pramā*. However, Vijñānabhikṣu favours the theory of considering the operation of *buddhi* as the *pramāṇa* and the *pramā* as located in the *Puruṣa*. He quotes the authority of Vyāsa that *pramā* is the *bodha* located in the *Puruṣa*. He further argues that it is right to consider the knowledge as located in *Puruṣa* because it is held in the Sāṁkhya that the operation of organs is to serve the purpose of *Puruṣa*.[64] He further quotes the authority of Vyāsa that the *Puruṣa* is the *pratisaṁvādi* of *buddhi*, which according to him means that *Puruṣa* is the location of the reflection of the *saṁvedanā* of *buddhi*.[65]

This also holds that Vijñānabhikṣu does not go against the immutable and the all-pervasive nature of the *Puruṣa*. The *Puruṣa* knows the object only through the *buddhi* with which he is associated and knows the object reflected into the *buddhi* which is reflected back into the *Puruṣa*. As such it does not involve the undesirable contingency of knowledge of everything at all times. The *Puruṣa* is unattached and as such it does not undergo modification into the form of the object. The reflection is really a modification of *buddhi* and is reflected into the *Puruṣa* just as the object gets reflected into the water but does not bring about change in it.[66]

---

64. *pātanjalabhāṣye tu vyāsadevai prametyuktaḥ, puruṣārthameva karaṇānāṁ pravṛtta phalasya puruṣaniṣṭhatāyā evaucityāt, ato atrāpi sa eva mukhyasiddāntaḥ* — *SPB*, 1.87.
65. *yogabhāṣyañca buddheḥ pratisaṁvedi puruṣa iti pratidhvanivat pratisaṁveda saṁvedanaprativimba tasyāśraya ityārtha* — *SPB*, 1.87.
66. *pratibimbaśca buddhereva pariṇāmaviśeṣa bimbākāro jalādigata iti mantavyaṁ* — *SPB* 1.87.

On the *pramāṇa* put forward by the Sāṁkhya-Yoga School the criticisms offered by Jayanta Bhaṭṭa and Vādidevasūri, the representatives of the Nyāya and the Jaina systems are taken into account. Jayanta Bhaṭṭa does not find the theory of the Sāṁkhya as convincing. The theory, states Jayanta Bhaṭṭa, implies two substrata of knowledge. The knowledge belongs partly to *Puruṣa* and partly to *buddhi* and completely to neither. The *mahat* which knows the object cannot be aware of it since it is non-sentient and the *Puruṣa* which becomes aware of the object cannot know because being immune to modifications it cannot be modified into the form of the object.[67] Vādideva also states that the agent of awareness does not know and the agent of knowing being insentient in nature cannot be aware of the object. Thus, the knowledge is not located in the *Puruṣa* and awareness of the object which is the result of *pramāṇa* is not found in *buddhi*.[68] Jayanta Bhaṭṭa further states that the theory of the Sāṁkhya involves the impossibility of rise of knowledge. On the same hand Vādideva also states that the Sāṁkhya themselves hold that the exchange of qualities between the *buddhi* and the *Puruṣa* is not actual but apparent.

Reviewing the above criticism we find that the main objection is against the locus of knowledge of Sāṁkhya-Yoga School which involves the problem of the relation of the *Puruṣa* with the *buddhi* and the attempt of the Sāṁkhya to retain the immutable nature of the *Puruṣa* and the modifiable nature of

---

67. *yahi jāmāti buddhyate adhyavasyati na tasya tatphalamartha-darśanamacctanattvānmahataḥ, yasya cārthadarśanam na sa jānāti na buddhyate nādhy avasayatiti bhinnādhikarṣṇattvaṁ pramāṇaphalayoḥ jñānādidharmayogaḥ pramāṇaṁ puṁsi na vidyate tatphalamarthadarśanaṁ buddhausnāsti* — NM, p. 24.

68. *[illegible]pi ca yojānati na tasyārthadarśanaṁ phalamacetanattvānmahataḥ, [illegible]sya vārthadarśanaṁ na sa jānātiti bhinnādhikaraṇattvaṁ [illegible]māṇaphalayo* — *SVR* Quoted in *SYDP*, p. 108.

the *buddhi*. It may be admitted that if the knowledge is related exclusively either to the *buddhi* or the *Puruṣa*, it becomes impossible to supply a proper explanation for the rise of knowledge. The Sāṁkhya, however, considers knowledge as belonging to the *buddhi* only, which, though essentially insentient, acts like a sentient entity with the sentience of the *Puruṣa* reflected upon it. Vijñānabhikṣu, however, goes a step further and holds that the *buddhi* having the reflection of the *Puruṣa* is again reflected back into the *Puruṣa*. In this way, the Sāṁkhya retains the immutable nature of *Puruṣa* and the combined activity of the sentient and the non-sentient entities. Jayanta Bhaṭṭa, of course, derives a wrong implication from the statement of the Sāṁkhyas that the *buddhi* is essentially non-sentient and the *Puruṣa* non-active. It does, however, not mean, as thought by Jayanta Bhaṭṭa, that the *buddhi* can never act like a sentient entity even when it comes in contact with the sentient entity. The mirror can illumine an object with the light of the lamp. An object can perform some activities with the properties of some other object. Vādideva also strains too much while deriving the implication that the Sāṁkhyas themselves have spoken of the untrue nature of *pramā* and *pramāṇa*.

From a closer study of the Sāṁkhya and Yoga epistemology it seems that the so-called valid knowledge is only valid in the limited sphere of existence. From the metaphysical standpoint, the so-called valid knowledge is illusory since transcendental consciousness is devoid of all attributes and changes. The above condition of the contact between the *buddhi* and the *Puruṣa*, according to Sāṁkhya refers to the empirical level of experiences and its denial by the Sāṁkhyas is always from the transcendental point of view. The reality of *pramāṇa* and *pramā* cannot be denied at the empirical level also.

According to the Buddhists, the distinction between *pramā* and *pramāṇa* is only imaginary. The author of *Yuktidīpikā* and Vācaspati Miśra draw a real distinction between *pramā* and *pramāṇa* that is fundamental. *Pramāṇa* is the unconscious mode of the intellect whereas *pramā* is the same mode illuminated. The relation of causality does not hold between *pramā* and *pramāṇa*, but *pramāṇa* is the logical condition of *pramā*. The Buddhists hold that a transient phenomenon of consciousness seizes the form of an object and *pramā* is the same consciousness that reveals the form. Therefore, the distinction between *pramā* and *pramāṇa* is only imaginary from the Buddhist point of view. But from the Sāṁkhya-Yoga point of view such distinction is not tenable since *pramāṇa* requires the grace of transcendental consciousness for its illumination. Thus, we see that the followers of Sāṁkhya and the Yoga School do not follow the footsteps of the Buddhist though they adopt the representative view of empirical consciousness. Thus, Sāṁkhya and Yoga systems offer an original definition of *pramāṇa* as the function of the *buddhi* or the *citta*.

The Number of Pramāṇas According to Different Systems

The schools of ancient Indian philosophy are not unanimous in their choice of the *pramāṇas*. In the matter of recognizing different *pramāṇas*, different schools of Indian philosophy adopted divergent schemes. The number of *pramāṇas* accepted by them vary from one to eight.[69] The Cārvākas accept *pratyakṣa* (perception) only as a single means of knowledge. The Vaiśeṣikas and the Buddhists recognize two — *pratyakṣa*

69. *pratyakṣamekaṁ cārvākā kaṇādaṣugatau punaḥ anumānañca taccātha sāṁkhyā śabdāñcate api nyāyaikadeśinoapyevamupamāṇañca kecanārthāpatyā sahaitāni catyvāryāha prabhākarāḥ, abhāva ṣaṣṭhanyetāni bhāttā vedāntina sthathā samvavatihyayuktāni tāni paurāṇikā jaguḥ* — *TR*, p. 56, cf. *BP*, p. 260.

(perception) and *anumāna* (inference). Sāṁkhya, Yoga, Viśiṣṭādvaita, Dvaita, Śuddhādvaita and Dvaitādvaita Schools of Uttara-Mīmāṁsā recognize *pratyakṣa* (perception), *anumāna* (inference) and *śabda* or *āgama* (verbal testimony) as the three means of knowledge. The Naiyāyikas recognize the above three with an addition, *upamāna* (comparison) as fourth. The Prābhākara School of Pūrva-Mīmāṁsā adds *arthāpatti* (presumption) to it. The Bhāṭṭa School of Pūrva-Mīmāṁsā and the Advaita School of Uttara-Mīmāṁsā recognize the above with the addition of *abhāva* (negation or non-apprehension). The Paurāṇikas admit the above six with the addition of *sambhava* (probability or inclusion) and *aitihya* (tradition or rumour). Some Tāntrikas recognize *ceṣṭā* (indication) also in addition to the above as the source of valid knowledge. Others add *pratibhā* (vivid imagination) as a source of valid knowledge to the list and thus the total number of *pramāṇa*s are ten.

The different *pramāṇa*s in short are as follows:

(1) ***Pratyakṣa* (perception)**: Knowledge which is produced by the contact of a sense-organ with an object. Perception gives a direct knowledge of reality, because by it we directly apprehend the reality, whereas other means give only an indirect knowledge. For example, when a jar directly comes in contact with the sense-organ, i.e. eye, there arises a perceptual knowledge of jar.

(2) ***Anumāna* (inference)**: *Anumāna* means literally measuring after something. *Anumāna* depends on previous experiences. This knowledge follows other knowledge, e.g., where there is smoke there is fire.

(3) ***Śabda* (verbal testimony)**: Knowledge depends on reliable authority and also depends on *ākāṅkṣā*, *yogyatā*

and *āsatti* of a sentence or different sounds arising from musical instruments, bamboos, etc.

(4) ***Upamāna* (comparison)**: The knowledge of similarity is generated by *upamāna*. Knowledge which arises from the presence of some common factors in a thing, which was experienced previously in another thing e.g., a citizen hears the word *gavaya* when he intends to go to a forest for the first time. Then he is instructed by an experienced inhabitant of the forest that a cow is similar to a *gavaya*. On seeing an unfamiliar deer resembling a cow he remembers the instruction of the forest dweller. He then ascertains the meaning of the word *gavaya* that the animal seen is denoted by the word *gavaya*.

(5) ***Arthāpatti* (postulation)**: *Arthāpatti* is the presumption of something for the explanation of a known fact. When one notices apparent contradiction in various forms of knowledge he presumes something to remove the apparent contradiction in it. What is presumed is said to be a distinct source of knowledge, e.g. when a particular person named Caitra known to be alive is not found in his house it is assumed that he must be somewhere outside.

(6) ***Anupalabdhi* (non-apprehension)**: Knowledge by which we immediately cognize the non-existence of an object, e.g. absence of rainfall indicates that the connection of cloud and the wind has not happened.

(7) ***Sambhava* (probability)**: The Paurāṇikas are the propounders of *sambhava* as an independent means of knowledge. If one says that he has a hundred rupees in his pocket, listening this the listeners remark that it

is highly probable that he has ten rupees in his pocket. The Paurāṇikas call this process of knowing as *sambhava*.

(8) ***Aitihya*** (**tradition**): The Paurāṇikas are the propounders of *aitihya* as an independent means of knowledge. "There is a ghost in this tree" is an example provided to explain the nature of *aitihya*.

(9) ***Ceṣṭā*** (**indication**): Some Tāntrikas recognize *ceṣṭā* also in addition to the above as the source of valid knowledge. Thus, by the movement of the hand one can make another understand "to go," or "to come" or by raising a finger or fingers one can make another understand, the numerical number "one," "two," "three," etc.

(10) ***Pratibhā*** (**imagination or intution**): Some thinkers consider *pratibhā* as one of the valid means of knowledge. One who has repeatedly experienced the particular objects as giving rise to pleasure, fear, etc. the knowledge of that object arises merely through the utterence of the word denoting that object even without the presence of that object. This is imagination. For example, when it is stated that a tiger lives here, the action as sweating and trembling body takes place merely through the earlier practice even without the presence of external objects. Again some thinkers consider *pratibhā* as the power of immediate understanding of something without conscious reasoning or study. It is a conviction of certainity that comes quite suddenly and instantly.

Forms of Invalid knowledge

Knowledge is a quality of the self, which inheres in it. It has the nature of manifestation. It manifests an object, physical or mental. The genus of knowledge inheres in it.[70] There are innumerable cognitions apprehending an infinite number of objects. But knowledge is mainly of two kinds, valid knowledge (*vidyā*) and invalid knowledge (*avidyā*). Valid knowledge is what apprehends an object in its real nature. Invalid knowledge is what apprehends an object as different from it.[71] Valid knowledge is a true and definite knowledge of some new facts. If any knowledge lacks definiteness or certitude or does not convey any new information or does not represent things as they really are, it is invalid.

There are some cases of knowledge which are presentational in character but not valid. These constitute the class of *apramā* or non-valid presentation (*ayathārthānubhava*) which includes all cognitions that are either false or not true but not false. Hence, under *apramā* Nyāya includes doubt (*saṁśaya*), with its varieties of conjecture (*ūha*) and indefinite cognition (*anadhyavasāya*) as well as error (*viparyaya*) and hypothetical reasoning.[72]

According to Kumārila there are three kinds of invalid knowledge, viz. error or illusion (*mithyājñāna*), non-cognition or ignorance (*ajñāna*) and doubt (*saṁśaya*).[73]

According to Vaiśeṣika philosophy invalid knowledge is of four kinds: (1) doubt (*saṁśaya*), (2) illusion (*viparyaya*),

---

70. *buddhitvasāmānyavati ātmāśrayaḥ prakāśo buddhiḥ* — *SP*, p. 47.
71. *tattvānubhavaḥ pramā, atattvajñānaṁ apramā* — *SP*, p. 59.
72. *ayathārthānubhavastrividhaḥ saṁśayaviparyayatarkabhedāt* — *TS*.
73. *SV*, 2.54.

(3) indefinite perception (*anadhyavasāya*) and (4) dream (*svapna*).

The Viśiṣṭādvaita theory of error is discussed by many exponents of the Viśiṣṭādvaita school and all of them, in common, hold that all judgements are true.[74] Viśiṣṭādvaita is not a distinct school of philosophy like Nyāya or Sāṁkhya or such other schools. It is only a particular interpretation of the original Vedānta school. The differences that are there among the various sects of the Vedānta are mainly rooted on some religious views regarding life and its destiny. While one sect, for instance, believes in creation to be an essential part of God (Rāmānuja), the other has a firm faith in complete difference between creation and God.

So far as Viśiṣṭādvaita is concerned, here it is not necessary to discuss its specific religious view of life. The main aim is to show how a problem like error is tackled by the Viśiṣṭādvaitin. In Indian philosophy generally the term *jñāna* is used in a wider sense so as to include true as well as false cognition. It is only the term *pramā* which is exclusively used for the judgement. All cases of *apramā*, hence, mean just the reverse. The Viśiṣṭādvaitins' remark "all judgements are true," (*yathārtha sarva vijñānaṁ*) seems to be directly opposite to this general trend of Indian philosophy. In fact, they do not distinguish between *pramā* and *apramā*. But how can the so-called *apramā* be interpreted to be the same as *pramā*? Here the Viśiṣṭādvaitins resort to what is known as the famous doctrine of *pañcīkaraṇa*.[75] This doctrine suggests that there is unity in everything. All things share in all things and contain common characteristics. Everything involves every other thing (*sarvaṁ*

---

74. *yathārtha sarva vijñānaṁ iti veda vidāṁ mataṁ — SaB*, I.1.1.

75. *pañcīkaraṇaprakriyā pṛthvyādi sarvobhūtānāṁ sarvatra vidyāmānatvāt* — *YMD*, p. 12.

sarvātmakaṁ). Things of the same element have structural affinity along with their own distinguishing features. The objects of the physical world, which are all compounds, contain all the five *bhūtas* or gross elements, though in varying proportions. Thus, in the case of the "mirage" what is being looked at is a heated sandy water which contains not only earth which is the preponderant part of it, but also water, however slight, and the apprehension of water there, it is said, is therefore what is actually presented to the eye.[76]

Any discussion of error in the context of Indian philosophy cannot be said as comprehensive unless one takes the Advaita account of error into discussion. In fact, it is Advaita alone which is found to have given maximum importance to the discussion of error for the construction of its own philosophical position. *Māyā*, the popular expression for error, has been so elaborately analysed and discussed in the entire Advaita literature that the whole system is called by many as Māyāvāda.

Māyā, in the usual sense of the term, stands for cosmic illusion. It is very often taken for granted that the Advaita, by the very discussion of error, comes to the conclusion that the whole cosmic existence is *māyā* or illusory in essence. Even the rivals of the Advaitins take this *māyā* to be the central thesis of the Advaita system. As a man, in the actual process of illusion, sees a second moon which does not exist, so also men see a visible world of many objects, which do not exist. The Advaita, as a distinct philosophical tradition, owes its origin mainly to the writings of Śaṅkara. Before him one of course finds the writings of Gauḍapāda, who is also known as the advocate of the Advaita doctrine of non-duality. But

76. *IPS*, p. 58.

the account of error in particular has not been so elaborately discussed by Gauḍapāda as it is found in Śaṅkara's works. In fact Śaṅkara insists that any enquiry into the knowledge of *Brahman* must necessarily be presupposed by a clear analysis of the concept of error, what he calls as *adhyāsa*.

In the Sāṁkhya and Yoga system of thought, apart from *pramā* many other states such as *viparyaya, smṛti, nidrā* and *vikalpa* are mentioned. From a closer study of the Sāṁkhya and Yoga epistemology the so-called valid knowledge is only valid in the limited sphere of existence. From the metaphysical standpoint the so-called valid knowledge is illusory since trascendental consciousness is devoid of all attributes and changes. When the mode of an intellect is revealed by catching the reflection of transcendental consciousness, transcendental illusion takes place. As a result of transcendental illusion the properties of the intellect are attributed to transcendental consciousness, and consciousness is attributed to the mode of the intellect, i.e. experience of an object. This transcendental illusion is unavoidable in all cases of empirical experience. Therefore, empirical experience being based on transcendental illusion is invalid from the metaphysical point of view. In this respect the Sāṁkhya and the Advaita Vedāntins of the Śaṅkara school advocate the one and the same hypothesis.

Illusory knowledge is, in Sanskrit, termed either as *bhrama* or as *viparyaya*. It is undoubted knowledge indeed, which does not agree with the true nature of the object.[77] Error (*bhrama*) is the reverse of valid knowledge. While valid knowledge is the presentation of an object as what it really is (*tattvānubhava*), erroneous knowledge is the cognition of an object as what it really is not (*atattvajñāna*). In error an object is cognized as having certain characteristics that really fall outside of its

77. *avadhāraṇa rūpatattvajñānaṁ viparyayaḥ* — *SP*, p. 72.

being. Hence, it has been described as the wrong apprehension (*mithyopalabdhi*) in which an object is taken for what it is not.[78] The cognitions of a shell as silver, of a rope as a snake, of a post as a man, are all cases of error or wrong cognitions. In each case there is the cognition of an object as other than what it really is. Hence, it may be said that error consists in attributing such characters to an object as are not to be really found in it.[79] Illusion or error represents an object in a form which does not belong to it. It reveals an object differently from what it actually is.[80]

Swāmī Dayānanda, a great philosopher of the nineteenth century, opines that illusion is due to ignorance, which arises because of defects or faults in senses and mental impressions (*saṁskāras*). Further elaborating the notion of true knowldge and ignorance, Swāmī Dayānanda points out that "that which creates awareness of the real nature of substances is true knowledge, while that which does not provide real knowledge of the substance or that which produces the knowledge of some other thing in some thing, is called ignorance."[81] If then ignorance is defined as false knowledge, such an argument amounts to dependent reasoning. Vyāsa declares in his commentary on the Yoga that "knowledge which is contrary to true knowledge, is ignorance."[82] The Vaiśeṣika refers to it as defective knowledge.[83] Śāṁkhya calls it non-discrimination and therefore considers it the cause of bondage.[84] But how

78. *atasminstaditi pratyayaḥ* — *NV*, 1.1.2.
79. *tadabhāvavati tatprakāraka* — *TS*.
80. *anyathāsantamākāramanyathā gṛhṇāti* — *NR* on *SV*, p. 118.
81. *SP*, p. 236.
82. *kintu vidyāviparītaṁ jñānāntaramavidyeti* — *YB* on *YS*, 2.5.
83. *tad duḥsataṁ jñānaṁ* — *VS*, 9-2-11.
84. *tad yoga apyavivekānnasamānatvam* — *SS*, 1-55.

does ignorance arise and what is its nature? Neither of these two questions is satisfactorily answered by such definitions. This question remained unanswered by Śaṅkara's philosophy. The Sāṁkhya philosopher Kapila attempted a solution. He states that "non-discrimination is the nature or innate tendency of internal organ and because of this it becomes conjoined with *Prakṛti* or matter and the other false apprehensions arise because of the companionship with matter."[85]

In the *Yogasūtra*, illusory knowledge is defined thus — *viparyayo mithyājñānamatadrūpa pratiṣṭhaṁ*.[86] Here the most common synonym of *viparyaya* is *bhrama*. The definition *mithyājñānam* which denotes such knowledge does not correspond to the object it reveals. The explanation of *mithyājñānam* has been given by the compound *atadrūpapratiṣṭham*. This compound word denies that the reference of the knowledge to its object is absurd, i.e. it does not refer to the object which should be well presented to consciousness.

The classification of illusory knowledge has been given in a detailed manner in the *Yogasūtra*, *Sāṁkhyakārikā* and *Sāṁkhyasūtra*. The *asmitā* is the first effect of basic illusory knowledge which mistakes the objects other than the soul for the soul and so on. In case of *asmitā* the modes of the intellect which are illumined are represented as identical with the experiencer, i.e. the subject represented in the narrow field of illusory knowledge. The illusory knowledge extends beyond the narrow sphere. We misidentify the soul with *avyakta*, i.e. Primordial Matter, the Intellect, the Empirical Ego and the five subtle elements. It envelopes the true knowledge and

85. *SS*, 1-57.
86. *YS*, I.8.

consequently it acquires an appropriate designation, viz. *tamas* (darkness). As darkness veils all the objects so the illusory knowledge covers the true object, i.e. the soul, and it admits of eightfold division.

Moha follows *tamas* as its corollary. The term *moha* denotes misrepresentation of the properties of the intellect as those of the soul such as a faculty of being very small or being very great and so on. The objects have been stated as ten. The passion for the enjoyment of these objects is called *mahāmoha*. This *mahāmoha* admits of tenfold division. Love is invariably connected with hatred. When one passionately loves an object of enjoyment he is afraid of its hindrance and the enjoyer generally becomes suspicious of molestation by other rivals and cherishes hatred against them. This hatred has been termed as *tāmisra*. This hatred admits of eighteen sub-divisions.

Fear apprehensive of loss of enjoyments has been expressed by the term *andhatāmisra*. The term *kleśa* means such states of mind which afflict the soul. This *kleśa* admits of five broad divisions — *avidyā, asmitā, rāga, dveṣa* and *abhiniveśa*. From a different angle of vision illusion has been treated by the Vedāntins, Naiyāyikas and the Buddhists. According to the Sāṁkhyists illusion has been divided into two broad divisions. It must be either conditional or unconditional. The conditional illusion has been termed as *sopādhika*. When an object is placed in close proximity to a transparent object the property of the object appears to be transferred to the transparent object. The transparent object is coloured by the colour of the adjacent object. This adjacent object which transfers its colour to another object is called *upādhi* — an adjunct. Under this condition illusion takes place. So it is called conditional illusion or *sopādhika bhrama*. Let us take an illustration. A red flower is placed on a spot where a piece of crystal exists. The piece of crystal appears to be red. When the red flower is removed from the spot the crystal gets back its original transparent colour. In order to remove such illusion removal of the adjunct is essential. Simply true knowledge cannot dispel illusion.

Another type of illusion is called *nirupādhika bhrama*, i.e. unconditional illusion. For example, the blue colour of the ocean. If we collect some portion of water in a bottle and pour it on our folded hands, we shall see that the water is not blue. No condition is found to explain it. So it is called as *nirupādhika bhrama*.

From the different point of view illusion may be classified namely *āhārya* and *aupādhika āhārya*. *Āhārya* means a deliberate misinterpretation of a fact in spite of our true knowledge of the fact. When we see a lean and thin person and we say deliberately that he is very strong and stout, it is a case of *āhārya bhrama*. Again if a man knows for certain that the moon is one, but deliberately wishes to see the double vision by pressing the eye ball with the tip of finger, it is an illustration of *sopādhika āhāryabhrama*.

The conditions of illusions have not been thoroughly discussed in the Sāṁkhya and Yoga literature. In the Nyāya and Vedānta literature this topic has been discussed to a great length. Sāṁkhya and Yoga literature do not throw sufficient light on the topic of illusion.

In Indian philosophical literature the typical theories of illusion have been discussed. The technical term they use is known as *khyātivāda*. The term *khyāti* from the philosophical point of view, implies knowledge, the faculty of discriminating objects by appropriate designation.[87] In case of *mithyājñāna* it is the discriminative faculty of knowledge which goes wrong

87. *TPSED*, vol. III, p. 641.

and hence the knowledge becomes false. To put it in a different manner, in all cases of valid knowledge (*pramā*) there is the appropriate discrimination or judging; and in cases of invalid knowledge there is misdiscrimination or misjudging. In this light it can be seen that the different *khyātivāda*s are merely different ways of explaining the discriminative or judging aspect of knowledge.

The classical philosopher, Vimuktātman mentions five theories of error out of which one is known as *asatkhyāti* and the rest are *ātmakhyāti, akhyāti, anyathākhyāti* and *anirvacanīya-khyāti*.[88]

ASATKHYĀTIVĀDA

The Mādhyamika Buddhists hold a mistaken view dubbed *asatkhyāti*, according to which error means judging something non-existent as existent.[89]

Asatkhyāti means that in erroneous perception there is merely the perception of something which is unreal (*asat*). In the shell-silver illusion the silver that is perceived is neither real as something external nor even real as something internal. Therefore, it is absolutely unreal. If the silver would have been externally real then there would not have been any scope for erroneous perception. If the silver would have been merely an internal idea then also there would have been no explanation with regard to its external manifestation. It is, as such, *asat* or *śūnya*.

---

88. *ātmakhyātir asatkhyātiḥsatkhyātiranyathā tathānirvacanīyakhyātir iti etat khyātipañcakaṁ — Vedānta Saṁjñāvali, Saṁjñā,* 170 cf ITE

89. *anye (śūnya vādino bauddhāḥ) asadviṣayaṁ jñānaṁ*
— *NVTT*, p. 72 (1.1.2).

The *Sāṁkhyasūtra* criticizes this view in its aphorism — *nāsataḥ khyānaṁ nṛśṛṅga vat.*[90] An unreal object is never presented to our consciousness. Nobody perceives the sky-flower, the horn of a man and so on. Similarly *rajatābhinna-śuktiḥ* being unreal cannot be experienced. The very premise of *asatkhyātivāda* is baseless.

ĀTMAKHYĀTIVĀDA

Yogācāra, the idealist holds the theory of *ātmakhyāti*. They are not satisfied with the metaphysical position of the Mādhyamika. According to them consciousness cognition or idea is the only metaphysical reality. Yogācāra states that error or illusion is the externalization or objectification of a subjective idea. Yogācāra Buddhists explain that the yields of externalisation of the reports of consciousness (*ālayavijñāna*) are, if properly understood, internal.[91] According to Yogācāra, all knowledge of the external world is erroneous and hence in the error "this is silver" the internal form of knowledge, i.e. consciousness itself is externalized as the silver.

The opponents deny the statement by saying that the knowledge which contradicts such error (*bādhakapratyaya*) can only show that the so-called external object (i.e., silver) is not present there, but it cannot demonstrate that it is all internal consciousness and there is no external consciousness.

ANIRVACANĪYAKHYĀTI

This theory of error is of the Advaita Vedāntins. According to this theory of error an object is presented to our consciousness. It is apprehended by the perceiver whereas another perceiver may perceive it differently. Therefore, the

---

90. *SS*, V.52.

91. *kecit (vijñāna-vādina ātmakhyātiṁ svīkurvāna bauddhāḥ), tu svākāraṁ bāhyatva-viṣayam jñānaṁ viparyayaḥ* — *NVTT*, p. 72 (1.1.2).

reality of the object lies in the presentation only. According to this theory when we mistake a shell for a piece of silver we are actually aware, for as long as our error persists, of a piece of silver which in some sense exists. It is presented but it is not real since the knowledge is false. In the rope-snake illusion the snake must actually be present where it is seen, though it enjoys merely a temporary existence so long as the illusion lasts, and because it can be neither absolutely real nor absolutely unreal, nor both together, it must be indefinable.[92] That which is absolutely real, e.g., the self, can never be sublated and that which is absolutely unreal, e.g., a man's horn, can never be perceived. The illusory snake is perceived for sometime and then sublated by a correcting experience. Therefore, it cannot be absolutely unreal or absolutely real. Hence, the illusory snake is indefinable. This *anirvacanīya* theory is elaborately explained by Maṇḍana Miśra in his *Brahmasiddhi* and henceforth the term later becomes the stock term for an Advaita theory of error. The term is used to indicate that the superimposition cannot be described either as real or unreal.[93]

The *Sāṁkhyasūtrakāra*, its Vṛttikāra Aniruddha Bhaṭṭa and Vijñānabhikṣu, the *bhāṣyakāra*, criticize the theory of Advaitins. According to them all supposition must be based upon facts. No indefinable fact is noticed in the universe. Therefore, the *anirvacanīyavāda* of the Vedāntists is baseless.

SATKHYĀTIVĀDA

Rāmānuja's theory of illusion is known as *satkhyātivāda*. According to him all knowledge are true. Even the object of

---

92. *nānirvacanīyasya tadabhāvāt* — *SS*, V.54.
93. *pratyekaṁ sadasattvābhyām vicāra-padavīm na yat gāhate tad anirvācyam āhur vedānta vedinaḥ* — *Cit*, p. 206.

illusory experience is real. In case of "this is silver," "this" a piece of mother-of-pearl is presented as "silver." The real silver has greater proportion of reality, whereas silver in a piece of mother-of-pearl has a small quantity of silver. This is the implied meaning of *satkhyātivāda*. *Sāṁkhyasūtra* criticizes this theory. According to them such a theory is not tenable. No real object in the universe is contradicted. Aniruddha Bhaṭṭa in his *Sāṁkhyasūtravṛtti* interprets the *sūtra* in a different way. In his opinion *satkhyāti* is another name of *asatkhyātivāda*. According to Prābhākaras there are extra-mental real objects in the Universe. Even illusion refers to such objects. *Akhyāti* means non-apprehension of differences between direct presentation and memory (*smṛti*). The memory of silver and the presentation of mother-of-pearl take place in quick succession. These two different activities of mind are not distinctly revealed because memory of silver always involves a reference to the past experience of an object, namely silver. Here the reference to experience-silver is deleted, so memory-silver does not possess the distinctive feature of memory. These two pieces of knowledge appear to be identical owing to non-discrimination of difference.

Aniruddha Bhaṭṭa criticizes this view. In his opinion the judgement of illusion is invariably contradicted. But if we accept the truth of the hypothesis of *akhyātivāda* such contradiction is not possible. No judgement can invalidate another true experience. *Akhyātivāda* as it stands has no element of illusion in it. Therefore, this hypothesis is contradicted by experience.

Vijñānabhikṣu in his *pravacanabhāṣya* on the *Sāṁkhyasūtra* interprets *satkhyātivāda* differently. He refers to the hypothesis of Rāmānuja. Some other early Vaiṣṇavas also hold a similar view. If the object of illusion is real it cannot be contradicted.

It is admitted by all that an illusory judgement is contradicted. As the basic nature of an illusion is not satisfied by this hypothesis, it is not acceptable.

ANYATHĀKHYĀTIVĀDA

This theory is upheld by the Nyāya and Kumārila Bhaṭṭa agrees with it. Śrīdhara refers to this view of error (*viparyaya*) as *viparītakhyāti*. He opines that misconception can arise even in the absence of any actual substratum, and says that even here something not existing is known as existing. To enunciate this opinion we may say that in illusion when there is an objective substratum, the similarities of things along with defects in the sense-organs cause error. Illusion according to Kumārila is not mere non-apprehension of the distinction between the perceived element and the remembered element, but a positive wrong knowledge due to false identification of the remembered element with the perceived element. Prabhākara regards error as due to omission while Kumārila regards it as one of commission.[94] This Bhāṭṭa theory of illusion is practically the same as the Nyāya theory except that the Bhāṭṭa does not account for illusion through extra-normal sense contact (*alaukika sannikarṣa*). This hypothesis has been accepted by Patañjali in his *Yogasūtra*.

The Sāṁkhyasūtrakāra criticizes this view in his *sūtra* — *nānyathākhyātisvavāco vyaghātāt*.[95] According to him, an object cannot be presented to consciousness as something else. Therefore, the very title of the hypothesis involves self-contradiction. An object is presented to our consciousness along with its peculiar individuality and its common element (universal). But it is never presented to our consciousness as something else.

94. *NR* on *SV*, Nirālambana, 117.

95. *SS*, V.55.

SADASATKHYĀTIVĀDA

Sāṁkhya's theory of illusion is known as *sadasatkhyātivāda*. According to this hypothesis the *sūtrakāra* admits the possibility of contradiction and at the same time advocates the non-contradiction of a real object. According to the *sūtra sadasatkhyātirbādhābādhāt.*[96] When an object is presented to our consciousness it has two elements, namely the subject and the predicate. The subject is called *dharmī* and the predicate is called *vidheya*. Here the relation between the subject and the predicate is not real. Some other relation is ascribed to the subject. "This is silver" is an illusory judgement. "This" is the subject, "silver" is the predicate and "is" is the copula. In case of true perception this copula stands for the relation of identity. "This" means the yonder object. And silver stands for silverness. "Silverness" is related to "this" by the relation of identity. "Is" stands for the relation which connects the subject with the predicate. In this particular instance it is the relation of identity. Identity may be actual or it may be attributed. The attributed relation is contradicted by a subsequent true judgement. The relation is only contradicted but not silverness. Therefore, in the illusory judgement the Sāṁkhyasūtrakāra mentions that contradiction plays some part here. But the sphere of this contradiction is very limited. It is only confined to the small circle of attributed relation. It should be remembered in this connection that silverness is not contradicted, i.e. its reality is not challenged. Silver has truth, i.e. it is a real and true object. When it is not manifested it is called *asat*. The term *asat* does not signify the unreal object. But it only denotes the unmanifest object. After destruction its reality is not contradicted. It simply changes its form and remains hidden in its cause. In *sadasatkhyāti, asat* has not been

---

96. *SS*, V.56.

taken to denote such unmanifest form of an effect. Therefore, contradiction and non-contradiction stand inseparably connected in the *sūtra* quoted above.

According to the Naiyāyikas, a judgement is only contradicted but not the real object. Let us take an example. "This is silver" is a judgement. This judgement is contradicted by a negative judgement namely, this is not silver. The first judgement is contradicted by the second one. Silver which has been used as a predicate in the above judgement is not materially contradicted. The Sāṁkhyists hold that only the attributed relation is contradicted. Similarly in the spiritual world when the "soul" is distinguished from *Prakṛti* it is held that the soul is not matter. The relation of ascribed identity is only contradicted. Matter and material world are not objectively contradicted by the true knowledge of the soul. After the realization of the soul, matter will also exist to evolve intellect and other evolutes gradually in proper order. The Sāṁkhyists draw a distinction between two categories of reality — (i) immutable or unchangeable reality and (ii) changeable reality. *Puruṣa* is unchanging reality and *Prakṛti* is changing reality. The effect is also real though in its unmanifest form and destroyed form it is called *asat*. The term *asat* does not mean that an effect is unreal.

The hypothesis of *sadasatkhyāti* is not of recent origin. Udayana in his *Tātparya-pariśuddhi* refers to this hypothesis. Padmapāda also refers to this hypothesis. He states that the Sāṁkhyists advocate the hypothesis of *saṁsargabhrama*.[97] Vijñānabhikṣu explains the *sūtra* in an exact manner and points out that the essence of *sadasatkhyāti* is constituted by *saṁsargabhrama*.

---

97. *atattve tattvajñānamiti śāstrakāreṇaiva darśitaḥ saṁsargabhramaḥ*
— Pañcapādikā. cf. *IPh*, p. 41.

Memory (Smṛti)

Memory is knowledge of one's own past. It is a representative cognition of past experience due solely to the impressions produced by them.[98] Memory plays an important role in the progressive world. In every walk of life memory is indispensable. Memory owes its existence to impression of the previous experience of an object. Impression is the most active factor which produces memory. Thus, we see memory reveals only the object which is already known but it does never reveal a new object. Now the question is why such faithful representation of an object should not be accepted as a form of valid knowledge. Some logicians accept its validity. The Jainas are the foremost among them. A section of modern logicians also accepts its validity. Those who deny validity to it are the Buddhists, the ancient logicians, the Advaitins, the Sāṁkhyists, the followers of Patañjali, the Naiyāyikas and both the Mīmāṁsā Schools of the Bhāṭṭas and Prābhākaras.

Memory according to the Nyāya and both the Mīmāṁsā schools of the Bhāṭṭas and the Prābhākaras is not valid knowledge because in it the remembered object is not directly presented since it is past but, only represented or recalled by the similarity and hence it is not a means of valid knowledge.[99] On this ground memory does not give us any new knowledge. Praśastapāda observes that memory is a true form of knowledge (*vidyā*) though he does not classify memory as a *pramāṇa*. He classifies memory as one of several varieties of true knowledge. Śrīdhara elucidates that, despite this, memory is not a means of valid knowledge, because it is dependent on perception and inference which initially makes us acquainted

98. *saṁskāramātrajanyaṁ jñānaṁ smṛtiḥ* — *TS*, p. 32.

99. *na pramāṇam smṛtiḥ pūrva pratipatter apekṣanāt, smṛtiḥ punaḥ pūrva saṁskārajaṁ jñānaṁ utpadayati* — *TS. PP*, 5.2, p. 104.

with the objects we can subsequently recall. According to Jayanta Bhaṭṭa memory is not to be counted as valid knowledge because its content is not among its causal factors.[100] The ancient Naiyāyikas also hold that memory is not produced by the object which is revealed by its recollections. We have already found that the Mīmāṁsakas offer a different theory to exclude memory, namely, that since all valid knowledge has as content objects not previously known, and since memory has as its content an object previously known, memory is not valid.[101]

According to Buddhists every object has only momentary existence. When the object is recollected it does not exist. Therefore, an object can never produce its recollection. Gaṅgeśa Upādhyāya argues in a different way. Every form of valid knowledge illuminates an object as present whereas memory invariably involves a reference to the past time. So according to him memory should not be included in the list of the species of valid knowledge.

In the Yoga system many illustrations have been given which involve complicated process of knowlege. Several memories of some parts or events may be combined by imagination in memory. Let us give an example of complicated memory. A person has seen his body including head in a mirror. He has seen a sword and also the act of cutting something. In dream he may produce an image with the combination of these pieces of recollection with the help of imagination. He sees in dream that he beheads himself with a sword. The *bhāṣyakāra* Vyāsadeva of *Yogasūtra* holds that all dream images are memory images. Vācaspati Miśra further

---

100. *tasmād anarthajatvena smṛti — prāmāṇya vāranād......*
— *NM.* (1), p. 21.

101. *ajñātā padenatra jñāta — viṣayayoḥ smṛtyanu vādayor nirāsaḥ*
— *MM*, p. 2.

says that memory does never reveal more than what is experienced though it may reveal less, i.e. omitting some portion it may reveal partial picture of the object.[102] In the *Sāṁkhyasūtra* no new information is given with regard to memory.

Dream

Dream means a vision which one seems to experience during sleep. It is in Sanskrit known as *svapna* which is derived from the root *svap* (to sleep). According to Nyāya dream cognitions are all memory cognitions and untrue in character.[103] They are brought about by the remembrance of objects experienced in the past, by organic disorders and also by imperceptible influence of past desires and actions (*adṛṣṭa*).[104] Dream knowledge, however, is intrinsically false. It is no doubt related to certain objects of the real world. But these objects as cognized in dream are not present to sense. They are either past or remote. Still in dream, objects are actually represented as present. Hence, there is in dream a false cognition of the real when it represents the not-present as the present, the "that" as "this." It may so happen that dreams sometimes turn out to be true and tally with the subsequent experience of waking life. But such correspondence between dream cognitions and waking experience is neither normal nor invariable. Hence, dream can never be called *pramāṇa*. Kumārila explains dream as the reflection of real objects seen before elsewhere. The objects may be seen either in the same life or in the other life. Though the object is not actually present at

---

102. *tadadhika viṣayaparigrahastu sampramoṣaḥ*
— *Tattvavaiśāradī* on *Vyāsa Bhāṣya*, Ch. I, II, p. 36.

103. *svapna tu sarvameva jñānaṁ smaraṇamayathārthaṁ ca* — *TB*, p. 30.

104. *svapnastu anubhūtapadārthasmaraṇaiḥ adṛṣtena dhātudoṣeṇa ca janyate* — *TM*. cf *NTK*.

the time of dreaming still it is something known before and now revived through some impression.[105] According to the Prābhākaras, dream is a distinct type of memory. This type of knowledge cannot arise, unless its object is previously known. But the mutilation of the known part and the knowledge that the object really exists occur only due to the demerit.[106]

The Prābhākaras' idea regarding dream is that true knowledge of memory is sometimes not recognized to be such, and that mutilated memories form the subjects of our dream.[107]

Doubt (Saṁśaya)

Doubt is a knowledge produced by inner sense-organ, mind. Doubt is the cognition of conflicting notions with regard to the same object.[108] It is the mental reference of two or more contradictory properties to the same object. In it mind oscillates between different alternate characterizations of some given object.[109] Doubt has been spoken of as incomplete or indecisive cognition (*anavadhāraṇātmaka*). But doubt is not merely the absence (*abhāva*) of assured cognition (*niścaya*). Doubt as knowledge cannot be called valid, because it is not certain knowledge. Such knowledge is contrasted with knowledge coming out of the ascertainment (*nirṇaya*).

---

105. *svapnādi pratyaye bāhyaṁ sarvathā nahi neṣyate sarvatrālambanaṁ bāhyaṁ deśakālānyathātmakam janmaryekatra bhinne vā tathā kālāntarepivā taddeśo vānyadeśo vā svapna jñānasya gocaraḥ* — *SV*, pp. 173-74.

106. *svapnastu smṛti eva na hyananubhūte sa samudeti* I *dosācca tattā pramoṣaḥ grahaṇākāraśca* II — *TR*, p. 4.

107. *evam svapne 'pi vastūni smaryamāṇāni santyapi anubhūtāṁśamoṣena bhāsante gṛhyamānavat* II *PP*, 3.44, pp. 54-55.

108. *NS*, 1.1.23.

109. *ekasmin dharmiṇī viruddhanānādharmavaiṣiṣṭya jñānaṁ saṁśayaḥ* — *TS*, p. 82.

Doubt is of five kinds. First, it may arise from the perception of such properties as are common to many things, as when we perceive a tall object at a distance and are not sure if it is a man or a post or a tree trunk, because tallness is common to them all. Secondly, it arises from the cognition of any peculiar and unique property, as when the cognition of sound makes us doubt if it is eternal or non-eternal, since it is not found in eternal objects like the soul and the atom nor in non-eternal things like water and earth. Thirdly, it may be due to conflicting testimony, as when the different philosophical theories of the soul leave us in doubt as to the real nature of the soul. Fourthly, it is caused by the irregularity of perception, as when we doubt if the perceived water really exists or not, since there is a perception of water both in a tank and a mirage. Lastly, doubt springs from irregularity of non-perception as when we are not sure if the thing we cannot see now really exists or not, since the existent also is not perceived under certain conditions.[110]

Vikalpa

According to the realists an unreal object is never presented to our consciousness. Nāgārjuna and his followers and some other logicians are of the view that an unreal object is presented to our consciousness. Yoga system combines these two opposite views and shows that an unreal object is communicated to other minds through the medium of words. There are certain verbal expressions which produce some knowledge which does not refer to an object. Let us illustrate the point with the example, "The son of a barren mother," *anutpattidharmāpuruṣaḥ, tiṣṭathi bāṇah* and so on. The son of a barren mother has no objective reference, still it suggests to

110. *NBh*, 1.1.23.

our mind that it is something real. According to Sāṁkhya and Yoga systems transcendental consciousness has neither attribute nor property. Therefore, the adjective *anutpattidharmā* simply suggests that it does not come into being. Thus, these words communicate some meaning having no corresponding object.[111] In this way through *vikalpa* one can communicate the unreal to the minds of the listeners.

Nidrā (Sleep)

The sleeping state of the intellect is not easy to explain. During the state *tamas* plays a prominent role. It subdues *sattva* and *rajo guṇa*s. When *tamas* subdues *sattva* and *rajas* and with their co-operation produces a distinct state of the intellect, it is called *nidrā* or sleep. The Vaiśeṣikas hold that sleep means absence of knowledge. But our experience contradicts such an explanation of sleep. When we awake we remember either of the three states of intellect, namely (i) we slept in the last night enjoying happiness or (ii) we remember that we slept feeling pain during the sleep or (iii) we remember that we slept with a sluggish mind and knew nothing. The cheerfulness of the intellect in the morning is not accidental state of mind. It is due to experience of happiness. According to the fundamental assumption of the Sāṁkhya and Yoga School of Logic, the mode of the intellect is only revealed by transcendental consciousness. Therefore, intellect also assumes the form of the state of the intellect which reigns supreme, during the state of slumber. From this standpoint Vijñānabhikṣu holds that during the state of imperfect slumber a person has experience. But during the state of perfect slumber no knowledge is possible. Because during that state all the states of intellect disappear since the intellect itself becomes merged in its cause. Balarāma Udāsīna, a sub-commentator of *Tattva*

---

111. *śabdajñānānupāti vastuśūnyo vikalpaḥ* — *YS*, ch. I.9.

vaiśāradī of Vācaspati Miśra, adds a very useful comment on the *sūtra* of Patañjali which defines sleep.[112] He first refutes the hypothesis of the Vaiśeṣikas. He, of course, criticizes the view of Udayana who is supposed to be the best exponent of the Vaiśeṣika system of thought. According to him, during the state of sleep soul has no experience at all. He points out defects in the argument of Udayana. Next, he criticizes the hypothesis of Vijñānabhikṣu.

In all the literature of Sāṁkhya-Yoga school, whether the experience of pleasure, pain, etc. during the state of slumber is valid or not is not discussed. During the state of slumber *ahaṁkāra* plays its part but whether *manas* plays a part or not is not discussed.

Tarka (Hypothetical Argument)

Tarka is a type of implicative argument by which we may test the validity of the conclusion of any reasoning (or of any judgement). It is defined as the *prasañjana* of an inadmissible negation from the two negations having equal force on account of their being in the same space and time.[113] For example, absence of smoke (*dhūmābhāva*) in the argument "if there were no fire there would be no smoke"[114] for, in the absence of the cause the effect is not possible.

Tarka is a distinct type of reasoning. It is not based on any perception. It is like this: we see a mass of smoke rising from a distant house and say that the house has caught fire. A friend contradicts this and says that there is no fire. Now we argue: if there is no fire there cannot be smoke. Thus, with regard to

112. *abhāvapratyayālamvanāvṛttirnidrā*, — *YS* ch., I.10.

113. *aniṣṭa-vyāpaka prasañjaṁ tarkaḥ tulyatvenābhā vayoḥ pratyābhāva vacanaṁ prasañjanam* — *SP*, p. 81.

114. *yadyatra vahnyābhāvaḥ syāt tarhyatra dhūmābhāvo 'pisyat* — *Ts.*

the inference of fire from the perception of smoke, there are two alternative positions, namely, that the smoky object is fiery, and that it is not fiery. From the latter position we deduce the proposition that the object is not smoky which is contradicted by our direct experience. This is expressed in the form of a hypothetical proposition, viz. if the object be fireless, it must be smokeless. Since reasoning like this is not to know the fire, but to confirm our previous inference of fire from smoke, it is not valid knowledge. Hence, Vātsyāyana thinks that it does not give us determinate knowledge, but it leads indirectly to valid knowledge. He observes that *tarka* is neither included in any means of valid knowledge nor a distinct one but by knowing the reality it assists the *pramāṇas*.[115] *Tarka* has been defined by the modern Naiyāyikas as the process of deducing from a mark that of which it is a mark, but it is false.[116]

Reinculcation (Saṁvāda)

Reinculcation is repetition of what is previously told. The invalidity of it is not acceptable to Nyāya school and others. But the Mīmāṁsakas do not accept the view. They argue that as the repetition does not possess any distinction from the previous knowledge either in the determination of facts or in empirical usage, it does not deserve the name of valid knowledge.[117]

---

115. *na tvavadhārayati na vyavasyati na niścinoti evam evedam iti* — *NBh*, p. 322 (1.1.40).

tarko na pramāṇa saṁgṛhīto na pramāṇāntaram pramāṇāmanugrāhakas tattva jñānāya kalpate — *NBh*, p. 53. (1.1.1.).

116. *vyāpyāṅgikāreṇa aniṣṭavyāpaka prasañjānarūpaḥ* — *TB*, p. 32.

117. *anuvādānām aprāmāṇyam tārkikādīnām nānumatam vayam tu brūmaḥanuvādo hyartha-pariccheda vyavahāre vā na pūrva jñānat kiñcid viśeṣam ādhatte ato. . . . anuvādo 'pi bahiṣkārya eva iti* — *MM*, p. 2.

3

Perception (Pratyakṣa Pramāṇa)

In Indian epistemology, two words are used to mean knowledge. They are *jñāna* and *pramā*. *Jñāna* means all kinds of knowledge, true or false. When reality reveals true knowledge it is called *pramā* or valid knowledge. Sources of right knowledge or means of cognition[1] are essential for the establishment of a valid knowledge. In this point almost all the thinkers of Indian systems are unanimous. But regarding the number of *pramāṇa*s they are different. Yet it is interesting that all the schools of Indian philosophy both *āstika* and *nāstika* are unanimous about perception or *pratyakṣa pramāṇa* as the first and foremost of all the *pramāṇas*.[2] Perception is the primary and fundamental of all the sources of valid knowledge and it is universally recognized. Perception is most powerful among the means of valid knowledge, because it gives a direct or immediate knowledge of reality of an object and therefore is the root of all other *pramāṇa*s. According to the Nyāya, perception is not the only source of our knowledge, but it is the basis of the other sources or means of knowledge. Hence, it has been said that all the other means of knowledge presupposes perception and must be based on knowledge derived from perception.[3] Perception is the basis on which we

1. *manādhīnā meyasiddhiḥ* — *SDS*, p. 235.
   lakṣaṇapramāṇābhyāṁ hi vastusiddhiḥ — *Ṛg. Bhā*, p. 2.
2. *pratyakṣasya pramāṇeṣu jyeṣṭhatvāditi* — *VP*, p. 6.
3. *sarvapramānānāṁ pratyakṣapūrvakatvāt* — *NVTT*. 1.1.3.

have a knowledge of other truths by inference as well as by comparison and testimony. Perception is the final test of all knowledge. One may question the truth of the knowledge derived from inference, testimony, etc. but the truth of perception is in a way beyond question. Perceptual verification is thus the final test of all other knowledge and as such, perception is the chief of all the sources of human knowledge.[4] It is widely accepted by all the philosophical systems since all the systems have to support their theories through perception in the arena of epistemological investigation. The very simple but correct definition of perception has been given by Śālikanātha Miśra when he says that perception is the direct apprehension.[5]

In European philosophy, the validity of perception as a source of knowledge is rather overstressed by the empiricists and some modern realists. According to them, the truth of perception is unquestionable and self-evident. Thus J.S. Mill remarks: "Whatever is known to us by consciousness (intuition), is known beyond possibility of question. What one sees or feels, whether bodily or mentally, one cannot but be sure that one sees or feels."[6] So also W.T. Mervin thinks that "perception is the ultimate crucial test, and as such, it does not presuppose its own possibility. It simply is; and the man who questions it assumes it in order to do the questioning."[7] Similarly Russell tells us repeatedly that the truths of perception are self-evident truths, for which we require no test at all.[8]

---

4. *sā ceyaṁ pramitiḥ pratyakṣaparā* — *NB*, 1.1.3.
5. *sākṣātpratītiḥ* — *PP*, V. 125.
6. *System of logic*, p. 4, cf. — *NTK*, p. 100.
7. *The New Realism*, pp. 66-67, *ibid.*
8. *Problems of Philosophy*, Ch. XI, p. 72, *ibid.*

The philosophers of Sāṁkhya-Yoga system have stated that perception has been treated as superior to all other forms of valid knowledge and they assign the following reasons — (i) perception as a form of valid knowledge has been accepted by all logicians, and (ii) other valid forms of knowledge presuppose perception whereas perception presupposes none of them.

The term *pratyakṣa* consists of two parts, *prati* and *akṣa*, *prati* means before or near or related to and *akṣa* means eye. The process through which immediate knowledge of an object arises or the instrument by which the object is conceived, is also called *pratyakṣa*. That is why perception is sometimes defined in terms of the process as well as instrument therein. There is differnce of opinion among the different systems of Indian philosophy regarding the definition of *pratyakṣa*.

Different Opinions of Pratyakṣa

CĀRVĀKA VIEW OF PRATYAKṢA

All the schools of Indian philosophy, both *āstika* and *nāstika*, accept *pratyakṣa* (perception) as a source of valid knowledge. Thus Cārvākas hold that perception is the only *pramāṇa* or dependable source of valid knowledge.[9] The perceptual knowledge is so vivid that there arises no question about its validity. External perception and internal perception are the two broad divisions of perception. External perception is that immediate knowledge which arises out of the contact of senses and object. And internal perception is the immediate perception of the mental states like pleasure, pain, etc. The internal perception depends on external perception. Anything beyond the range of perception is not real. The world of our perception is the only reality. Hence, the Cārvākas reject the reality of heaven and hell as they are not objects of our perception.[10]

---

9. *pratyakṣamekaṁ cārvākaḥ* . . . . — *TK*, vide *BP*, p. 260.

10. *na svargo nāpavargo vā naivātmā pāralaukikaḥ* — *SDS*, p. 16.

The Cārvākas do not consider the validity of *anumāna* and *śabda*. The author of the *Mahābhārata* says that the Cārvākas do not treat *anumāna* or inference and *āgama* or authority as *pramāṇas*. He states that both *anumāna* and *āgama* are based on *pratyakṣa* and this is the reason why the Cārvākas do not consider them as the means of valid knowledge.[11] The author of the epic also states that these philosophers do not recognize *anumāna* as *pramāṇa* for another important reason. The reason is that they cannot assert the validity of the *vyāpti* or the invariable concomittance which plays the most significant part in inference.[12] The materialists do not consider this *vyāpti* as infallible. Therefore, the author of the *Mahābhārata* observes that the materialists do not recognize *anumāna* as a *pramāṇa*.[13]

Actually, it is not always possible to attain the correct knowledge of something with *anumāna*. Similar is the case of *upamāna*, etc. But the fact cannot be denied that one cannot totally dispense with *anumāna* in his practical life. Sometimes, it is found that *pratyakṣa* alone does not serve the purpose. The author of the *Nyāyakusumāñjali* observes that if a Cārvākā depends entirely on *pratyakṣa* he will invite his own miseries due to his dogmatic view. According to the author, when Cārvākā will go away to a remote place by leaving his wife and children at home, naturally, he will be unable to perceive them from that place. Thus according to his own standpoint, they will be non-existent to him and hence he will have to lament for their loss.[14] A section of later Cārvākās probably

---

11. *pratyakṣaṁ hyetayor mūlaṁ . . . na kiñcana* — Śāntiparva, *MBh.*, pp. 218-27.

12. *Ibid.*, pp. 218-26.

13. *anumānena yad gatyādidarśanaṁ tadapi asati lakṣaṇe jñāpake hetau .... vyabhicārādarśanāt . . . na kim api* — NC on *MB*.

14. *darśanadaśāyaṁ bhāvaniścayāt . . . śokavikalo vikrośet* — *NKM*, p. 355.

realized this problem. Therefore, Guṇaratna informs that the Cārvākas recognize *anumāna* also as a *pramāṇa* for practical purposes. Guṇaratna says that these philosophers agree to accept such an inference only as is essentially necessary for proving the existence of fire in a hill with the help of a column of smoke. But they do not recognize such extrasensory inference (*alaukika anumāna*) as are commonly accepted by some other philosophers to establish the existence of heaven, *adṛṣṭa* etc.[15] Purandara also says that the Cārvākas recognize *laukika anumāna* or popular inference as a *pramāṇa*.[16]

THE JAINA VIEW OF PRATYAKṢA

From the viewpoint of the Jainas valid knowledge has been treated in two ways, namely, Āgamic tradition and logical tradition. From the Āgamic point of view, determinate knowledge has been divided into five types, namely *mati, śruta, avadhi, manaḥ-paryāya* and *kevala*.[17]

From the viewpoint of logical tradition, valid determinate knowledge has been classified into two: *pratyakṣa* or direct and *parokṣa* or indirect.[18] Bhadrabāhu in his *Āvaśyaka-nirukti*, follows the Āgamic tradition, while *Nyāyāvatāra* of Siddhasena Divākara follows the logical tradition. Umāsvāti in his *Tattvārthādhigamasūtra* has followed both these traditions, and his method has been borrowed by Mādhavācārya in his *Sarvadarśanasaṁgraha*. According to this classification, knowledge has first been divided into five types, namely, *mati*,

---

15. *cārvākair lokayātrānirvāhanapramāṇaṁ dhūmādyanumānamisyate,* etc. — *SSM*, p. 457.

16. *purandarastvāha lokaprasiddhaṁ anumānaṁ cārvākairapisyata eva. . . . kamalaśīla.* — *TS*, p. 526.

17. *moti śrutāvadhi-manaḥparyāya kevalāni jñānam* — *TAS*, 1.9.

18. *tad dvibhedaṁ pratyakṣam parokṣam ca* — *PNT*, 2.1.

śruta, avadhi, manaḥ-paryāya and *kevala*.[19] Then they have been brought under two main heads of *pramāṇas*: *pratyakṣa* or direct and *parokṣa* or indirect. *Mati* and *śruta* have been included in the *parokṣa* class, while the rest are regarded as belonging to the *pratyakṣa* class.[20] Here, *pratyakṣa* means that knowledge which is directly acquired by the self (*akṣa*) without the mediation of the mind or the senses, and *parokṣa* is that knowledge which is acquired by the self through the mediation of the mind and the senses.[21]

The Jaina logicians define perception as clear knowledge. According to Vidhyānandi *pratyakṣa* is the knowledge which is clear. Aklaṅka says *pratyakṣam viṣadam*.[22] Mānikyanandi, Vādideva and Hemacandra also define perception as clear knowledge.[23] Thus according to the Jainas, perception is clear knowledge. Perception is defined as distinct knowledge. Distinctness consists in the apprehension of an object with its specific qualities without the mediation of any other knowledge. *Pratyakṣa* is classified into two: (i) empirical (*saṁvyavahārika*) and transcendental (*pāramārthika*). Empirical perception is uncontradicted perception which prompts successful action in the form of attainment of a desired object or rejection of an undesired object. It depends on sense-organs

---

19. *etac ca dvividhaṁ indriyajam anindriyajam ca dvayamapīdam mati śruta bhedād dvidhā* — *TB*, 1.5.

20. *ādye parakṣaṁ* — *TAS*, 1.11.
pratyakṣaṁ anyāt — *ibid.* 1.12.

21. *akṣnoti vyāpnoti jānāti iti akṣah ātmā* — *SS*, 59.
yat parato vijñānaṁ tat tu parakṣam iti bhanitaṁ artheṣu,
yadi kevalena jñātam bhavati hi jivena pratyakṣam —*PS*, 1.58.

22. *NKC*, 1.3.

23. *viṣadam pratyakṣam,* — *PKM*,
spaṣtam pratyakṣm — *PNT*.

and other conditions. Transcendental perception, on the other hand, does not depend on sense-organs or any condition. Again the empirical perception has two forms: (i) sensuous and (ii) non-sensuous perception. Sensuous perception is due to the external sense-organs stimulated by external objects. Non-sensuous perception is mental perception. It apprehends pleasure, pain, etc. through the mind which is not a sense-organ. Distinct apprehension of an object with its infinite qualities and relations is not possible with sensuous and non-sensuous perception.

BAUDDHA VIEW OF PRATYAKṢA

The Buddhists define perception as the unerring cognition of a given sensum in complete isolation from all ideata.[24] In it the object of cognition is a unique individual and the process of cognition is a mere sensing without any element of ideation (*kalpanā*) in it. Vasubandhu, a Bauddha logician of the Yogācāra School, characterizes perception as a cognition that is directly produced by the object, of which it is the cognition.[25] The cognition of fire, for example, is a perception. Diṅnāga, the greatest Bauddha logician, brings out the implications of Vasubandhu's definition of perception. According to Diṅnāga, *pratyakṣa* is different from imagination and has no connection with names, genus, etc.[26] Dharmakīrti defines *pratyakṣa* as non-erroneous cognition of a given sensum in complete isolation from all constructions (*kalpanā*). He further states that *kalpanā* is a distinct cognition (*pramītiḥ*) of a mental reflex (*pratibhāsa*) which is capable of being united with verbal designation. *Pratyakṣa* is such knowledge as is free from such construction

---

24. *pratyakṣam kalpanāpodhamabhrāntam* — *NB*, I.
25. *tatorthādvijñānam pratyakṣam* — *NV*, 1.1.4.
26. *pratyakṣam kalpanāpoḍham nāmajātyādyasaṁjutam* — *PSa*, Ch. I.

when it is not affected by an illusion produced by colour-blindness, rapid motion, travelling on board a ship and other causes.[27]

THE VIEW OF ADVAITA VEDĀNTA

Śaṅkara refers to three sources of valid knowledge: perception, inference and scriptural testimony. Later writers add comparison, postulation and negation. In the Advaita Vedānta, perception as a *pramāṇa* is the unique cause of perception as a form of valid knowledge. In this sense the sense-organs constitute the *karaṇa* or the unique cause of perceptual cognition. According to Advaita Vedānta perception is the direct consciousness of objects[28] obtained generally through the exercise of the senses. It is the knowledge acquired through the operation of *antaḥkaraṇavṛtti*. In perception the transparent *antaḥkaraṇa* goes out through the sense-organs, pervades the object, say, the pot and assumes the form of that object. This transformation of the internal organ in the form of the object is called *antaḥkaraṇavṛtti*.[29] Perception is the immediate knowledge in which the mental modification is non-different from the object and is lit up by the self's light. When the eye is fixed on a jar the internal organ is supposed to go out towards it, illuminate it by its own light, assume its shape and cognize it. This inner activity is assumed to account for the transformation of the physical vibration into mental states. If one simply stares at the blue sky one cannot perceive anything.

---

27. *abhilāpasaṁsargayopratibhāsam pratītiḥ kalpanā, tayā rahitam timirāśubhramaṇanauyānasaṁkṣobhā dyanāhita bibhramam jñānam pratyakṣam* — *NB*, 1.4.5.

28. *pratyakṣapramāyāḥ karaṇam pratyakṣapramāṇam* — *VP*, p. 15.

29. *tathā taijasam antaḥkaraṇamapi cakṣurādidvārā nirgatyā ghaṭādi viṣayadeśam gatvā ghaṭādiviṣayākaraṇa pariṇamaje sā eva pariṇāmo vṛttirityucyate* — *VP*, p. 33.

The internal organ functions like light, its *vṛtti* moves outwards in the form of ray of light. The *vṛtti* identifies itself with the object, and its identification might spread over the whole surrounding scene. What one perceives depends on the nature of the mode. If the mode takes the form of the weight of the object, one perceives weight, if of colour, one perceives colour. In the case of perception of the jar, the consciousness determined by the jar is found to be unified with that determined by the *vṛtti* of the internal organ falling on that jar, even as the space enclosed within a jar in the room is unified with that enclosed within the room itself. The two limiting conditions of ultimate consciousness, the modification and the object do not produce a difference. This unification makes the cognition of the jar perceptual in character. Perception is distinct from memory, since only past events are recollected. A further qualification is mentioned, that the object and the mental mode must belong to the present time (*vartamānatvam*).

VAIŚEṢIKA VIEW OF PRATYAKṢA

According to Vaiśeṣika valid knowledge is what apprehends an object in its real nature. Invalid knowledge is what apprehends an object as different from it. Four kinds of valid knowledge are admitted according to Vaiśeṣikas which are perception (*pratyakṣa*), inference (*laiṅgika*), remembrance (*smṛti*) and intuitive knowledge (*ārṣajñāna*). Perception enables us to apprehend substances, qualities and actions. Praśastapāda defines perception as the cognition that is dependent on sense-organs.[30] *Pratyakṣa* according to Vaiśeṣika is external or internal. Internal perception is due to conjunction of the self with the internal organ. Cognition, pleasure, pain, desire, aversion and

30. *akṣamakṣampratītyotpādyate iti pratyaksam* — *VB* (Pratya).

volition are apprehended by internal perception. External perception is of five kinds, olfactory, gustatory, visual, cutaneous and auditory. The Vaiśeṣika admits yogic perception, by which the perceptual cognition of the soul (*ātmapratyakṣa*) arises.

THE MĪMĀṀSĀ VIEW OF PRATYAKṢA

Jaimini's aphorism — *sat saṁprayoge puruṣasyendriyānām buddhi janamatat pratyakṣam animittam vidyamānopalambhanāt* — forms the basis of the Mīmāṁsā theory of perception.[31] There are, however, divergent views regarding the interpretation and application of this aphorism. Some commentators such as Śabara hold that the entire aphorism is simply a pointer to establish the fact that *dharma* cannot be known by perception.[32] According to Kumārila Bhaṭṭa, perception is a knowledge which is the result of the right functioning of the sense-organ with reference to their objects.[33] The Prābhākara School of Pūrva-Mīmāṁsā has presented a peculiar theory of perception called the *tripuṭipratyakṣavāda* (the theory of triple perception). Prabhākara has propounded this theory in his *Bṛhati,* which has been again eleborated by Śālikanātha Miśra in his *Ṛjuvimalā* and *Prakaraṇapañcikā.* In the *Amṛtakalā Prakaraṇa* of his *Prakaraṇapañcikā*[34] Śālikanātha has stated that perception is the direct knowledge which pertains to apprehend object (*meya*), the apprehending person (*mātā*) and to the apprehension itself (*miti*). In each act of perception the idea of each of these comes to be its constituent factor. This definition of perception gives

31. *MS,* 1.1.4.

32. *satindriyārthasaṁbandhe yā puruṣasya buddhirjāyate tat pratyaksam* — *SB,* 1.1.4.

33. *SV,* pp. 38-39.

34. *sākṣāt pratītiḥ pratyakṣaṁ meyamātṛpramāsu sā meyeṣvindṛyayogatta dravya jātiguṇeṣu sā* — *PP,*V.125.

us the theory of triple perception and in the *Pramāṇa Parāyaṇa* chapter of the *Prakaraṇapañcikā* also, we have the reference to this peculiar theory.[35]

THE SĀṀKHYA-YOGA VIEW OF PRATYAKṢA

The Sāṁkhya system consists of three different traditions in defining perception, viz. (i) the one initiated in the *Sāṁkhyasūtra* probably by Kapila himself, (ii) the one propounded by Vindhyavāsin and (iii) the one proposed by Īśvarakṛṣṇa. The *Sāṁkhyasūtra* defines perception as that discernment which being in conjunction of an object portrays the form thereof.[36] A popular definition of perception as the "operation of cognitive organs, ear and the rest" is ascribed to the followers of Vārṣagaṇya.[37] Pulinbihari Chakraborty thinks that Vindhyavāsin revised the definition given by Vārṣagaṇya by embodying the epithet *avikalpikā*.[38]

As regards the classical sources of Sāṁkhya-Yoga, Patañjali does not define perception. Hence, the *Sāṁkhyakārikā* of Īśvarakṛṣṇa is the earliest classical source about the definition of perception. In the *Sāṁkhyakārikā* the term *dṛṣṭa* has been used instead of *pratyakṣa*. None of the commentators of the *Sāṁkhyakārikā* explain why the author of the *Sāṁkhyakārikā* used the term *dṛṣṭa* instead of the term *pratyakṣa*. But the term *dṛṣṭa* is very significant. All cases of immediate experience are not due to sense-object contact. The experiences namely "I am happy," "I am sorry" etc. do not require the help of sense-organs and *manas*. Thus the term *pratyakṣa* is not applicable in

35. *sarvavijñānahetuttha mitau ca pramā sākṣātkartittvasāmānyāt pratyakṣatyenasammatā* — *PP*, V.137.

36. *yatsambandhasiddhaṁ tadākārollekhi vijñānaṁ tat pratyakṣam* —*SS*, 1.89.

37. *śrotrādivṛttiḥ pratyakṣam* — *YD*, 5.

38. *ODSST*, p. 137.

these cases because though the experience is immediate, it is not sensuous. In order to cover such cases, the term *dṛṣṭa* is only appropriate. Unfortunately, the author of the *Sāṁkhyasūtra* does not take notice of the inner significance of the term *dṛṣṭa* used by Īśvarakṛṣṇa. The term *pratyakṣa* used in the *Sāṁkhyasūtra* denotes only a small portion of immediate experience. The experience of inner phenomena remains outside the range of the definition of *pratyakṣa.*

The Sāṁkhyakārikā of Īśvarakṛṣṇa gives the definition of *dṛṣṭa* in the following way — perception is a determinate knowledge in respect of every individual object.[39] The definition when interpreted independently of the commentaries of the *Sāṁkhyakārikā* reveals that there is no reference to sense-object contact. Further Īśvarakṛṣṇa unlike Vārṣagaṇya defines perception in terms of knowledge. This knowledge is qualified by "pertaining to individual object." Such a definition also is unique in the arena of Indian philosophy. Knowledge of all kinds, according to Īśvarakṛṣṇa, is the function or attribute of *buddhi.*[40] *Buddhi* is taken in the sense of both — actual agent of knowing and means of knowledge.[41] Thus the question naturally arises as to what is the factor which differentiates perception from sources of non-valid knowledge accepted by Sāṁkhya. The expression "determinate knowledge" differentiates it from doubtful knowledge, the word *object* from already perceived knowledge and the word *prati* from memory etc.[42]

---

39. *prativiṣayādhyavasāyo dṛṣṭam* — *SK*, 5.

40. *adhyavasāyo buddhi dharma jñānam virāga aiśaryam sāttvikametad rūpaṁ tāmasamasmāt viparyastam* — *SK*, K. 23.

41. *sa adhyavasāyo buddherasādhāraṇa vyāpāro, tadvedā buddhiḥ* — STK, K. 23.

42. *STK*, 5.

There is a set of scholars who do not interpret *prativiṣaya* as cognitive organ. However, they introduce sense-object contact through importation. Māṭhara[43] followed by Gauḍapāda[44] interpret one definition offered by the *Sāṁkhyakārikā* as perception is the knowledge with reference to particular object. Here Māṭhara seems to define perception in terms of indeterminate perception as determinative knowledge cannot arise in cognitive organ. Thus Māṭhara and Gauḍapāda import *indriyānaṁ* in the above definition given by the *Sāṁkhyakārikā.* The Jayamaṅgalā, however, imports *indriyadvāreṇa* and explains the above definition as perception is the knowledge of the objects like word, etc. through cognitive organs like ear,[45] etc.

Interpreting the definition of Īśvarakr̥ṣṇa, Vācaspati states that perception is a modification of the mind which gives definite cognition of objects affected by the sense-object-contact. In his opinion, through intellect (*buddhi*), ego (*ahaṁkāra*), mind (*manas*) and the senses, external object is apprehended by the subject. When an object incites the senses the *manas* arranges the sense impression into a percept, the ego refers it to the self and the intellect forms the concept. The author of *Yuktidīpikā* elucidates Īśvarakr̥ṣṇa's definition and holds that the term *viṣaya* refers to the objects of cognition, the word *prati* in the definition stands for proximity and the word *adhyavasāya* implies the function of the intellect. The author of the *Yuktidīpikā* splits up *prativiṣayādhyavasāya* into two component parts — the first *prativiṣayādhyavasāya* covers the perception of external objects and the second *prativiṣayādhyavasāya* covers the immediate experience of the

43. *MV*, 5.

44. *GB*, 5.

45. JM, 5.

inner phenomena. He holds that it is a case of *ekaśeṣa,* i.e. one component factor which is similar to the next one is dropped according to the rule of grammar.[46] Though one word is dropped, its meaning is conveyed by the remaining component. It denotes its own meaning as well as that of the other (the dropped one). Regarding the number of the word, the author of the *Yuktidīpikā* does not explain why singular number has been used instead of the dual one. The *Yuktidīpikā* further shows the significance of the word *prativiṣaya* in the definition. The word *adhyavasāya* excludes application of the definition to the knowledge of absolutely non-existent objects like mirage, the circle of fireband and the city of the Gandharvas. If the definition would have been worded as *adhyavasāyadṛṣṭaṁ* it will include non-existent objects also because one will get determinate knowledge of these objects. According to *Yuktidīpikā* the word *viṣaya* only can exclude the knowledge of the above non-existent objects from the domain of perception as these are mental concepts and not the objects in reality. The word *prati* in the definition excludes inferential knowledge from perception. The word *prati* means near and thus, denotes sense-object contact which is not found in inference. Again the *Yuktidīpikā* states that the word *prati* is used in the definition to exclude understanding of mutual intention by the cognitive organs.[47] In Sāṁkhya philosophy when one sense-organ cognizes its object, the other understands its intention and takes action. For example, when colour of a ripe mango is observed by the eyes, the organ of taste attains eagerness for that after understanding the decision of the eyes. Thus understanding of mutual intention arises in

46. *evam tarhi prativiṣayādhyavasāyascā prativiṣayādhyavas sāyaśca prativiṣayādhyavasāyat iti sārupāṇāmekaśesakarisyate* — *YD* on *SK*, 5.

47. *YD*, 5.

organs through their mutual contact and not through the contact of organs with the object cognized. Therefore, the term *prati* excludes understanding of mutual intention by the cognitive organs.

The *Sāṁkhyasūtra* defines perception as the knowledge which portrays the form of object coming in contact with it.[48] Here, knowledge according to Vijñānabhikṣu stands for *buddhivṛtti*. The *buddhi* goes to the object with the respective cognitive organ and gets the form of that object. This is perception.[49] The essence of the definition is that perception is *vṛtti* of *citta* followed by its contact with the object and through the cognitive organ.[50] According to Jwalaprasad the definition has two special features: (i) that the knowledge called *pratyakṣa* is regarded more as an act than as a product and (ii) that it is the form of object (*tadākāra*) which is cognized and not the object itself.[51] Here it is noticed that knowledge in Sāṁkhya is itself an act as well as a result in the form of a particular modification or state of *buddhi*. As to the second observation, *buddhi* which is a determining principle is a form which is not imaginary but real, and thus, what is cognized is the object only and not the form created with mental imagination as supposed by the Buddhists. According to *Sāṁkhyasūtra* the above definition cannot apply to perceptive knowledge of *yogin*s as also to the perception of Īśvara. In their opinion perception defined here is the external perception while the perceptive knowledge of *yogin*s does not come under the

---

48. *yat sambandhasiddham tadākārollekhi vijñānam tat pratyakṣam* — *SS*, 1.89.

49. *sambaddhavasttvakāradhāri bhavati yadvatijñānaṁ budhivṛttiḥ tatpratyakṣam pramāṇamityarthaḥ* — *SPB*, 1.7.

50. *Ibid.*

51. *HIE*, p. 195.

purview of it.[52] Again to avoid the defects of the definition they try to explain that *yogins* due to their exaltation can come in contact with the objects lying in their cause in the past and future states also. As to the defect of its non-applicability to Īśvara's perception the *Sāṁkhyasūtra* states that existence of Īśvara is not proved.[53]

After Īśvarakṛṣṇa we come across the definition of perception in the *Yogabhāṣya* of Vyāsa. In the Yoga system of Patañjali, there is no definition of perception. The *sūtra* mentions only perception as one of the three valid forms of knowledge. According to Vyāsadeva, the *bhāṣyakāra* on the *Yogasūtra*, the mode of the intellect goes out through the channel of sense-organs and becomes united with the object by means of its mode.[54] The mode is the part and parcel of the intellect itself. It is like the rays of the sun that go out and catch the form of the object with which they are united. In perception, the particular is emphasized though the universal element in the object used is not overlooked. Vācaspati brings out the following implications of the definition: since perception is knowledge of a real object, it is free from all unreal mental imagination imposed upon it. The statement that *citta* is coloured by the form of an object implies that knowledge existing in *citta* comes in contact with external object. Though there is no direct contact of *citta* with the object known yet the cognitive organ serves as the medium. Perception apprehends chiefly the specific nature of an object. It implies that although generic nature also is apprehended in

---

52. *yogināmbayapratyakṣatvād na dosaḥ* — *SS*, 1.90.

53. *īśvarāsiddhe* — *SS*, 1.92.

54. *indriyapraṇālikayā cittasya vāhyavastuparāgāt tadviṣayaḥ sāmānya viśeṣātmano arthasya viśeṣāvadhāraṇapradhāna vṛttiḥ pratyakṣom pramāṇam.* — *YB*, 1.7.

perception yet it is subordinate to specific nature.[55] Vijñānabhikṣu observes that the expression after its being coloured with the form of external object through cognitive organs should not be considered a part of the definition. It speaks of merely the cause of perception.[56] Otherwise the definition will not be applicable to perceptive knowledge of soul, etc. as also perception of Īśvara for the former does not stand in need of colouring of *citta* by external object and Īśvara has no cognitive organ.[57]

For a citical estimate of the Sāṁkhya-Yoga position, it will be worthwhile to consider the criticism of these definitions. The definition offered by Vindhyavāsin is criticized by Jayanta Bhaṭṭa and Hemacandra; that given by Vārṣagaṇya, by Aklaṅka, Diṅnāga, Udyotakāra and Vācaspati Miśra; and that offered by Īśvarakṛṣṇa is criticized by Jayanta Bhaṭṭa followed by Hemacandra. The definition given by the *Sāṁkhyasūtra* is not criticized by the ciritics of Sāṁkhya. It seems that the *Sāṁkhyasūtra* is a later composition and hence could not draw the attention of eminent old logicians.

Jayanta Bhaṭṭa criticized Vindhyavāsin's definition on the ground that it is having much in common with the Buddhist definition and is refuted with the Buddhist definition itself. Here the similarity with the Buddhist definition is with reference to the condition of being "free from imagination." Hemacandra criticizes the definition mainly from Jaina point of view. He presupposes that means of knowledge must be conscious only. The senses are unconscious and conse-quently

55. *yadyapi sāmānyamapi pratyakṣe pratibhāsate tathāpi viśeṣam pratyupasarjanibhūtamityarthaḥ* —*TV*, 1.7.

56. *ātmādipratyakṣavyāpanādiśvarapratyakṣā vyāpanācca tasyajanattvāt* —*YV*, 1.7.

57. *Ibid.*

their function will also be unconscious. As such they cannot be the means of knowledge. The definition offered by the followers of Vārṣagaṇya as the function of (cognitive organ) ear and the rest has invited severe criticism from Diṅnāga, Aklaṅka, Uddyotakāra and Vācaspati Miśra. The points of their ciriticism are given below:

Diṅnāga finds following faults in the definition: The Sāṁkhyas hold that perception is the function of cognitive organs to apprehend a specific object. The object of apprehension is composed of three *guṇas*. However, if a particular cognitive organ cognizes a particular proportion of the *guṇas*, there will arise the undesirable contingency of acceptance of many cognitive organs, as the objects in particular proportion of the *guṇas* are innumerable. Aklaṅka rejects the above definition on the ground that it would apply even to the erroneous knowledge. Uddyotakāra rejects the definition on the ground that the Nyāya position is the only correct one and that which differs from it is unacceptable and incorrect.[58] Vācaspati Miśra adds that the above definition is wrong because it is equally applicable to doubtful knowledge, etc.[59]

Jayanta Bhaṭṭa, followed by Hemacandra, expresses his dissatisfaction over Īśvarakṛṣṇa's definition of perception. Īśvarakṛṣṇa defines perception as determinate knowledge of objects. Jayanta Bhaṭṭa states that the above definition is not correct as it does not mention sense-object contact as a necessary condition of perception. Consequently, it becomes too wide as it is applicable to the other *pramāṇas* like *anumāna* which are also the means of definite knowledge.[60]

58. *evamānena nyāyena yānyapyanuktāni tanyetasmālak ṣanānna bhidyamānāni na lakṣaṇanti* — *NV*, 1.4.

59. *NVTT*, 1.4.

60. *anumānādivijñānānāmapi viṣayādhyavasāyasvabhāvattvenātivyāptaḥ* — *NM*, p. 100.

The above discussion leads to the following conclusions: Sāṁkhya-Yoga had its own tradition of defining perception which was not originally influenced by other systems. It has undergone various changes during its development. The earliest available definition was offered by Vindhyavāsin which was revised by the followers of Vārṣagaṇya. The condition of being free from imagination was dropped mainly because it was not necessary from Sāṁkhya point of view and because it could not stand the critique also. The definition of Vārṣagaṇya was rejected by the later Sāṁkhyas because it is not applicable to the internal perception as also to the extraordinary perception of *yogins*. Īśvarakr̥ṣṇa defines perception in terms of determining an individual object. The logicians of other schools have criticized these definitions on various grounds but most of the objections can be easily alleviated by Sāṁkhya-Yoga.

Role of Senses in Perception

Perception is primarily unconditioned by the activity of the senses in relation to some objects. Hence, perception is usually defined in terms of sense stimulation. Everyone admits sense activity as a factor conditioning all perception. But there is some difference of opinion as to the exact nature of the senses and their functions in perception. According to the Buddhists, the senses are the external organs occupying different parts of the surface of the body.[61] The visual sense for example is the pupil of the eye, since objects can be seen only when the pupil is in order but not otherwise. For the Jainas a sense is the physical organ with a specific energy.[62] According to the Sāṁkhyas, the senses are not physical bodies like the pupil of

61. *golakasyendriyatvamiti bauddhāḥ* — *NSV*, 3.1.30. cf. — *NTK*, p. 142.

62. *PKM*, p. 61.

the eye, but modifications of the subtle material principle called *ahaṁkāra*. They think that a physical organ cannot account for the perception of distant objects. In perception the senses must function in direct contact with the objects of perception. But a physical organ like the eye-pupil cannot have direct contact with an object lying at a distance or behind a glass. This is possible only if the sense-organ be all-pervading in character and not a limited physical substance. So the Sāṁkhyas think that the senses are modifications of a subtle all-pervading matter and are themselves all-pervading in character.[63]

The Nyāya rejects both the Bauddha and the Sāṁkhya views about the nature of the senses. It agrees with Mīmāṁsā and the Vedānta in holding that the senses are neither the end-organs nor modifications of any all-pervading subtle matter. According to these systems the external senses are material substances constituted by the physical elements and localized in the different end-organs.[64] Another definition of sense given by some Naiyāyikas is that it is the medium of a contact between the mind and an object to produce such knowledge as is different from memory.[65] This definition, however, is not applicable to mind as a sense since it cannot be said to be the medium of contact between itself and objects like pleasure and pain. The *Śāstradīpikā*[66] defines sense as what produces a clear and distinct knowledge of the object it is brought in contact with. This definition holds good with regard to all the senses including the mind.

According to the Nyāya and Mīmāṁsā, there are six sense-organs. Of these some are called external and some internal.

63. *ahaṁkāropādānakamindriyam* — *TK*, p. 26, cf. *NTK* p. 143.

64. *NS*, 1.1.12.

65. *SM*, p. 58.

66. *SD*, p. 36.

There is only one internal sense called *manas* or mind. There are five external senses namely, the olfactory, the gustatory, the visual, the cutaneous, and the auditory. These senses are physical in character, because they are constituted by the physical elements. The olfactory sense is the organ of apprehending smell. The gustatory sense is the condition of taste sensations. The visual sense is the ground of colour sensations and is itself coloured. The cutaneous sense is the source of touch sensations and temperature sensations. The auditory sense is the source of sensations of sound. To the above list of the six senses, recognized by the Nyāya and the Mīmāṁsā, the Sāṁkhya system adds five other senses. These are the five senses of action (*karmendriya*). They are called speech, hands, feet, rectum and the sex-organ and perform respectively the functions of speaking, prehension, locomotion, evacuation and reproduction.[67] The Vedānta accepts this with one exception. It excludes the mind or *antaḥkaraṇa* from the list of the senses.[68]

Function of the Senses

The function of the senses is to produce perception of objects. For a sense-organ, to function is to give us immediate knowledge about certain objects. According to the Buddhists the senses function without direct contact with the objects of perception. They are all "distance receptors" (*aprāpyakāri*) and do not require immediate contact with their objects. This is especially seen in the case of the senses of sight and hearing.

67. (a) *budhindriyāni cakṣuḥśrotraghrāṇarasanasparśanakāni vākpāṇipādapāyupasthān karmendriyāni ityāhu* — *SK*, K. 26.

(b) *śabdādiṣu pañcānāmalocanamātramiṣyate vṛttiḥ vacanādānaviharaṇat sargānandāśca pañcānāṁ* — *SK*. K, 28.

68. *VP*, Ch. VII.

We see far off objects that cannot have any direct or approximate contact with the eyes. We hear sound produced at a long distance from our ears. Similarly the eye perceives objects much larger than itself and so incapable of being covered by it. Many of us can, at the same time, see the same object or hear the same sound from different places. Conversely, one man can, almost at the same time, see two things or hear two sounds, quite apart from each other. This shows that the senses of sight and hearing may function without actual contact with their respective objects.[69] According to the Nyāya, Sāṁkhya, Mīmāṁsā and Vedānta systems, the senses can perceive only such objects as are in direct or indirect contact with them (*prāpyakārin*). This is obvious in the case of the so-called lower senses, namely, touch, taste and smell. Sensations of touch and taste arise only when the sense-organs are in immediate contact with their respective objects. To taste a thing is to place it in direct contact with the tongue. To touch a thing is to bring it in contact with the skin. If the smelling object be in our immediate surrounding, there is obvious contact of it with the olfactory organ. In the case of the lower senses all systems of philosophy admit a direct sense-object contact. The remaining two senses of sight and hearing also act in contact with their objects, although not quite as directly as the rest. According to the Vedānta, the sense of hearing travels to the sounding objects and gives us sensations of sound.[70] The Nyāya, however, agrees with modern science in holding that sound waves sent by the object are received into the ear-passage and these are perceived as sound.[71]

---

69. *NV*, 1.1.4.
70. *VP*, Ch. 1.
71. *BP*, 165-66.

Modes of Perception

Broadly speaking, there are three divergent views regarding the modes of perception, viz. (a) The Buddhist view, according to which *nirvikalpaka* is the only mode of perception and there is no such thing as *savikalpaka pratyakṣa,* (b) The Grammarians' view, which is diametrically opposed to the Buddhist position, refers to *savikalpaka* as the only possible form of perception and rejects *nirvikalpaka* altogether. The Cārvākas and the Madhva and Vallabha sects of Vedānta also fall in this category, and (c) The majority view, according to which both *nirvikalpaka* and *savikalpaka* are the valid modes of perception.

THE BUDDHIST VIEW

According to the Buddhists *nirvikalpaka* is the only type of valid perception. It is such cognition of an object as contains no element of thought or ideation in it (*kalpanā poḍhaṁ*).[72] Ordinarily knowledge involves two elements namely, the given or sensed and the meant or ideated. The Buddhists hold that what is given is a unique individual that belongs to no class and is not related to anything.[73] One can call it by a name, bring it under a class and think of it as having certain qualities, actions and relations. But its name, class, quality, action and relation are not any part of what is directly given. These are the contributions of our mind (*kalpanā*) to the given experience. Hence, *nirvikalpaka* perception is a cognition which is not modified by any idea or concept like those of its name, class, etc. *Nirvikalpaka* perception is not a verbalized experience. As contrasted to this, *savikalpaka* perception is a verbalized experience in which the object is determined by the concepts of name, class, relation, etc. Here we think of the objects having

---

72. *PSa,* Ch. I.

73. *apare tu svalakṣaṇamātragocaraṁ nirvikalpakamicchanti* — *SD,* p. 41.

attributes, bearing certain name and having certain relations. Such knowledge, however, is false, since it is not due to the given object, but due to our conceptual construction of it. Thus the Buddhists reduce *nirvikalpaka* to pure sensation which is valid but blind and *savikalpaka* to conceptual knowledge which is definite but false.

THE GRAMMARIAN'S VIEW

According to some linguistic thinkers there cannot be any *nirvikalpaka* perception in the sense of an unverbalized experience. They hold that we cannot think of things except through words. All objects are inseparably connected with the words by which they are denoted. To cognize a thing is to know it as such and to relate it to a denotative word. Likewise, we can act in relation to a thing only when we know it precisely as of this or that kind, i.e. determine it by means of a class-name. In fact, all our cognitions are embodied in verbal propositions, such as "I know a colour," "I have a taste," "it is a smell" and so on. All cognitions being thus inseparable from verbal expressions, there can be no *nirvikalpaka* or unverbalized cognition. According to the Cārvākas, the Jainas, the ancient Śābdikas and the Viśiṣṭādvaita Vedānta of Rāmānuja, all perceptions are *savikalpaka* or determinate and that there is no such thing as a perfectly indeterminate perception. According to Rāmānuja, to know a thing is to know it as possessed of certain attributes. A thing's existence cannot be separated from its nature and attributes. There being thus no absolutely indeterminate knowledge, the distinction of *nirvikalpaka* and *savikalpaka* perception is a relative distinction. While in *nirvikalpaka* the object of perception is partially determined, in *savikalpaka* it is determined more fully and clearly.

The Cārvākas, the Śābdikas and the Jainas go further than Rāmānuja and hold that *nirvikalpaka* perception is not real in any sense. According to the Jainas all true knowledge must be a definite and an assured cognition of objects. What distinguishes true knowledge from doubt, error and the rest is the fact that it is a firm belief which is also true. It is a definite judgement of an object as this and not as that.[74] In it there is a definite affirmation or denial that an object is or is not. In the so-called *nirvikalpaka* perception, however, there is no such definite assertion of anything about any object. Hence, it cannot be recognized as a form of valid knowledge. In perception there need not be a transition from an initial stage of vague and unorganized sense-impressions to that of distinct and determinate knowledge. All true perceptions are, therefore determinate (*savikalpaka*) cognitions of objects as they really are in themselves.[75]

THE MAJORITY VIEW

According to the Mīmāṁsā, the Sāṁkhya, the Nyāya-Vaiśeṣika, any perception, *nirvikalpaka* or *savikalpaka*, is a direct cognition of the real individual which is a unity of the universal and the particular. It is probably Kumārila who has initiated the proper analysis of the problem of indeterminate and determinate forms of perception of Indian philosophy. He refers to *nirvikalpaka* as mere apprehension (*ālocana*) and a non-reflective knowledge, which resembles the cognition of a child or of a mute and is caused by the mere object. He admits reflective knowledge (*savikalpaka*) but condemns it as a second stage of perception.[76] The Prābhākara School also admits two forms of *pratyakṣa*. They agree with the Bhāṭṭa School but their expressions differ in the nature of *nirvikalpaka* perception. According to Kumārila, the particular and generic characters

---

74. *tanniścayātmakaṁ samaropaviruddhatvādanumānavat* — *PKM*, p. 3.
75. *Ibid.*, p. 8.
76. *ITK*, pp. 114-21.

are not perceived at the first moment while according to Prabhākara they are perceived but not as particular and generic characters. The Vedānta also refers to two types of perception: (i) *savikalpaka,* and (ii) *nirvikalpaka.*[77] Gautama introduces the epithets *avyapadeśya* and *vyavasāyātmaka* in the definition of perception. Vācaspati holds that the Sūtrakāra refers to *nirvikalpaka* and *savikalpaka* forms of perception through these words. However, there is some difference of opinion as to the nature and structure of *nirvikalpaka* perception between the Bhāṭṭa Mīmāṁsā and Sāṁkhya systems on the one hand and the Prābhākara and Nyāya-Vaiśeṣika systems on the other.

According to the Sāṁkhya and the Bhāṭṭa Mīmāṁsā both *nirvikalpaka* and *savikalpaka* are equally valid and necessary modes of perceptual knowledge. By *nirvikalpaka* they mean that cognition which spontaneously arises at the first moment of contact between sense and object.[78] It is a knowledge of the object as one individual whole of generic and specific attributes. There is no differentiation between the universal and the particular that are combined in the body of the individual. Hence, there is only an apprehension of the individual as an indefinite object, but no definite understanding of it as this or that kind of object.[79] *Nirvikalpaka* perception thus resembles the perception of the children and dumb persons.

According to Nyāya-Vaiśeṣika and Prābhākara Mīmāṁṣa ordinary perception is of two kinds, namely *nirvikalpaka* and *savikalpaka*, both of which are equally valid and grounded in

---

77. *tacca pratyakṣaṁ dvividhaṁ savikalpaka* and *nirvikalpakabhedāt* — *VP*, p. 63.

78. *akṣasannipātānantaramaiviviktasāmānyaviśeṣa vibhāgaṁ saṁmugdhavastumātragocaramālocanajñānaṁ* — *SD*, p. 40.

79. *saṁmugdhaṁ vastumātrantu prāggṛhṇantyavikalpitam tatsāmānyaviśeṣābhyāṁ kalpayanti manīṣinaḥ* — *TKD*, p. 27.

reality. They hold that *nirvikalpaka* is not merely a cognition of the bare particular (*svalakṣaṇa*) since it manifests the universal as well. If the universal is not cognized at the *nirvikalpaka* stage; our knowledge of it at a subsequent *savikalpaka* stage becomes inexplicable. According to Naiyāyikas, *nirvikalpaka* is a real but not a perceived fact (*atindriya*).[80] It is conscious but not a self-conscious state.

The Sāṁkhya-Yoga text accepts two kinds of perception: normal (*laukika*) and abnormal (*alaukika*). The former requires a particular process in sense-object contact with the respective sense-organ. Vācaspati refers to Yogic perception as abnormal (*alaukika*) kind of perception. The *yogin*s can perceive the objects like subtle elements (*tanmātra*s) which are not the object of sense perception for ordinary people.[81] The perception of *yogin*s unlike that of normal persons does not depend upon the contact of their external organs with objects.

Śrīkr̥ṣṇa Vallabhācārya states that in addition to yogic perception Sāṁkhya-Yoga accepts *jñānalaksaṇa* type of abnormal perception. It is the perception of an object which is not directly connected with the sense but through a previous knowledge of that object. For example, after perceiving a piece of sandalwood one comes to have the knowledge of its fragrance. The past experience of fragrance in sandalwood serves as contact between sense and the object. The texts of Sāṁkhya-Yoga do not discuss abnormal kind of perception. Vācaspati gives the reason for such an absence. Sāṁkhya-Yoga system is meant for understanding by common people. The supernormal knowledge of *yogin* is not useful for common

---

80. *jannirvikalpākhyam tadatindriyamiṣyate* — *BP*, p. 58.

81. *asmadādināmaviṣayaśca tanmātralakṣaṇā yogināmūrdhasrotasāṁ ca viṣayāḥ* — *STK* under *SK*. 5.

people. The absence of such a discussion does not mean its non-existence. Such a yogic perception must be admitted.

The Sāṁkhya accept *nirvikalpaka* and *savikalpaka* as two stages of perception. They refer to indeterminate perception as the immediate, pure and simple cognition of an object. It presents a vague idea of the object. Determinate perception, on the other hand, is the definite cognition of an object related to its properties and qualified by its generic and specific characteristics. In Sāṁkhya works, Vācaspati Miśra is the pioneer to subdivide perception into two sub-classes, namely (i) *nirvikalpaka* (indeterminate perception) and (ii) *savikalpaka* (determinate perception). Vācaspati Miśra follows the footsteps of Kumārila Bhaṭṭa in this respect. He quotes verses from *Ślokavārttika* of Kumārila Bhaṭṭa to define indeterminate and determinate perception.[82] But no such terms are found in the authoritative Sāṁkhya works. The word *ālocana* has been used in the *Sāṁkhyakārikā*. Vācaspati Miśra interprets *ālocanajñānam* as indeterminate perception which does not discriminate the two elements of an object namely the particular from the universal. In the very definition of *dṛṣṭa*, the term *adhyavasāya* has been used. *Adhyavasāya* is defined by Vācaspati Miśra himself as the form of determinate knowledge. Vācaspati Miśra admits that *ālocana* is indeterminate. So far as we understand the sense of the definition of *pratyakṣa* as given by the *Sāṁkhyakārikā*, it is always indeterminate. Vācaspati Miśra in his classification includes indeterminate perception in the class of perception but does not justify its possibility. If we go through the explanation of the author of *Yuktidīpikā*, we find

82. *asti hyālocanam jñānam prathamam nirvikalpakakam* ।
bālamukhādi vijñānasadṛśam vastujātam ॥
tataḥ param punarvastudharmairjatyādi bhiryayā ।
buddhyā vasiyate sāpi pratyakṣatvena sammata iti ॥
— *SV* as quoted in *STK*, 27.

that he explains *ālocana* as equivalent to the form of the object as seized by the sense-organ.

The determinate perception is due to the operation of *manas*, as Vācaspati Miśra interprets. *Manas* alleviates the doubt regarding the definiteness of the object cognized. At this stage genus and particular qualities of an object are decided. *Ahaṁkāra* then determines the relation of an object with the cognizer. Finally, *buddhi* decides whether to accept or to reject the object. This is the final state called *adhyavasāya*. At this stage knowledge is turned into determinate.[83] Here we can say that the above process differs from that given by the Naiyāyikas regarding determinate perception. According to the Naiyāyikas vague apprehension is turned into determinate knowledge at the stage of *manas*, while according to the Sāṁkhyas determinate knowledge takes place at the stage of *buddhi*. The author of the *Sāṁkhyasūtra* and Vijñānabhikṣu are wise enough not to discuss the problem of the classification of *pratyakṣa*. They do never utter a word like *nirvikalpaka* or *savikalpaka pratyakṣa*. Vijñānabhikṣu criticizes Vācaspati Miśra very often on different topics but the classification of perception as given by Vācaspati Miśra escapes his notice and he kept silent on this topic.

The above discussion is according to Sāṁkhya system. In the system of Yoga we come across a different account of process in perception. Vyāsa states that *citta* goes to the external object through senses and gets the form of that object. According to Vijñānabhikṣu *citta* goes to the external object along with the senses.[84] The statement "through the senses"

---

83. *saṁkalpena rūpena manolakṣyate ālocitamindriyena vastu idam iti sammugdham idamevam naivam 'iti samyak kalpayati, viśeṣaṇaviśeṣyabhāvena vivecayatīti yāvat* — *STK* under *SK*, K. 27.

84. *cittasyendriya sāhityenaivārthākāraḥ pariṇāmo bhaveti* — *YV*, 1.7.

does not mean that *citta* alone travels to the objects cognized. The fact that the defect of eye like jaundice affects perceptual knowledge and the *citta* is modified into the form of object along with the sense-organ.[85] Vijñānabhikṣu further states that this *citta* or *buddhi* again reflects its modification into the *Puruṣa* after getting the reflection of *Puruṣa* earlier. There arises the apparent knowledge in *Puruṣa* through this reflection.

Perception in this way depends upon the contact of sense-organs with the object on the one hand and with the internal organs on the other. When the object is clearly visible or when one feels fear or the like, the contact of external sense with the object and among internal senses is simultaneous. For example, when one sees a lion facing him, operation of the aggregate of internal organs and the external sense is simultaneous. There is, however, difference of opinion amongst the Sāṁkhyas in this respect. The *Yuktidīpikā* maintains that the theory of simultaneous action is not the view of Sāṁkhya. Īśvarakṛṣṇa treats it as a *prima facie* view and rejects it for establishing his theory of successive action of senses.

On the basis of the nature of objects perceived, perception comes to be of two kinds: external and internal. The former depends upon the intercourse of external senses with objects, while the latter requires the intercourse of organs with the objects which are also situated internally and are beyond the reach of the senses which are extrovert in nature. It comprehends the qualities of *buddhi* like pleasure, pain, desire, aversion etc. In this there is no need of postulating indeterminate perception because being found at the stage of senses it does not have any scope there. The nature of intercourse between *buddhi* and the object cognized is *tādātmya*

85. *nayanādigatapittādyanaya vyetirābhyām* — *YV*, 1.7.

in the case of perception of its quality and that of *tādātmya* in the perception of generic feature of the quality.

The Sāṁkhyas strongly advocate the intercourse between sense and object. They also insist that the function of every sense-organ, or in other words the sense-organ itself moves to the object cognized. The Naiyāyikas and the Mīmāṁsakas, however, feel that such a case does not hold in case of perception of sound. The view of the Sāṁkhyas differs from the Naiyāyikas in two respects. Firstly, unlike the Sāṁkhyas, the Naiyāyikas hold that sound reaches auditory sense and not vice versa. One sound produces the other in the manner of a wave giving rise to another wave (*vicitaraṅganyāya*). The last one is produced in the ether enclosed by the cavity of the ear. Secondly, according to the Naiyāyikas, the auditory sense perceives sound through the relation of inherence (*samavāya*) while the Sāṁkhyas think that the auditory sense perceives sound through contact. The Mīmāṁsakas like the Naiyāyikas and unlike the Sāṁkhyas hold that the sound travels to the ear. Thus it is observed that while there is no difference between act and its agent in the theory of Sāṁkhya, other schools of philosophy raise objections pertaining to this very theory of the Sāṁkhya of non-difference between function and its agent.

Vijñānabhikṣu and his follower Bhāvagaṇeśa discussed one problem of perception. Actually Bhāvagaṇeśa repeats the view of Vijñānabhikṣu in this regard. According to Vijñānabhikṣu the sense-organ goes out but not get detached from the body. It prolongs itself and the prolonged part remains united with the sense-organ. It goes straight to the object and catches the form of the object with which it becomes united. The prolonged part is called *vṛtti*. Since a distant object is perceived small, the question arises whether the sense-organ goes out through *vṛtti*. The object remaining at a distant place is not really small. The observer perceives it small. One simultaneously perceives the lightpost and the Sun. The distance between the observer and the lightpost is little but the distance between the Sun and the same observer is far greater. It is to be discussed whether the same *vṛtti* can be united with both of them at the same time. If it cannot do so, the two objects cannot be perceived at the same time. Neither Vijñānabhikṣu nor Bhāvagaṇeśa utters a single word to explain these difficulties. Again all the sense-organs excepting the visual one do not go out in order to be united with their objects. Therefore, Vijñānabhikṣu's discussion on this topic is not at all complete.

Another problem of perception has not been discussed either in the Sāṁkhya works or in the Yoga works. The problem is, in case of illusory perception, is it partially or entirely illusory? The perceptual judgement has three parts — subject, copula and predicate. If the predicate is only illusory it is questionable whether this wrong predicate invalidates the whole judgement. But none of the authors discussed this matter.

Internal Perception and Its Objects

Internal perception is due to the internal sense or *manas*. Hence, it is called *mānasa* or *āntara pratyakṣa*. It is the knowledge of mental facts brought about by their contact with the inner sense or *manas*. Thus *mānasa* or internal perception is, like introspection, the source of our direct knowledge about mental or subjective facts. But while modern introspectionists take introspection as mind's knowledge, the Naiyāyikas treat internal perception as knowledge of certain subjective facts other than, but due to the mind as a sense. Generally speaking, the self and its contents are the objects of internal perception. These are perceived when they come in contact with *manas* or the mind. In introspection the mind or self turns back on itself and perceives what is going on there without requiring any sense.

Among the objects of *mānasa-pratyakṣa* or internal perception, the *Bhāṣāpariccheda* mentions the feelings of pleasure and pain, desire and aversion, cognition or knowledge and all kinds of mental effort or volition.[86] All of these are perceived when there is contact between them and the internal sense of *manas*. According to the Vedānta, pleasure, pain, desire, aversion and volition are perceived but their perception requires no sense-organ like *manas* or the mind. They are the different parts or aspects of the *antaḥkaraṇa*. As such, there is a natural identification between these and the *antaḥkaraṇa* or the mind. This identification means a perception of all that is identified with the *antaḥkaraṇa*. It can be said that mental states are perceived facts because they are mental and so do not require any sense to perceive them.[87]

As to the question how cognition or knowledge is known, there is a sharp difference of opinion among the philosophers. According to Sāṁkhya, the Prābhākara Mīmāṁsā and the Advaita Vedānta, knowledge is known by itself. Cognition or knowledge is a conscious fact and it is the very nature of consciousness to be aware of itself. The point has been elaborated by the Prābhākaras in the theory of *tripuṭisaṁvit*. According to it every knowledge manifests itself at the same time that it manifests an object and the knowing subject. It is at once a manifestation of three things, namely, knowledge, the object and the knower. The Jainas also take a similar view with regard to the nature of knowledge. The Advaita Vedānta

---

86. *manogrāhyam sukham duḥkhamicchā dveṣo matiḥ kṛtiḥ* — *BP*, p. 57.

87. *VP*, Ch. I.

takes knowledge or intelligence to be the essence of the self, the very stuff of it. As such, knowledge is self-manifest and self-shining. It does not require anything else to manifest or know it. According to the Bhāṭṭa Mīmāṁsā, knowledge cannot be directly known. We can never know any knowledge immediately by itself or by any introspection called internal perception.

Recognition (Pratyabhijñā)

Recognition is also another kind of perception. Recognition may be understood in two senses. In the wider sense recognition means understanding the nature or character of a thing. In this sense to recognize a thing is to know it as such. In the narrower sense however, recognition means knowing a thing as that which was known before. *Pratyabhijñā* is recognition in this sense. It consists in knowing not only that a thing is such and such but that it is the same thing that we saw before. For example, "This is that Devadatta." According to Naiyāyikas recognition is a kind of qualified perception, in which the present object is qualified by a distinct recollection of its past experience. The Mīmāṁsakas and the Advaita Vedāntins also hold that recognition is a kind of perception. The Mīmāṁsakas, however, do not distinguish it from an ordinary *savikalpaka* perception. According to them, recognition is that kind of perception in which the object is determined by the name by which it is called, e.g., "this is Devadatta."[88] For the Advaitin, *pratyabhijñā* is a perception of the *nirvikalpaka* kind, since there is in it no prediction of anything about the perceived object, but an assertion of its identity amidst changing conditions.[89]

88. *SD*, p. 42.

89. *V.P.* Ch. I.

According to Sāṁkhya and Yoga systems *pratyabhijñā* or recognition is a kind of perception. It is possible becuase *buddhi* is eternal, and quite different from the momentary cognitions of individuals. The eternal *buddhi* undergoes modifications, by virtue of which it becomes connected with the different cognitions involved in recognition. This would not be possible of the self which is unmodifiable.

According to the Sāṁkhya, a cognition is not perceived by another cognition but is perceived by the self. For cognition is regarded as a function of *buddhi*, which is unconscious and so it cannot be its own object, but can only be apprehended by the self.[90]

Non-Sensuous Perception in Philosophy

The concept of non-sensuous perception is found in most of the systems of Indian philosophy. All Indian systems except the Cārvākas and the Mīmāṁsakas believe in Yogic perception. The non-sensuous perception is called *atindriya pratyakṣa*. It is intuitive experience which arises in the self. In the first place such perception is not caused in the ordinary way. The sense-organs do not play a role in its production. Secondly, there is no limitation of space, time and place for it. One who has the power to acquire the non-sensuous perception, can know the objects of the past, present, future, far and near. Again the systems, which believe in *atindriya pratyakṣa* accept that it arises in the self directly when the ignorance is destroyed by the regular practice of mental and bodily discipline. The self shines by the light of great knowledge in the state of purification or perfection and some supernormal powers or the *siddhi* or *labdhi* arise in the self. These are not forms of miracle, but the power of the self itself which arises by the destruction of ignorance.

---

90. *Y.B.*, IV.9.

The aim of the *yogī* is not to acquire the supernormal power. He practises for his purification in an effort to get freedom from the bondage of the world.

THE NYĀYA THEORY OF ALAUKIKA PRATYAKṢA

The modern Naiyāyikas classified perception into two types, *laukika* or ordinary perception and *alaukika* or extraordinary perception. The first type of perception is based on the sense-object contact. In the second type of perception, the objects are not actually present to the senses, but are experienced through an extraordinary medium. All the various kinds of extraordinary sense-object contacts are called *alaukika-sannikarṣa*. Extraordinary perception is of three kinds, namely, *sāmānyalakṣana, jñānalakṣana* and *yogaja*. The perception of the generic character is called *sāmānyalakṣana* perception. Sense-object contact not only gives us the knowledge of the object, but we become immediately aware of the class essence (*sāmānya*) existing in the object. On looking at a particular animal we can perceive it as a cow, because we directly perceive "the cowness" in that cow. "Cowness" is the generic character (*sāmānya*) of cow.

The second type of extraordinary perception is called *jñāna lakṣana*. It is the perception of an object which is in contact with sense through a previous knowledge of itself.[91] When on seeing something one says: "I see a piece of fragrant sandal-wood," he has an immediate knowledge or perception of its fragrance. This cannot be explained without the help of *jñāna laksaṇa*. It is extraordinary perception, because in it the quality of the object is perceived by the sense-organ which is not competent to give us that knowledge. Here our past experience of fragrance in the sandalwood does the work of contact

91. *viṣayī yasya tasyaiva vyāpāro jñānalakṣaṇaḥ* — *BP*, 65.

between sense and object. Our past knowledge of fragrance brings about the present perception of it, although it is not actually smelt by us.

The third kind of extraordinary perception is called *yogaja*. It is the intuitive perception of all objects — past, distant and future due to some super-normal powers generated in the mind by devout meditation (*yogābhyāsajanitodharma viśeṣaḥ*). The reality of *yogaja* perception is generally accepted in Indian philosophy on the authority of the scriptures.[92] *Yukta* and *yuñjāna* are the two kinds of *yogaja* perception. In the case of *yukta* who have attained spiritual perfection, intuitive knowledge of all the objects is constant and spontaneous. The second i.e. *yuñjāna* is the intuition of a *yogin* who is practising *Yoga* to attain union with God but has not yet attained it. Those who are on the way to perfection, it requires the help of concentration as an auxiliary condition.[93] From the chart shown on next page one can have the perception of Nyāya philosophy:

THE ADVAITA THEORY OF NON-SENSUOUS PERCEPTION

According to Śaṅkara, *Brahman* is present in every man and is the universal self in all. *Brahman* is reality but different from the phenomenal world and not sensible. *Brahman* is of the nature of consciousness. Knowledge is its essential property. It is *sat* (real), *cit* (consciousness) and *ānanda* (bliss). One cannot attain the knowledge of reality or the *Brahman*, so long as one is subject to *avidyā* or ignorance. *Vidyā* gives the highest conceptual knowledge of *Brahman*. There is no difference between *Brahman* and *ātman*. *Ātman* is *Brahman*. The *anubhava* of *ātman* or the integral experience is a type of intuitional

92. *BP*, 65-66.

93. *Ibid*.

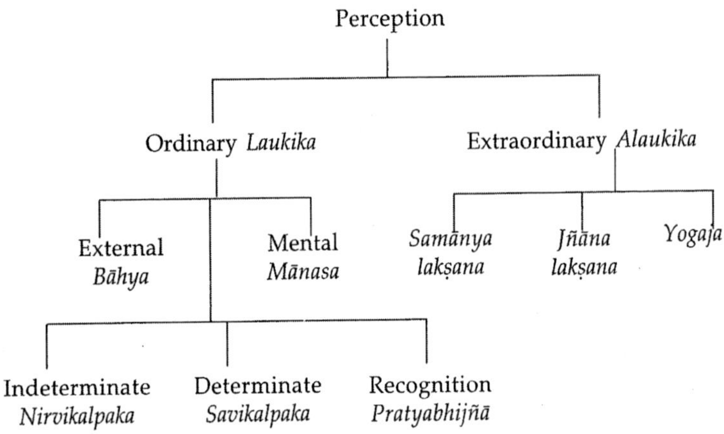

consciousness which may be called the knowledge of *Brahman*, in which the individual self feels the identity with *ātman* or *Brahman*. It is the inexpressible experience beyond thought and speech. It is *sākṣātkāra* or direct perception of the awareness of the empirical self and the *ātman*. One can get this intuition of *ātman* by faith, devotion, meditation, study and by a preparation of mind.

THE VAIŚEṢIKA VIEW

The Vaiśeṣika too believes in the capacity of *yogins* to perceive things which are beyond the reach of ordinary people. Praśastapāda says that *yogins*, acquire extraordinary excellence resulting from the practice of Yoga and during the state of ecstasy, perceive through their minds alone. He further holds that in the post-ecstatic state, not only the mind but even the external senses acquire excellence and *yogins* can perceive subtle and remote objects with their help.

THE BUDDHIST VIEW OF YOGĪ-PRATYAKṢA

Dharmakīrti defines *yogī pratyakṣa* as the knowledge which is manifested in the highest state of deep meditation on transcendental reality.[94] Dharmottara says that when concentrative contemplation (bhāvanā) reaches the point of perfection, mystics have a vivid vision of objects as if they were lying behind a transparent wall of mica. The cognitions of mystics are perceptual in character because they are direct, distinct and devoid of subjective images.[95]

THE JAINA VIEW

According to the Jaina view souls in their natural condition are omniscient. It is due to the accumulation of karmic matter during transmigratory state that they lose omniscience and consequently they know only so much as is permitted by the sense-organs. But when through the practice of right conduct the veil of karmic matter is destroyed they regain omniscience. Knowledge in their state depends purely on the soul and it is called transcendental perception (*pāramārthika pratyakṣa*). Transcendental perception does not depend on sense-organs or any condition. The ominiscience of a soul liberated from the bondage of *karma* is called transcendental perception. Transcendental perception is either incomplete (*vikalpa*) or complete (*sakalpa*). Incomplete transcendental perception is of two kinds — *avadhi* and *manaḥparyāya*. (1) Due to the partial removal of the *karma* matter that obstructs knowledge, the self perceives remote sensible objects. This perception is independent of the sense-organs or mind. But as this perception is limited, it is called *avadhijñāna* or limited knowledge. (2) When a man gets rid of jealousy, hatred and other like passions, he attains the power of entering the minds of others and knowing their thoughts directly without the help of any sense-organ or mind. This is called *manaḥparyāya*.

---

94. *bhūtārthabhāvanāprakarṣaparyantajam yogījñānam ceti*, — *NB*, p. 14.

95. *PNT*, pp. 102-20.

When all the *karma* matters obstructing knowledge are removed once for all, the self attains its natural power of omniscience. This is called *kevala jñāna*, and this is known as *sakalpapāramārthika pratyakṣa* or complete transcendental perception.

THE SĀṀKHYA VIEW

Yogic perception is admitted by the Sāṁkhya, which holds that all things exist involved or evolved at all times. The mind of the *yogin* can come into contact with the past and the future objects, which exist at present in a latent condition, by virtue of certain powers produced by meditation.[96] Yogic perception produced by the powers of mind is unlike sense perception.

The Supernormal Powers in Yoga System

Through the practice of Yoga, the *sādhaka* acquires some supernormal powers in particular state of the *yaugika sādhanā*. These are called *siddhi* or the supernormal powers, and a knowledge of supernormal objects. Through it the *yogī* or the *sādhaka* knows the inmost core of objects and reaches the great light of wisdom (*prajñāloka*). He acquires heightened powers of the senses by which he can see and hear at a distance, have direct knowledge of the past, and can acquire knowledge of others' mind (*paracittajñānam*). He can also know past, present and future by the supernormal power. The *yogī* can make his body invisible also and by the realization of the difference between the self and the outer world he gains omniscience. A *yogī* can acquire all those supernormal powers by the discipline of body and mind. The aim of a *yogī* is not to acquire them but he tries to make his self perfect and to get freedom. According to the Yoga system of philosophy, these supernormal powers are not considered as miracles, because they hold that the

96. *SPB*, I.91.

world open to one's senses is not the whole world of nature. One's physical senses do not have the power or capacity to perceive the whole world. The world beyond one's capacities has its own science and laws, which are apprehended by the supernormal power of the *yogī*. A *yogī* acquires this capacity by discipline and meditation.

The Mīmāṁsakas do not recognize the yogic perception. In the yogic perception, the *yogin*s have some extraordinary yogic power through which they can perceive the past and future, imperceptible and distinct. This intuition is either sensuous or non-sensuous. If the former, then, since the senses cannot come into contact with past, future and distinct objects, there can be no cognition of them. Even the internal sense of *manas* can produce only cognitions of the mental states of pleasure and pain. It is meaningless to argue that the senses can comprehend objects without coming into contact with them when they attain a high degree of development, because no amount of development can change the nature of the sense-organs. If the yogic intuition apprehends things perceived in the past, then it is a case of memory. If it apprehends objects that have not been perviously apprehended, then its validity is doubtful. A knowledge of past, distinct and future objects can be got only through the Vedas and nothing else.

Theory of Perceptual Error

The systems of Indian philosophy have divergent views on the issue of process and causes of erroneous knowledge in perception. Their theories are popularly stated to be *ātmakhyāti* held by Yogācāra School of Buddhism, *asatkhyāti* held by Mādhyamika School of Buddhism, *akhyāti* held by Prābhākara School of Pūrva-Mīmāṁsā, *anyathākhyāti* held by the Naiyāyikas, the Vaiśeṣikas, the Bhāṭṭa Mīmāṁsakas, Yoga and the Jaina systems and *anirvacanīyakhyāti* held by the Śāṅkara

School of Uttara-Mīmāṁsā. According to the first, *ātman* or *buddhi* (knowledge) itself appears erroneously in the form of object. The second explains that the object erroneously perceived is actually non-existent (*asat*). The upholders of the third maintain that in fact there is no erroneous knowledge at all. In the cases like "this is silver" where shell erroneously appears to be silver, what directly perceived is "this," the silver is only remembered and in fact due to its confusion with memory it looks to be silver. According to the fourth some object is erroneously perceived in the form of some other object. For example, due to similarity of shell with silver, silver situated at some other place is remembered and is imposed on the shell and thus the shell is erroneously perceived to be silver. Fifthly the followers of Advaita Vedānta think that the object erroneously perceived is undefinable.

Knowledge in Sāṁkhya-Yoga briefly means taking the form of an object by *buddhi*. In the case of perception such a modification of *buddhi* is brought about by sense-object contact.[97] Thus when the form of object in *buddhi* corresponds to the object known, the knowledge is right; when it is different the knowledge is wrong. Perceptual error is thus, non-correspondence of the form of *buddhi* to the object when that knowledge involves sense-object contact. The Sāṁkhya theory of perceptual error did not assume a concrete form in the early texts of the Sāṁkhyas. It is for the first time found mentioned in the *Sāṁkhyasūtras*.[98] The *Sāṁkhyakārikā* of Īśvarakṛṣṇa which is the earliest Sāṁkhya work available, does not explicitly deal with the problem but implies some theory

97. *upāttvaviṣayanāmindriyānām vṛttau sattām buddhesthomoabhibve sati ya sattvasamudrekaḥ sa adhyavasāya iti, vṛttirīti, jñānamīti cākhyāyate* — *STK*, under *SK*, K5.

98. *naikasyānandacidrūpattve dyoyorbhedāt* — *SS*, 5.66.

of perceptual error while dealing with error. One can consider the theory of error in two aspects, why does it occur and how does it occur. As to the first, it is lack of knowledge which gives rise to complete non-perception or partial perception. The reasons for lack of knowledge are great distance, extreme proximity, defects of organs, non-steadiness of mind, minuteness, interposition, predominance and intermixture.[99] The consequence of partial knowledge is that *buddhi* fails to distinguish between real and unreal. As a result, *Puruṣa* appears to be active and *buddhi* appears to be sentient. The *Sāṁkhyakārikā* does not directly deal with the second aspect of the problem and does not explicitly mention the process of erroneous perception but a *kārikā* in it implies that the object observed is mistaken to be of different nature due to its resemblance through the memories of past experience. When *Puruṣa* which is sentient and inactive and *buddhi* which is insentient and active come in mutual contact, the former looks active and the latter looks sentient. Here the *kārikā*[100] deals with the erroneous identification of *Puruṣa* with *buddhi.*

The Yoga system unlike Sāṁkhya and like Nyāya-Vaiśeṣika, does not accept the partial or incomplete knowledge as leading to erroneous perception. It believes in *anyathākhyāti* in which error is not due to lack of knowledge but due to positive superimposition of something else on an object. Vijñānabhikṣu draws this conclusion from the descripton of *avidyā* in the *Yogasūtra*. In Yoga, *avidyā* is not lack of knowledge, but a positive misconception leading to perverted knowledge. But there is a difference between Yoga and Vaiśeṣika systems.

---

99. *atidūrāt sāmipyādindriyaghātānmano anavasthānāt saukṣmād vyavodhānādabhibhavāt samānabhihārā* — SK, K.7.

100. *tasmāt tat samyogādacetanam cetanāvadiba liṅgam* ǀ *guṇakartitve api tathā karteba bhāvatyudāsīnaḥ* ǁ — SK. K.20.

In the cases like erroneous perception of shell as silver, the Vaiśeṣikas think that the external real silver is attributed on the shell while Yoga holds that it is the conception or idea of silver inside the body which is attributed on the object. Vijñānabhikṣu supports this view on the following grounds: Firstly, the theory of Vaiśeṣika philosophy on this aspect is not clear because the knowledge of the object of shell, which is placed near is not taken into account in case of erroneous perception while the silver is placed far away. Secondly, when some object is perceived in dream and is realized to be non-existent after waking up from that stage, we cannot say that it was the real object placed somewhere which appeared erroneously in dream. In the opinion of Vijñānabhikṣu, Yoga system is not interested in discussing the cases of worldly perceptual error. Since the worldly examples do not help to attain liberation which is the sole aim of Yoga philosophy those are not discussed in this system in detail.

In conclusion, it can be said that the problem of perception in Sāṁkhya and the Yoga works has not been discussed in its full length. The reason for incomplete discussion is that the philosophers of both the Sāṁkhya and Yoga Schools are interested in self-realization. Logic plays a subordinate role in their metaphysical and ethical science.

4

Inference (Anumāna Pramāṇa)

ALL the systems of Indian philosophy except the Cārvākas hold that *anumāna* (inference) is a distinct means of valid knowledge, and hence every system has tried to discuss it in the light of its own metaphysical background. The word *anumāna* is generally translated in English as inference. It is used to indicate two components viz. inferential cognition (*anumiti*) and the instrument of inferential cognition (*anumiti-karaṇa*). In this way, when the word *inference* stands for an abstraction, it means inferential cognition and when it stands for the instrument, it means a source of inferential cognition. Inference is indirectly accepted as an independent means of knowledge even by Cārvākas who deny to accept it since the rejection of inference by Cārvākas itself implies the acceptance of inference by them because the rejection is through the inference itself.

Anumāna literally means such knowledge that follows some other knowledge. It is the knowledge of an object due to a previous knowledge of some sign or mark.[1] The previous knowledge is the knowledge of the *liṅga* or mark as having a universal relation with the *sādhya* or major term and as being present in the *pakṣa* or minor term.[2] Hence, *anumāna* has been defined in the Nyāya system as the knowledge of an object,

1. *mitena liṅgena liṅginorthasya paścātmānamanumānam* — *NBh*, 1.1.3.
2. *vyāptiviśiṣṭapakṣadharmatājñānajanyam* — *TCM*, II, p. 2.

not by direct observation, but by means of the knowledge of a *liṅga* or sign and that of its universal relation (*vyāpti*) with the inferred object.[3] *Anumāna* as a *pramāṇa* is, therefore, the source of our knowing through the medium of a sign or mark that a thing has a certain character. It leads to the knowledge of a thing as possessing a character, say fire, because of its having another character, smoke, which we apprehend and which we know to be always connected with it. Thus, in *anumāna* we arrive at the knowledge of an object through the medium of two acts of knowledge or propositions.

The term *anumāna* is derived from *anu* followed by the root *mā* with the suffix *lyut*. *Māna* means an apprehension or a way of apprehension of an object and the prefix *anu* denotes after. So, the result of such knowledge is called *anumiti* which is the knowledge of an object due to a previous knowledge of some mark having the universal relation with the *sādhya* and being present in the *pakṣa* and *anumititva* is a kind of genus or universal.[4] Hence, inferential knowledge is produced not by direct apprehension but by means of knowledge of proban and that of the universal relation with the inferred object.[5] Inferential knowledge is definite knowledge produced by knowing the special coherence or proban concerning the major term that resides in doubtful substratum of major term to one who previously grasped coherence.[6]

All systems of Indian philosophy agree in holding that *anumāna* is a process of arriving at truth not by direct

---

3. *NM*, p. 109.
4. *anumititvam jātiviśeṣaḥ* — *PR*, p. 44, cf. *SPR*, p. 168.
5. *anumānam jñātasambandhasyaikadeśa darśanād eka deśāntare sannikṛṣṭe 'rthe buddhiḥ* — *Mb*, p.11.
6. *vyāpya darśanād asannikṛṣṭārthajñānam anumānam* — *PP*, p.196.

observation but by means of the knowledge of *vyāpti* or a universal relation between two things.

The Views of Anumāna According to Different Systems

THE VIEW OF THE CĀRVĀKAS

The Cārvākas do not consider the validity of *anumāna* and *śabda*. The author of the *Mahābhārata* says that the Cārvākas do not treat *anumāna* or inference and *āgama* or authority as *pramāṇas*. He states that both *anumāna* and *āgama* are based on *pratyakṣa* and this is the reason why the Cārvākas do not consider them as the means of valid knowledge.[7] The author of the epic also states that these philosophers do not recognize *anumāna* as *pramāṇa* for another important reason. The reason is that they cannot assert the validity of the *vyāpti* or the invariable concomitance which plays the most significant part in case of inference.[8] The materialists do not consider this *vyāpti* as infallible. Therefore, the author of the *Mahābhārata* observes, the materialists do not recognize *anumāna* as a *pramāṇa*.[9]

Actually it is not always possible to attain the correct knowledge of something with *anumāna*. Similar is the case of *upamāna*, etc. But the fact cannot be denied that one cannot totally dispense with *anumāna* in his practical life. Sometimes, it is found that *pratyakṣa* alone does not serve the purpose. The author of the *Nyāyakusumāñjali* observes that if a Cārvāka depends entirely on *pratyakṣa* he will invite his own miseries due to his dogmatic view. According to the author when a Cārvāka will go away to a remote place by leaving his wife

---

7. *pratyakṣam hyetayormūlam . . . na kiñcana* — Śāntiparva, *MBh*, 218-27.
8. *Ibid*., 218-26.
9. *anumānena yad gatyādidarśanam tadapi asati laksaṇe jñāpake hetau . . . vyabhicāradarśanāt . . . na kimapi* — *NC* on *MBh*.

and children at home, naturally he will be unable to perceive them from that place. Thus, according to his own standpoint, they will be non-existent to him and hence he will have to lament for their loss.[10] A section of later Cārvākas probably realized this problem. Therefore, Guṇaratna contends that the Cārvākas recognize *anumāna* also as *pramāṇa* for practical purposes. He says that these philosophers agree to accept such an inference only as is urgently necessary for proving the existence of fire on a hill with the help of a column of smoke. But they do not recognize such extra-sensory inference (*alaukika anumāna*) as is commonly accepted by some other philosophers to establish the existence of heaven, *adṛṣṭa*, etc.[11] Purandara is also of the view that the Cārvākas recognize *laukika anumāna* or popular inference as a *pramāṇa*.[12]

THE BAUDDHA VIEW

Diṅnāga, chief of the early Buddhist logicians and author of the *Pramāṇa Samuccaya*, described two means of knowing — perception and inference, and two corresponding objects are realized through them — the particular and the universal. The universals are cognized by inference and the particulars by perception.[13] Diṅnāga described the characters of the middle term (*hetu*) and we may form a definition of inference from these characters. Inference is the valid knowledge of an inferable property (*sādhya*) from the knowledge of a mark of inference which is invariably related to the *sādhya* and which abides in the minor term or subject of the inference (*pakṣa*).

10. *darśanadaśāyāṁ bhāvaniścayā . . . śokavikalovikrośet* — *NKM*, p. 355.
11. *cārvākair lokayātrānirvāhena pramāṇam dhūmādyanumānamisyate* etc. — *SSM*, p. 457.
12. *purandarastvāha lokapasiddham anumānam cārvākairapisyata eva . . .* — *Kamalaśila; TSa*, p. 526.
13. *PSa*, 2.1.

Dharmottara, however, states that this definition refers to the source and not to the essence of an inference. According to Dharmakīrti, author of the well-known *Nyāyabindu* and *Pramāṇavārttika*, *anumāna* is of two varieties: (1) inference for one's own sake (*svārthānumāna*) and (2) inference for the sake of others (*parārthānumāna*). Dharmakīrti defines *anumāna* thus: inference to the cognition of the inferrable from the sign having a three fold character.

THE JAINA VIEW

The Jainas, however, add *anumāna* to the list of *pramāṇa*s. The definition of *anumāna* according to the Jainas, is the knowledge of the major term derived from the knowledge of the middle term. Fire is inferred from smoke. Smoke is the middle term, and fire is the major term. *Anumāna* is based on *vyāpti* derived from induction (*tarka*). *Vyāpti* is the invariable concomitance between the middle and the major term. In inference, there are three terms — the middle term (*hetu* or *sādhana*), the major term (*sādhya*) and the minor term (*pakṣa*). The middle term is that which is definitely known to be inseparably connected with the major term. If the major term does not exist, the middle term cannot exist. If the middle term exists, the major term must also exist. This is the only mark of middle term.

NYĀYA VIEW OF ANUMĀNA

According to the Naiyāyikas, *anumāna* is the knowledge of an object through the medium of the knowledge of some mark by virtue of a relation of invariable concomitance between the two. Gautama does not define *anumāna*. He simply holds that inference presupposes perception. It is of three types.[14] Vātsyāyana, author of the *Nyāyabhāṣya*, a well-known

---

14. *atha tatpūrvakam trividhamanumānam pūrvavaccheśavat sāmānyatodṛṣṭaṁ ca* — *NS*, 1.1.5.

expostition on Gautama's *Nyāyasūtra* deals with the etymological aspect of the term *anumāna* and states that it is the knowledge of *liṅgī* arising after the knowledge of *liṅga*.[15] According to Vātsyāyana "no inference can follow from the absence of perception." Only when the observer has perceived fire and smoke to be related to each other, he is able to infer the existence of the fire and on the next occasion he perceives smoke.[16] According to Jayanta, *anumāna* is the instrument of knowledge of an unperceived probandum through the apprehension of a probans with fivefold characteristics together with the recollection of the relation of invariable concomitance between the two.[17] Bhāsarvajña in his *Nyāyasāra* defines inference as the means of knowing a thing beyond the range of the senses through its "inseparable connection (*samavāya sambandha*) with another thing" which lies within their range. Gaṅgeśa[18] following Śivāditya[19] defines inferential knowledge as knowledge produced by other knowledge.

VAIŚEṢIKA VIEW OF ANUMĀNA

Kaṇāda, founder of the Vaiśeṣika system, holds that *anumāna* is the knowledge of probandum derived from the knowledge of the probans. Praśastapāda defines *anumāna* as the knowledge which results from the apprehension of a sign (*liṅga*). He explains *liṅga* as that which is related to the probandum and which has co-presence and co-absence with

---

15. *liṅgaliṅginaḥ sambadhyayo darśanena liṅgasmṛtiravisaṁbadhyate smṛtyā liṅgadarśanena cāpratyakṣorthonumiyate* — *N.Bh.* 1.1.5.

16. *NBh* under *NS*, II.1.31.

17. *liṅgalinginoḥ sambandhyayo darśanena liṅgasmṛtirāvisambadhyate smṛtyā liṅgadarśanena cāpratyakṣortho numiyate* — *NBh*, 1.1.5.

18. *TCM*, ii, p.2.

19. *SP*, 146.

the probandum. According to Vaiśeṣika the knowledge of *anumāna* is derived from the mark, from which the existence of the probandum is inferred as its effect, or cause or conjunct or antagonist. From a heavy rainfall in the source of a river, flood in the river is inferred. From smoke the existence of fire is inferred. From the infuriated serpent, the existence of a mongoose hidden behind a bush is inferred. Thus, it can be said that mark is the means of inference which is based upon the relations of causality, conjunction, etc.

MĪMĀṀSĀ VIEW OF ANUMĀNA

The definition of *anumāna* as propounded by Śabara, a renowned commentator on the *Mīmāṁsāsūtra*, is that when a certain fixed relation has been known to subsist between two things, so that if we perceive any one of these things we have an idea of the other thing, this latter cognition is called inferential knowledge.[20] Kumārila Bhaṭṭa explains the compound *jñātasambandhasya* in four alternative ways, viz. (1) as referring to a person who knows the invariable relation between two things, e.g. smoke and fire, or (2) as referring to the substratum where the relationship, e.g. of smoke and fire is apprehended, (3) as referring simply to a known relationship or (4) as referring to both the *liṅga* and *liṅgin* together. Smoke and fire are parts (*ekadeśa*) of a logical whole.[21] Prabhākara on the other hand, holds that the word *jñātasambandhasya* qualifies the term *ekadeśa* in the compound *ekadeśadarśanāt* and refers to that whose invariable concomitance with another is known.[22]

---

20. *anumānam jñātasambandhasya ekadeśadarśanātekadeśāntare asannikṛṣṭe arthe buddhiḥ* — *SB* under *MS*, 1.1.5.

21. *TVa*, 2.3.

22. *jñātasambandhaniyamasya ekadeśasya darśanādekadeśāntare sannikṛṣṭe arthe yā buddhiḥ* — *PP*, p. 196.

Thus, though there are points of difference between Bhāṭṭa and Prābhākara schools of thought, a comprehensive definition of *anumāna* can be found out from the Mīmāṁsā standpoints based on Śabara's definition of *anumāna* in the following form: *anumāna* is the knowledge of a thing, not in contact with the sense-organs from the perception of another object when an invariable relation is known to hold between them.

VEDĀNTA VIEW

Inference (*anumāna*), according to Vedānta, is made by the notion of concomitance (*vyāpti jñāna*) between two things, acting through specific past impressions (*saṁskāra*). The notion of concomitance is generated by the perception of two things together, when no case of the failure of concomitance is known (*vyabhicāra jñāna*) regarding the subject.

SĀṀKHYA-YOGA VIEW OF ANUMĀNA

The most authentic work on Sāṁkhya logic is the *Sāṁkhyakārikā*. In the system of Sāṁkhya-Yoga, the definition of inference is influenced by the *Nyāyasūtra* of Gautama. The *Sāṁkhyakārikā* defines *anumāna* as the knowledge derived from sign and signate.[23] Vācaspati Miśra explains the definition elaborately. He states that *liṅga* means pervaded (*vyāpya*) and *liṅgī* means pervasive (*vyāpaka*).[24] These may, in other words, be called probans and probandum. He states that in the wording of *Sāṁkhyakārikā* probans and probandum stand for inferential knowledge. Thus, inferential knowledge arises through the knowledge that probans like smoke is pervaded and probandum like fire is pervasive.[25] Vācaspati Miśra further

23. *prativiṣayādhyavasāyo dṛṣṭaṁ trividhamanumānamākhyātam* I
talliṅga liṅgīpūrvakamāptaśrutirāpatavacanantu II — *SK.* K.5.

24. *liṅgam vyāpyam liṅgī vyāpakam* — *STK* under *SK.* K.5.

25. *dhūmādirvyāpya vahnyādirvyāpaka* — *STK* under *SK,* 5.

realizes that mere knowledge of invariable concomitance cannot lead to inferential knowledge. Everything like light on burnt up ashes existing on the mountain is not helpful in inferrring fire from smoke. Therefore, it requires, in addition, an application of probans on the subject or the place whence probandum is inferred. Here, Vācaspati Miśra states that the word *liṅgī* in the text of the *Sāṁkhyakārikā* should be considered as an example of *ekaśeśa*. While explaining the *kārikā*, it should be repeated. The first gives an idea of pervasive *vyāpaka* or probandum forming the part of invariable concomitance while the second means that (subject) which is possessed of probans, thus leading to the idea that probans is endowed with the condition of being present in subject (*pakṣadharmatā*).

The *Sāṁkhyacandrikā* also explains *liṅga* as probans and the *liṅgī* as probandum. The perception by the means of probans and probandum is deliberation that the *pakṣa* is possessor of the probans which is pervaded by probandum. This deliberation is inference.[26]

Māṭhara[27] and Gauḍapāda[28] also establish the necessity of both probans and probandum for inference but they draw further conclusion that sometimes *liṅga* leads to the knowledge of *liṅgī* and sometimes *liṅgī* to the knowledge of *liṅga*. For example, sometimes *liṅga* like *tridaṇḍa* lead to the knowledge of mendicant and sometimes *liṅgī* like mendicant leads to the knowledge of *liṅga* like *tridaṇḍa*.

---

26. *SC* under *SK*, K. 5.

27. *talliṅgaliṅgīpūrvakamiti liṅgena tridaṇḍādi darśanenadṛṣṭo api liṅgī sādhyate nūnamasau parivrāḍasti yasyedam tridaṇḍamiti*

— *MV* under *SK*, K.5.

28. *liṅgena liṅgī anumīyate yathā daṇḍena yatiḥ*............... *liṅginā liṅgamanumiyate yathā dṛṣṭvā yatimasyedam tridaṇḍamiti*

— *GB* under *SK*. K. 5.

The *Sāṁkhyasūtra* defines *anumāna* as knowledge of invariably associated *vyāpaka* through the knowledge of invariable association.[29] It seems that the *Sāṁkhyasūtra* defines it in terms of inferential knowledge of which invariable association serves as the cause. The definition is similar to the definition offered by Vindhyavāsin. Aniruddha, however, offers a different interpretation. He interprets *pratibandhadṛśaḥ* as "a case of a man who has known the invariable association." He imports the word *vyāpyajñānāt* (through the knowledge of pervaded) in his interpretation. The inference according to Aniruddha is "the knowledge of pervasive after knowing the pervaded in case of one who has observed the invariable concomitance between the two."[30] Vijñānabhikṣu interprets the *sūtra* as "inference is the knowledge of pervasive, through observing the invariable concomitance."[31]

In the system of Yoga, the definition of *anumāna* is found in the *Yogabhāṣya* of Vyāsa. Vyāsa defines inference as modification of *citta* brought about by the relation which exists in objects of homogeneous nature and does not exist in objects of heterogeneous nature, and ascertains chiefly the generic nature of an object.[32] The distinguishing factor of inference lies in the fact that such modification is caused by the knowledge of relation. The knowledge of *sambandha* and *pratibandha* (relation) is the commonly used expression in definition of inference by Vārṣagaṇya, Vyāsa and the *Sāṁkhyasūtra*. *Sambandha* means relation or invariable

---

29. *prativandhadṛśaḥ pratibaddhajñānamanumānam* — *SS*, 1.100.

30. *avinābhāvadarśino vyāpyajñānadanu vyāpakajñānamanumānam* — *SSV*, 1.100.

31. *vyāptidarśanād vyāpakajñānamanumānam*, — *SPB*, 1.100.

32. *anumeyasya tulya jātiyeṣu anuvṛttau bhinnajātiyebhya vyāvṛttaḥ sambandho yastadviṣayā sāmānyā vadhāraṇa pradhānā vṛttiranumānam* — *YB*, 1.7.

concomitance. Hence, it can be said that the definition of inference in Sāṁkhya-Yoga means the modification of *citta* brought about by invariable concomitance.

Distinction Between Perception and Inference

Both perception and inference are equally valid sources of knowledge. But perception is independent of any previous knowledge, while inference depends on previous perception. Inference is a knowledge which is preceded by perception. It depends on perception for the knowledge of *liṅga* or the middle term as subsisting in the *pakṣa* or the minor term. It depends on perception for the knowledge of *vyāpti*. Thus, inference is knowledge derived from some other knowledge. That is, inference is mediate knowledge and perception is immediate knowledge of an object. All perception is of one kind that is the knowledge of what is given. But there are different kinds of inferences based on different kinds of *vyāpti* or universal relation. Perception takes place between the contact of sense-organs with the objects. It gives the knowledge of only those objects which lie within the range of the senses. Hence, it is limited to present objects. But the knowledge of inference is due to the knowledge of *vyāpti* or universal relations among objects. It is by means of such universal relations that inference gives us knowledge of objects beyond the reach of our senses. It extends our knowledge from the present to the past, distant and future.

The Constituents of Inference

From the definition of inference it is noted that an inference is a distinct means of knowledge, because it gives us knowledge concerning things we are not immediately acquainted with, but the things in question must be such that we can immediately be acquainted with them. From the definition of inference it will appear that there must be three propositions and three terms in any inference. In inference one arrives at the knowledge of some unperceived character of object through the knowledge of some *liṅga* or sign in it and *vyāpti* or a universal relation between the sign and the inferred character. There is first the knowledge of *liṅga* in relation to the *pakṣa* or the subject of inference. Secondly, inference requires the knowledge of *vyāpti* or a universal relation between the *liṅga* and the *sādhya* or the middle term and major term. This knowledge of the *liṅga* or middle term as always related to the *sādhya* or major term is the result of the previous experience of their relation to each other. Thirdly, the inferential knowledge results from the previous knowledge of the *liṅga* and that of its universal relation with the *sādhya*. Corresponding to the minor, major and middle terms of the syllogism, inference in Indian logic contains three terms, namely, *pakṣa*, *sādhya* and *hetu*. The *pakṣa* is the subject in the course of the inferential reasoning. It is that individual or class about which we want to establish something or predicate an attribute which is suspected but not definitely known to be present in it.[33] While the *pakṣa* is the subject, the *sādhya* is the object of inference. It is *sādhya* which we want to know or prove by means of any inference. The *sādhya* is that character of the *pakṣa* or minor term which is not perceived by any one but indicated by some sign present in it. Regarding the exact nature of the *sādhya*, there is some difference of opinion among the different systems of Indian philosophy. According to the Advaita Vedānta what is inferred is the unperceived character of the subject or minor term of inference. In the inferential knowledge that the hill is fiery, it is not the hill which is inferred though it is perceived. Actually "the fire" is inferred.

---

33. *saṁdigdhasādhyavān pakṣaḥ* — *TS*, p. 44.

According to Buddhists "the fire" cannot be the object of inference from smoke. One can know it just when one knows the smoke as related to fire. The term *relation* cannot be used unless there are two things to be related. But in inference only one thing, i.e. the hill is perceived. The hill being perceived cannot be said to be the object of inference. Therefore, "the hill as possessed of fire" is inferred. According to Mīmāṁsakas the subject or minor term which is related to the predicate or the major term is inferred.[34] The Naiyāyikas, however, maintain that the object of inference may be different in different cases. What is inferred may be either the subject or minor term as related to the major term, or the major term as related to the minor, or the middle term taken as a particular individual and related to the major term.[35] The third term of inference is called the *liṅga* or sign because it serves to indicate that which one does not perceive. It is also called the *hetu* or *sādhana* insofar as it is the ground of the knowledge of *sādhya* or what is inferred. It is found once in relation to the *pakṣa* or minor term and then in relation to the *sādhya* or the major term. It is through an universal relation between the *hetu* and the *sādhya* or the middle and major terms that the *pakṣa* or minor term which is related to the middle, becomes connected with the *sādhya* or major term. There are five characteristics of the middle term. The first is *pakṣadharmatā*, or its being a character of the *pakṣa*. The middle term must be related to the minor term, e.g. the hill is smoky. The second is *sapakṣatva* or its presence in all homogeneous instances in which the major term exists, e.g. all smoky objects are fiery. The third is *vipakṣatva* or its absence in all heterogeneous instances in which the major term is absent, e.g. whatever is not smoky is not

---

34. *tasmāt dharmaviśiṣṭasya dharmiṇaḥ syāt prameyatā* .
— *SV*, ch. on Inference.

35. *NBh*, 1.1.36.

fiery. The fourth is *abādhitaviṣayatva* or the uncontradictoriness of its object, e.g. the middle term must not establish absurd and contradictory objects as the coolness of fire, etc. The fifth character of the middle term is *asatpratipakṣatva* or the absence of counteracting reasons leading to a contradictory conclusion.

The logicians have put forth several views regarding the number of these components. A variety of opinions are also observed in the system of Sāṁkhya-Yoga. The *Yuktidīpikā* enumerates ten components of inference. Māṭhara records five components of inference. Vijñānabhikṣu and Aniruddha also recognize the five components of inference. The ten components of inference enumerated by *Yuktidīpikā* are the following — inquisitiveness, doubt, purpose, conjecturing, throwing aside doubt, proposition, probans, example, application and conclusion.

The Ground of Inference

In inference the knowledge of the *sādhya* or major term as related to the *pakṣa* or minor term depends on the knowledge of *vyāpti* between the middle and major terms. It is on the ground of *vyāpti* or a universal relation that the middle term leads to the knowledge of the inferred object. *Vyāpti* and *pakṣadharmatā* are the two main grounds of inference. If fire is inferred on the hill when smoke is perceived in it, it is *pakṣadharmatā* and when universal relation between fire and smoke is taken into consideration it is called *vyāpti*. *Vyāpti* literally means the state of pervasion, i.e. one of the facts pervades (*vyāpaka*) and the other is pervaded (*vyāpya*). A fact is said to pervade another when it always accompanies the other. Contrariwise, a fact is said to be pervaded by another when it is always accompanied by the other. Etymologically *vyāpti* is a special relation between two facts which is universal in its nature. This special relationship has been referred to by various seemingly synonymous words such as *liṅga-liṅgī sambandha, sādhyasādhanabhāva, gamakagamyabhāva, avinābhāva-niyama, prasiddhi, pratibandha, avinābhāva*, etc. Though the Indian thinkers who regard inference to be a means of knowledge unanimously accept the principle of invariable concomitance (*vyāpti*) as an indispensible condition for inference, yet they differ with regard to its function, denotation, nature and the ways of its ascertainment. According to the Jainas, *anumāna* is based on *vyāpti* derived from induction (*tarka*). *Vyāpti* is the invariable concomitance between the middle and the major term. According to the Buddhists, *vyāpti* is the inductive relation. It is the relation of invariable concomitance between the middle term (*hetu*) and the major term (*sādhya*). Arcata, the Buddhist philosopher in *Hetubinduṭīkā*, states that *vyāpti* is the character of the probans as well as of the probandum. Kaṇāda seems to be aware of invariable concomitance of the probans with the probandum and its necessity for inference. He, however, calls it *prasiddhi*.[36] Praśastapāda mentions *vidhi* as a general principle of invariable concomitance derived from the observation of particular instances of co-presence and co-absence of the probans and probandum.[37] The Naiyāyikas hold the necessity of invariable concomitance or *vyāpti*. Udayana holds the invariable concomitance, *vidhi*, as non-separateness of the probans from the probandum.[38] Śabara introduces the element of invariable relation in the definition of inference. Kumārila Bhaṭṭa holds that the term *sambandha* in the definition of *anumāna* in the *Śābarabhāṣya* refers to the invariable

---

36. *prasiddhipūrvakatvādapadeśasya* — *VS*, 3.1.14.

37. *vidhistu yatra dhūmastatrāgniragnyabhāve dhūme api na bhavati* — *VB* (Anu).

38. *vidhistu avinābhāvagrahaṇaprakāraḥ* — *KV*, p. 295.

concomitance (*vyāpti*) of the middle term with the major term.[39] According to Advaita Vedānta *anumāna* is produced by the knowledge of invariable concomitance (*vyāpti jñāna*) of the *sādhana* or middle term with the *sādhya* or major term. The knowledge of *vyāpti* is the instrumental cause of inference. According to them *vyāpti* is the co-existence of the middle term and the major term in all the substrata of the middle term. It is known by observation of concomitance of the middle term with the major term and non-observation of their non-concomitance.[40]

In Sāṁkhya-Yoga philosophy, Vācaspati's discussion of pervaded and pervasive gives an idea of *vyāpti*. He explains the term *vyāpya* (pervaded) as that which is invariably and naturally associated with the nature of an object, without involving certain conditions suspected or ascertained.[41] The term *vyāpaka* (pervasive) is that with the nature of which the former is related.[42] The relation stands here for invariable association which is denoted by the term *vyāpti*. The case of relation involving condition can be explained thus: one infers smoke from fire. But it is observed that fire is not naturally related to smoke. If fire would have been invariably associated with smoke, it would always be accompanied with smoke and would never have been found without smoke. But in some cases like iron ball fire exists without smoke. Therefore, the association of fire with smoke involves condition. The fire

---

39. *sambandho vyāptiriṣṭātra liṅgadharmasya liṅginā vyāpyasya gamakattvam ca vyāpakaṃ gamyamiṣyate* — *SV*, p. 14.
40. *sā ca vyabhicārajñāne sati sahacāradarśanena gṛhyate* —*VP*, ii.
41. *saṁkitasamāropitopādhinirākaraṇena vastusvabhāva prativaddham vyāpyam* — *STK* under *SK*. 5.
42. *yena ca pratibaddham tad vyāpakam* — *Ibid.*

requires wet fuel in addition to itself to give rise to smoke. Thus, fire does not accompany the smoke naturally. On the contrary it involves further condition of wet fuel. It may be clarified with one example. The example given in the sub-commentary of Balarāma Udāsīna on the *Tattvakaumudī* is very appropriate. Suppose a lady named Maitreyī has nine sons. One comes to see eight of them and finds all of them are black in complexion. From this he comes to the conclusion that black complexion is associated with the fact of being the son of Maitreyī. But, however, such a conclusion, i.e. the black complexion associated with the son of Maitreyī is based upon a wrong notion. The eating of green vegetables, etc. is a condition for black complexion. This fact is deduced from the fact that the ninth son of Maitreyī is of fair complextion. If there would have been natural and unconditional relation between being the son of Maitreyī and darkness of complexion the ninth son would also be dark in complexion.[43] The condition involved in this can be conjectured or ascertained. In the case of the complexion of son of Maitreyī the condition, viz. eating green vegetables is conjectured because it is not ascertained through some means of knowledge or reasoning. The case of ascertained condition is the inference of smoke from fire. It is ascertained through perception that smoke is invariably associated with wet fuel while fire exists without that also. It may be observed that Vācaspati Miśra assimilated the view of the Bauddhas and the Naiyāyikas while offering the definition of *vyāpti*. According to the Bauddha, *vyāpti* means the natural relation (*svābhāvika-sambandha*) while according to the Naiyāyikas it is the unconditional relation (*nirupādhika-*

---

43. *yathāmitrātanayatvena śyamātve sādhye sākādyāhārā pariṇatijatvam iti sa śyāmo mitrātanayatvādṛṣṭa śyāmatva, visiṣṭamitrā tanayavat,*
— *VT* on *STK* 5.

sambandha). Both of these views are brought together in the *Sārabodhinī* while discussing the definition of *vyāpti*.[44]

The *Sāṁkhyasūtra* defines *vyāpti* as invariable concomitance of properties in case of two or one of them.[45] The part of the definition in case of both refers to the case of equal pervasion (*samavyāpti*); while the latter half, viz. in case of one of them refers to the cases of unequal pervasion (*viṣamavyāpti*).

The Jayamaṅgalā enumerates seven kinds of relation between sign and signate:[46] (i) master and servant, (ii) original and its modification, (iii) cause and effect, (iv) pot and its possessor, (v) association as between *cakra* bird and its mate, (vi) opposition, as between cold and hot and (vii) the object and the being for which it is meant as between an object of enjoyment and its enjoyer.

In the *Sāṁkhyasūtra*, some more details are found regarding pervasion (*vyāpti*). According to them *vyāpti* is not a different category from the co-existence of properties, otherwise it would lead to the cumbrousness of self-evident fact as it would compel to consider *vyāpti* as an independent category.[47] According to Aniruddha, if *vyāpti* is considered as an independent category the invariable association would require separate mention. Therefore, it is said that invariable association itself is *vyāpti*.[48] Vijñānabhikṣu adds that if *vyāpti* is an additional entity to those admitted by Sāṁkhya, it would lead to the acceptance of the substratum of *vyāpti* as another

---

44. Vide *STK*, pp. 136-37.

45. *niyatadharmasāhityamubhayorekatarasya vā vyāptiḥ* — *SS*, 5.29.

46. *kadācilliṅga pūrvakam kadācilliṅgipurvakam dṛśyate. . . . gamyagamakatvam satisambandhe* — JM on *SK*, 5, p. 8.

47. *na tattvāntaram vastukalpanāprasakteḥ* — *SS*, 5.30.

48. *tattvāntarasvīkāre apyavyabhicāro vaktavyaḥ* — *SSV*, 5.30.

additional entity and it would be difficult to carry.[49] In the opinion of some *ācāryas vyāpti* is the result of the power of objects and as such an additional entity which is quoted in the *Sāṁkhyasūtra*.[50] On this point Aniruddha states that *vyāpti* is the power in pervasive and pervaded and is observed through observing the two. In the opinion of Vijñānabhikṣu *vyāpti* should be considered as arising of power of pervasive and pervaded and not that of objects. Pañcaśikha holds that *vyāpti* means the relation connected with power of being sustained.[51] In the Sāṁkhya system every effect exists in its cause before its manifestation and after unmanifestation. So the cause is having a power of sustaining the effect while the effect has got a power of being an object located. *Vyāpti* is the power of being associated in the pervaded. Aniruddha justifies the meaning of the word *ādheyaśakti* in the definition. It should be the power of being related as pervaded and not the object itself, otherwise just after seeing the object even a person ignorant of particular power of a particular object would consider the object capable for a particular thing. According to Pañcaśikha, *vyāpti* means possession of power of being related as a sustained and hence not an independent category in form of the power essentially belonging to objects, before its manifestation. In fact, the view of Pañcaśikha differs from that of the other teachers mainly in two respects. Firstly, unlike other teachers, Pāncaśikha does not consider *vyāpti* as a separate concept. Secondly, Pañcaśikha considers that *vyāpti* is *vyāpakatva* or the state of being pervaded and is found in case of pervaded only. The other teachers, however, relate *vyāpti* to both the associates.

---

49. *niyatadharmasāhityātirikta vyāptirṇa bhavati vyāptitvāśrayasya vastuno 'pi kalpanāprasaṅgāt* — *SPB*, 5.30.

50. *nijasaktyudbhavamityacāryāḥ* — *SS*, 5.31.

51. *ādheyaśaktiyogena iti pañcaśikhaḥ* — *SS*, 5.32.

Ascertainment of Vyāpti

Indian systems of philosophy take inference as a process of reasoning which is not only formally valid but also materially true. This inference depends on *vyāpti* (universal relation). So, the most vital question regarding inference relates to the way of getting the universal proposition. One intends to know the process of knowing *vyāpti* so as to realize how one can pass from particular cases of the relation between smoke and fire in the kitchen, etc. to the universal proposition such as all cases of smoke are fire.

THE CĀRVĀKA VIEW

All Indian thinkers other than the Cārvākas have discussed the ways of ascertaining *vyāpti*. The Cārvākas do not accept *anumāna* as a source of valid knowledge. For them perception is the only source of knowledge. In their opinion, it is impossible to ascertain that smoke is invariably and universally accompanied by fire because if it is accepted that a person knows all cases of smoke in the past and present, future cases will remain outside the limits of his knowledge. So, in their opinion, a universal relation, i.e. *vyāpti* cannot be ascertained.

THE BUDDHIST VIEW

The Buddhists accept *vyāpti* as a ground of inference and have propounded the theory of identity and causality in this regard. They maintain that a universal relation can be ascertained without considering all its past, present and future cases if it is proved that the referred cases are related either through causality or through identity of essence.

THE JAINA VIEW

The Jaina logicians refer to *tarka* as a means of ascertaining *vyāpti*. *Tarka* is regarded as a way of knowing the invariable concomitance of the middle term with the major term in the past, in the present and in the future arising from the observation of their co-presence and co-absence.

THE VAIŚEṢIKA VIEW

Praśastapāda holds that the invariable concomitance between the probans and the probandum is known by the repeated observation of their agreement in presence and agreement in absence.

THE BHĀṬṬA VIEW

According to Kumārila Bhaṭṭa, *vyāpti* is known through repeated observation. By *vyāpti* he means a necessary relation generally between two particulars. *Vyāpti* is established by the joint method of agreement and difference. Kumārila holds that *vyāpti* is induction from a limited number of observed cases.

THE PRĀBHĀKARA VIEW

According to Prabhākara, though the knowledge of *vyāpti* is gained by a single act of sense perception in the very first observation, e.g. of smoke and fire, subsequent observations confirm the *vyāpti* apprehended in the first observation. The Prābhākaras refer to repeatẹd observation but they assign separate roles to the first and the subsequent observation.

THE VEDĀNTA VIEW

According to the Vedānta, *vyāpti* or a universal proposition is the result of an induction by simple enumeration. It rests on the uncontradicted experience of agreement in presence between two things. When one finds that two things go together and that there is no exception to their relation, one may take them as universally related.

THE NYĀYA VIEW

The Nyāya agrees with the Vedānta in holding that *vyāpti* is established by means of uncontradicted experience of the relation between two things. It is based not on any principle like causality or identity, but on the uniform experience of concomitance between two objects. The Nyāya goes further than the Vedānta and supplements the uncontradicted observation of agreement in presence by that of agreement in absence and *tarka* or indirect proof.[52]

THE SĀṀKHYA-YOGA VIEW

In Sāṁkhya-Yoga philosophy also the question naturally arises as to how can such an invariable association between two objects be ascertained. One cannot personally experience all the cases of two objects found together. In the opinion of Vijñānabhikṣu such an invariableness should be apprehended through appropriate confutation (*anukūlatarka*).[53] He explains it in this way: If one has to know the relation of smoke with fire, one observes smoke associated with fire and starts thinking that smoke is invariably associated with fire; if smoke would not have been invariably associated with fire, it would have been perceived without fire, but such a case is not observed, and so there is no possibility of smoke without fire. Therefore, the invariableness is ascertained through such a confutation.

As regards the kinds of *vyāpti*, the Sāṁkhya-Yoga texts do not discuss the problem explicitly. While discussing the nature of inference, the *Yogabhāṣya* differentiates the *vyāpti* into positive invariableness (*anvaya vyāpti*) and negative

52. *VP*, Ch. II.

53. *niyamaścānukūlatarkeṇa grāhya iti na vyāptigrahāsambhava iti bhāvaḥ* — *SPB*, 5.29.

invariableness (*vyatireka vyāpti*). Inference is said to be caused by the relation which is found present in the similar cases and absent in the dissimilar cases.[54] The difference between *anvaya vyāpti* and *vyatireka vyāpti* is simple. In the case of the *anvaya vyāpti,* existence of probans and probandum at the same place is stressed and illustrated, while in the case of the *vyatireka vyāpti,* their negation is stressed and illustrated. While discussing the nature of *vyāpti,* the *Sāṁkhyasūtra* gives another division of *vyāpti.* Aniruddha[55] and Vijñānabhikṣu[56] enumerate two kinds of *vyāpti* as *samavyāpti* (equal pervasion) and *viṣama vyāpti* (unequal pervasion). When the space or time of the pervader and the pervaded is similar it is *samavyāpti* and when the pervaded occupies lesser space or time it is termed as *viṣamavyāpti.*

The Types of Anumāna

In Indian logic, *anumāna* has not been divided into formal and material or deductive and inductive or mediate and immediate or pure and mixed types. The Indian logicians are, no doubt, aware of the varieties and subvarieties of *anumāna.* But the principles upon which the varieties of *anumāna* are based are different from those of Western inference. In Indian philosophy, *anumāna* has been classified in various ways, for example (a) *pūrvavat, śeṣavat* and *sāmānyatodṛṣṭa,* (b) *kevalānvayī, kevalavyatirekī* and *anvayavyatirekī,* (c) *svārtha* and *parārtha* and (d) *vīta* and *avīta.*

Various divisions of *anumāna* based on various principles are found in the system of Sāṁkhya-Yoga. The *Sāṁkhyakārikā*

---

54. *tulyajātieṣvanuvṛtto bhinnajātīyebhyo vyāvṛttaḥ sambandho* — *YB*, 1.7.

55. *ubhayorīti samavyāptikayoḥ . . . viṣamavyāptikasya* — *SSV*, 5.29.

56. *ubhayorīti samavyāptipakṣe proktam* — *SPB*, 5.29.

refers to the division of *anumāna* into three kinds,[57] which according to its commentators refer to *pūrvavat, śeṣavat* and *sāmānyatodṛṣṭa*. In addition to the above three kinds, Aniruddha mentions other three kinds, viz. *kevalānvayī kevalavyatirekī* and *anvayavyatirekī* raising the number of kinds of *anumāna* to six.[58] While discussing *anumāna,* the *Yuktidīpikā* and Māṭhara divide inference into one's own self (*svārtha*) and that for others (*parārtha*). However, the *Yuktidīpikā*[59] and Vācaspati[60] incorporate division of inference into *vīta* and *avīta.*

PŪRVAVAT, ŚEṢAVAT AND SĀMANYATODṚṢṬA

The *Sāṁkhyakārikā* refers to the division of *anumāna* into three kinds which is propounded by Gautama in his *Nyāyasūtra.*[61] Vātsyāyana offers two alternative explanations of the nature of *pūrvavat,* etc. The commentators of the *Sāṁkhyakārikā* follow either of the two explanations offered by Vatsyāyana. Therefore, it will be worthwhile to discuss Vātsyāyana's explanation of the nature of these varieties before discussing them on the basis of the commentaries of *Sāṁkhyakārikā.*

According to the first explanation, the *pūrvavat* is that in which an effect is inferred from its cause, e.g. from the rise of cloud it is inferred that it will rain. The *śeṣavat* is that in which the cause is inferred from its effect, e.g. seeing the water of

---

57. *trividhamanumānamākhyātam*........... — *SK. K,* 5.

58. *anenānvayī, vyatirekī, anvayavyatirekī, pūrvavat, śeṣavat, sāmānyatodṛṣṭañca saṁgṛhītam* — *SSV,* 1.100.

59. *tatra prayogamātrabhedāt dvaividhyam vītaḥ avītaḥ iti* — *YD* under *SK,* 5.

60. *tābaddvividham vītamavītañca,* — *STK* under *SK,* 5.

61. *atha tatpūrvakam trividhamanumānam pūrvacche ṣavatsāmānyatodṛṣṭañca* — *NS,* 1.1.5.

river as different from that in the past, as also the fullness of the river, i.e. stream and the swiftness of the current, it is inferred that it had rained. The *sāmānyatodṛṣṭa* is illustrated as the perception of something at some other place is caused by movement, as the sun is observed at different places. Therefore, it is inferred that there is movement of the sun, though imperceptible. Another interpretation of the term *pūrvavat* as suggested by Vātsyāyana is that it is a type of inference in which out of two things one that is not perceived is inferred from the perception of the other on the basis of a former perception of both of these things together, e.g. inference of unperceived fire from perceived smoke on the basis of the previous perception of fire and smoke together. As an alternative interpretation of the term *śeṣavat*, Vātsyāyana states that it may also signify as remainder. There could be many possibilities with regard to the explanation of a fact. When all the possibilities except one are rejected, the remaining one is cognized through the means of *śeṣavat* inference, e.g. sound is distinct from the categories of generality, individuality and inherence. The second explanation offered by Vātsyāyana refers to *sāmānyotodṛṣṭa* as an inference in which the relation between the antecedent and the consequent, not being a matter of perception, is established. On the ground of an abstract similarity with something else, e.g. inference of soul on the basis of the fact that desire, etc. are qualities and that qualities must abide in some substance namely the self.

The *Yuktidīpikā* states that the term *pūrva* means cause and *pūrvavat* means that which has a cause as a probans. It means the inference in case of which after observing the cause one comes to know the future effect.[62] For example, one apprehends

---

62. *tatra pūrvavat yadā karaṇamavyuditam dṛṣṭvā bhaviṣyattvaṃ kāryasya pratipadyate* — *YD* under *SK*, K. 5.

future rains after observing the rise of cloud. The author of *Yuktidīpikā*, however, realizes the difficulty in the above example. The valid probans by its very nature should necessarily lead to the probandum and failing it the probans ceases to be a probans. But the above example lacks in the above condition and hence ceases to be a proper example. The rise of cloud is not necessarily the cause of rain. There is no invariable relation between rise of clouds and rains, because there is the possibility of obstruction by wind and the rest. Hence, the *Yuktidīpikā* defines *pūrvavat* thus — *pūrvavat* is that through which observing the causal power arrested amongst the assisting powers free from obstructing elements one comes to know future rise of effect just as after observing the clay possessed by the potter who is active and having the instrument like the iron rod and the rest one comes to know the future preparation of a pot. According to Vijñānabhikṣu and Māṭhara, *pūrvavat* depends upon the past experience. For example, one infers the future rain through particular rise of cloud. Gauḍapāda follows the *Yuktidīpikā* in explaining it as the inference which has cause as the probans.

Śeṣavat is variously interpreted in three ways: (i) from effect to cause, (ii) from one part to the rest, and (iii) through elimination. The *Yuktidīpikā* gives the first interpretation. The *Yuktidīpikā* defines *śeṣavat* as that in which after observing the accomplishment of an effect one comes to know the prior existence of its cause. For example, one comes to know the meeting of the couple after seeing a boy. The *Yuktidīpikā* however, feels that such an example is also not faultless. There is no invariable relation between meeting of a couple and birth of a boy. The birth of Droṇa is heard to be without meeting of the couple. Therefore, the example is rejected by the *Yuktidīpikā*. The *Yuktidīpikā* gives a faultless example as after seeing the leaf one comes to know the root of water lily or after seeing the sprout one comes to know the seed.[63] Māṭhara[64] and Gauḍapāda[65] give the second of the interpretations mentioned above. For example, after finding a drop of water from the sea to be saltish one infers that the rest of the water is also saltish. Vācaspati Miśra gives third of the above-mentioned interpretation. He quotes the *Nyāyabhāṣya* of Vātsyāyana that *śeṣavat* is the definite knowledge with reference to the residual after eliminating the undesirably involved objects when there remains no undersirable involvement of something else.[66]

The *sāmānyatodṛṣṭa* type of *anumāna* is understood in two ways: (i) based upon analogy and (ii) inferring a characteristic in other cases after observing it in one case. Some of the commentators of the *Sāṁkhyakārikā* give both of these interpretations while some give one of them. Māṭhara gives the latter interpretation. For example, observing the mango tree having flower, one infers the flowers on other trees as well.[67] Gauḍapāda gives both of the above interpretations. For the former he gives the following example: the moon and stars have movement because they change the place. Whatever changes the place has movement just as Caitra.[68] For the latter he gives the same example as offered by Māṭhara. The

---

63. *parṇam dṛṣṭvā śālukam pratipadyate aṅkuram vā dṛṣṭvā vījamiti tadā śeṣavat* — *YD* under *SK*, K. 5.

64. *samudrodakavindum prāśya śeṣasya lavaṇabhāva anumīyate iti śeṣavat* — *MV* under *SK*, K. 5.

65. *samudrādekam jalavalam lavaṇamāsādya śeṣasya 'pyasti* — *GB* under *SK*, K. 5.

66. *śiṣyate pariśiṣyate iti śeṣaḥ sa eva viṣayatayā yasyāstyanumānajñānasya taccheṣavat* — *STK* under *SK*. K.5.

67. *puṣpitāmradarśanāt anyatra puṣpita āmarā iti* — *MV* under *SK*, K. 5.

68. *deśāntarāddeśāntaram dṛṣṭam gatimaccandratārakam, caitra* — *GB* under *SK*, K. 5.

Yuktidīpikā discusses the *sāmānyatodṛṣṭa* more elaborately. It states that after observing the invariable association of two objects one comes to know the invariable association of the objects of same group at some other place at some other time.[69] For example, after observing the relation of smoke and fire one comes to know at other time the existence of some other fire through some other smoke.

SVĀRTHA AND PARĀRTHA

Though the division of *anumāna* into *svārtha* and *parārtha* is not found in the *Nyāyasūtra* or *Vaiśeṣikasūtra*, Praśastapāda has mentioned it on the *Vaiśeṣikasūtra*. This division is accepted by Buddhists also. Etymologically what is intended for oneself is *svārthānumāna* and what is intended for others is *parārthānumāna*. In the *svārthānumāna*, premises are known from our own experience, while in *parārthānumāna* premises are discovered by one man and imparted to another through the medium of language. *Parārthānumāna* is, however, based upon *svārthānumāna* in the sense that one cannot convince other if he himself is not convinced. The *Sāṁkhyakārikā* does not discuss the division of *anumāna*. The *Yuktidīpikā* and Māṭhara seem to imply such a division in their discussion of inference.

KEVALĀNVAYĪ, KEVALAVYATIREKĪ AND ANVAYAVYATIREKĪ

Uddyotakara is the first logician to introduce *kevalānvayī*, *kevalavyatirekī* and *anvayavyatirekī* as the varieties of inference.[70] If a middle term is positively related to the major term it is called *kevalānvayī*. If the middle term is negatively related to the major term it is called *kevalavyatirekī*. If the middle term is

69. *sāmānyatodṛṣṭam nāma yatraikadā arthayorvyabhicāra mupalabhy deśāntare kālāntare ca tajjātīyayoravyabhicāraṁ pratipadyate*
— *YD* under *SK*, K. 5.

70. *trividhamiti anvayī vyatirekī anvayavyātirekī ceti* — *NV*, 1.1.5.

positively and negatively related to the major term in an inference then it is called *anvayavyatirekī*. Aniruddha mentions *kevalānvayī, kevalavyatirekī* and *anvayavyatirekī* in addition to the three kinds of inference, i.e. *pūrvavat, śeṣavat* and *sāmānyatodṛṣṭa*. In the case of *kevalānvayī* the *vyāpti* is affirmative only and there is no possibility of counter example. In the case of *kevalavyatirekī* the *vyāpti* is negative only and there is no possibility of homogeneous example, while in the case of *anvayavyatirekī* the *vyāpti* can be stated in both the forms. The example of *kevalānvayī* is: Man is mortal because he is born. The example of *kevalavyatirekī* is: the cloth does not differ from threads, because it is of the nature of threads. In this case there is no possibitity of homogeneous instance. An instance of the third kind of inference, i.e. *anvayavyatirekī* is fire through smoke.

VĪTA AND AVĪTA

Vīta and *avīta* mean direct inference and inference through elimination. The Sāṁkhya texts specially the *Yuktidīpikā* has given importance to *vīta* and *avīta* type of *anumāna* and has discussed the characteristics of these two in detail. In his *Sāṁkhyatattvakaumudī* Vācaspati discussed the division of *vīta* and *avīta* types of *anumāna* correlating it with the other division of *anumāna* like *pūrvavat*, etc. But the discussion of *vīta* and *avīta* types of *anumāna* is not found in some other texts of Sāṁkhya-Yoga. The division has found an important place in the system of Nyāya also. In the system of Nyāya, Uddyotakara is the earliest logician to discuss the division of *anumāna* into *vīta* and *avīta*. The *vīta* gives rise to the knowledge of an object when employed in its own essential form while the *avīta* does so through refuting the other's stand. The former establishes an object in a positive way. The *avīta*, however, works through rejection or negation.

The Sāṁkhya has given importance to the division of *anumāna* as *vīta* and *avīta*. The *Yuktidīpikā* in its opening verse compares the Sāṁkhya system with an elephant having *vīta* and *avīta* as its tusks and thus easily enjoying in the forest of subject (*pakṣatā*). The *Yuktidīpikā* divides *anumāna* into two types: *vīta* and *avīta*. According to the *Yuktidīpikā, vīta* is that when the probans is applied in its very form and the *avīta* is through elimination when other possibilities are eliminated. The *Yuktidīpikā* states that the essential form of probans can be of two kinds — generic and particular. In the case of *vīta* the probans is employed in its essential without a reference to the exclusion of the other's stand. This is *vīta* division of *anumāna*. In the case of *avīta* the probans does not prove the probandum directly but wards off the other possible alternatives. Vācaspati Miśra in his *Nyāyavārttikatātparyaṭīkā* and also in his *Sāṁkhyatattvakaumudī* mentions the two-fold division of *anumāna,* viz. *vīta* and *avīta*. According to him *vīta* means that which is available in various ways, i.e. besides its presence in *pakṣa* it is present in *sapakṣa* and is absent in other dissimilar cases (*vipakṣa*), e.g. whatever is smoky is fiery, the hill is smoky, therefore, the hill is fiery. The *avīta* is different from it. *Avīta* is not found in *sapakṣa*. In the Nyāya system, however, they are *anvayī* and *vyatirekī*. Vācaspati Miśra reconciles the above division with the other three divisions, i.e. *pūrvavat, śeṣavat* and *sāmānyatodṛṣṭa*. According to him *anumāna* is firstly of two kinds, *vīta* and *avīta*. He defines *vīta* as that which gives rise to the inferential mainly through positive invariable concomitance and which leads to positive result. *Vīta* should not be understood as identical with *kevalānvayī*. It is applicable to both the *kevalānvayī* and *anvayavyatirekī*. The *vīta* is of two kinds, *pūrvavat* and *sāmānyatodṛṣṭa*. The *avīta* is opposite to *vīta* in nature. It is defined as that which gives rise to the inferential knowledge through negative invariable concomitance and which stresses the negative aspect. Vācaspati states that it is a case of *kevalavyatirekī*. He further states that *avīta* is identical with *śeṣavat* type of *anumāna*. For example, sound is specific quality of ether because it is not a specific quality of earth, water, fire, air, space, time, *manas* and the self. By elimination of other alternatives it is inferred that sound is the specific quality of ether which is the only remaining substance.

Fallacy

The term fallacy is associated with reasoning. Reason is regarded as true or valid when it has threefold property or character, lacking one of which means false or invalid reason. The triple nature of valid reason is as follows: (1) Its definite presence in the subject of inference, substratum, e.g. smoke must be present in the hill. It means that reason must be present in the subject of inference. The presence in the subject, i.e. *pakṣadharmatā*, is the first characteristic of valid reason. (2) Its definite presence must be in all the objects similar to substratum (*pakṣa*). The middle term must be present in all positive instances as in the kitchen where fire exists. (3) Its definite absence in the negative instances, that is, the middle term must be absent in the negative instances. This is the third nature of valid reason named *vyatireka*. Thus, the three characteristics are conditions of valid reason. Therefore, their inversion of either one or two characteristics turns the probans, as Kaṇāda observes, into fallacy. According to Gāgabhaṭṭa, the valid knowledge of the counter correlate which presents as inferential knowledge is called fallacy. The discussion on fallacy is not found in the *Mīmāṁsāsūtra* and *Śabarabhāṣya*. Kumārila and Prabhākara explain it. Kumārila admits three types of fallacy. Gautama in his Nyāya philosophy finds five varieties of fallacy.

But in the extant text of the Sāṁkhya-Yoga, the subject "fallacies in *anumāna*" is not discussed. The *Māṭharavṛtti* makes reference to them without explaining them. The *Māṭharavṛtti* states that there are thirty-three fallacies of *anumāna*. Further discussions about these fallacies are not found in the extant texts of Sāṁkhya-Yoga. Various important issues on inference are not discussed in the Sāṁkhya-Yoga text. However, it seems that such a silence could be due to the fact that these problems were discussed by some earlier texts of the Sāṁkhya-Yoga unfortunately lost to us.

5

Verbal Testimony (Śabda Pramāṇa)

ETYMOLOGICALLY the word *śabda* means sound (*dhvani*).[1] *Śabda* literally means verbal knowledge. It is the knowledge of objects derived from words or sentences. In the domain of linguistics again, the word *śabda* is found to be used to signify a *pada* (word). A *pada*, however, consists of certain letter or letters (*varṇa*).[2] A letter is undoubtedly a special kind of sound. So even in linguistics *śabda* keeps in fact its basic character of being a sound. The word *śabda* again is technically used in the school of Nyāya in the sense of a *pramāṇavākya*. A sentence is undoubtedly a specific collection of words. So, a sentence is inevitably a special collection of sounds, i.e. mutually related articulate sounds. This *śabda* in its basic character of *dhvani* is a *guṇa* (quality) and not a *dravya* (substance). Being a *guṇa*, it must belong to a substratum. The substratum to which *śabda* belongs is the *ākāśa*. This is the view of the Nyāya-Vaiśeṣika. *Śabda*, the sound, according to them, is the specific or differentiating quality of *ākāśa*. Here the Naiyāyikas differ from the Mīmāṁsakas, who understand *śabda* as a *dravya*.[3] Epistemologically *śabda* refers to a source of knowledge namely verbal testimony (*śabdapramāṇa*). It consists in the

1. *kastarhi śabdaḥ . . . tasmāddhvaniḥ śabdaḥ* — *MBh*, 1.1.1.
2. *varṇātmakānām śabdānām . . . samāharam padam* — *MM*, p. 226.
3. *śabdasya ca . . . vyabhicārāt*, etc. — *TP, BHC*, p. 16.

assertion of a trustworthy person.[4] All verbal knowledge, however, is not valid. A verbal statement is valid when it comes from a person who knows the truth and speaks the truth about anything for the guidance of other persons. But it is a matter of common observation that a sentence or a statement is not sufficient to denote any knowledge of things. Nor the mere perception of words of a sentence does give any knowledge about objects. It is only when one perceives the words and understands their meanings that he acquires the knowledge of a verbal statement. Hence *śabda* or testimony as a source of valid knowledge consists in understanding the meaning of the statement of a trustworthy person.[5] It is, however, in the context of verbal testimony that *śabda* has aroused a long discussion in the domain of Indian philosophy. The Sāṁkhya-Yoga admits verbal testimony as an independent means of knowledge in addition to perception and inference.[6]

Verbal testimony consists of verbal statements of people intended to express certain facts. Testimony is an important source of knowledge. A major portion of a person's stock of knowledge is acquired from the oral or written testimony of other persons. The verbal testimony requires an understanding of the meaning conveyed by words without which there is no possibility of verbal communication. The words of a foreign language carry no sense unless their meanings are clear. Thus, verbal testimony depends upon employment of words and understanding of their meanings. In verbal testimony knowledge arises through words, and this fact differentiates it from the other two means of knowledge, i.e. percepetion

---

4. *āptapadeśaḥ śabda* — *NS*, 1.1.7.
5. *vākyārthajñānam śabdajñānam* — *TS*, p. 73.
6. *dṛṣṭamanumānamāptavacanam ca sarvapramāṇasiddhatvād* ।
tṛvidha pramāṇamiṣṭam prameyasiddhiḥ pramāṇadhi ॥ — *SK*, K. 4.

and inference. Verbal testimony as a source of knowledge is accepted by the Jainas, Sāṁkhyaists, Vedāntins, Mīmāṁsakas as well as by the Naiyāyikas. Verbal testimony is designated in various ways by the different schools of Indian system. Thus, it is *śabda*, according to the Naiyāyikas, *śāstra* to the Mīmāṁsakas, *āptavacana* to the Sāṁkhyaists, *āgama* to Vedāntins, Yoga thinkers and Jainas also while it is *nigama* to the Bhāgavata.[7] Except the Cārvākas, the Buddhists and the Vaiśeṣikas all Indian philosophers have recognized verbal testimony as an independent source of knowledge.

The Denial of the Validity of the Verbal Testimony by the Cārvākas

The Cārvākas have not recognized verbal testimony as a source of valid knowledge. The Cārvākas reject testimony in general because, according to them, it does not give rise to valid knowledge, and scriptural testimony in particular, because Vedic knowledge in his opinion is "all fraud, a device of the cunning priests to earn their livelihood by cheating the ignorant persons."[8] "They are false because they make statements which are false. They are contradictory because they make statements which are incompatible with one another. A Vedic text declares: "one who desires a son should perform the *putreṣṭī* sacrifice." Yet it is found that a son is not born after the sacrifice has been performed. The text is false. If a text is false with regard to perceptible results, the text with regard to imperceptible results must be false. The three Vedas are inventions of cheats, knaves and demons. The rites and ceremonies enjoined by the Vedas are the inventions of

7. *pratyakṣenānumānena nigamenātmasaṁvidā* ।
ādyantavadasaj jñātvā niḥsaṅgo vicarediha ॥ — *BM*, 11.28.9.

8. *troya vedasya kartāraḥ*
bhaṇḍa-dhūrtaḥ-niśācarāḥ — *SDS*, p. 14.

the brāhmaṇas, who cheat the other castes to earn their livelihood. Religion is priestcraft. If a beast killed in a sacrifice goes to heaven, why does not a person sacrifice his own father. The rites are the inventions of imposters for their livelihood."[9] Again, according to the Cārvākas, there is no logical ground or justification for believing in anything simply on the statement of another person because in that case, they think that they would have to believe the utterance of absurd and fictitious objects of any fool. If, however, *śabda* or testimony is restricted to the statements of a trustworthy person, it would be, in their opinion, at best included in inference. But in the opinion of the Cārvākas, inference cannot be accepted as a valid source of knowledge. Hence, *śabda* or testimony should not be recognized as a *pramāṇa* or valid method of knowledge.[10]

Bauddha View of Verbal Testimony

According to the Buddhist logicians, *śabda* is not an independent source of knowledge, but a form of perception or inference. According to the Bauddhas, there is no relation of a word and an external object referring to it. If there were a relation between them, it would be either identity (*tādātmya*) or causality (*tadutpatti*). The relation of identity cannot distinguish a word and its object because these two are quite distinct from each other. A relation of identity is called oneness and if oneness is accepted among the two distinct objects, then cow and horse would be one. Again there is not any relation of causality between a word and an object. Because, between word and object relationship neither a positive relation of agreement nor a negative relation of difference is understood. For example, a pot is produced with a lump of

9. *SDS*, Cārvāka, p. 83.
10. *SDS*, Ch.I.

clay, a stick, water, wheel, etc. without the operation of words. If it is assumed that there is a different kind of relation other than identity and causality between a word and an external object, it would follow that a man without knowing the significance of the meaning can get the definite meaning of a word just as a jar is cognized when it is illuminated by a lamp. But this may not happen for a stranger who does not grasp any meaning from the word *vahni* (fire) when he hears it for the first time. A word denotes an object when the denotation and signification (*saṅketa*) is known. This contention is untenable because it cannot be upheld by any reason, for any signification can be applied to any object. After examining all the factors it is found that there is no justification for the settlement of a relation between a word and an object meant. The Bauddhas do not accept the validity of the Vedas and do not believe in the Vedic assertion of a seer. The Vedas deal with other worldly objects like heaven, hell, etc. e.g. the performance of *agnihotra* sacrifice will lead a person to paradise. The Buddhists rely on objects which are either perceived or inferred. If by *śabda* it means the statement of trustworthy persons, it is reduced to inference.[11] If, however, it is used to prove that these are actual facts corresponding to a statement, Bauddhas reduce it to perception.[12] So they do not admit the validity of the verbal testimony.

The Vaiśeṣika View of Verbal Testimony

The Vaiśeṣikas do not accept the verbal testimony as an independent source of knowledge although they agree with the Naiyāyikas and the Bhāṭṭas on the validity of the verbal

---

11. *bauddhās tu padārtha bodham api padyānyanumānavidhayā janayanti* — *PR*, p. 65. cf. *SPR*, p. 198.

12. Cf. *NTK*, p. 348.

testimony. The Vaiśeṣikas include verbal testimony within inference. Praśastapāda says that *śabda* and other sources of knowledge belong to inference because these sources involve invariable coherence with a perception free from doubt.[13] Śrīdhara says that there is no natural relation between word and its object, i.e. the meaning of the words is but conventional in origin. Verbal testimony is an inference because we understand the meaning only through coherence, as smoke indicates fire in the hill.[14] According to the Vaiśeṣikas, *śabda* as a form of knowledge is to be included in inference, since the ground of our knowledge is the same in both. Just as in inference one knows an unperceived object from the perception of something which is related to it, so in *śabda* from the perception of words one knows the objects which are unperceived but related to the words perceived by us.[15]

Establishment and the Nature of Verbal Testimony

Verbal testimony has been recognized as a separate *pramāṇa* by almost all the important schools of Indian philosophy.

JAINA VIEW OF VERBAL TESTIMONY

In the Jaina system, *śabda* or verbal testimony is recognized as a separate *pramāṇa* or source of knowledge. It consists in the knowledge derived from words which, when properly understood, express real objects and are not inconsistent with

---

13. *śabdādīnām apyanumāne 'ntarbhāvaḥ samānavidhitvāt yathā prasiddha-sāmayasyāsandigdha liṅga darśana prasiddhyanusmaraṇābhyām atindriye arthe bhavatyanumānam evam śabdādibhyo 'pīti*
—*PB*, p. 512.

14. *śabdonumānam vyāptibalenārthapratipādakatvād dhūmavat*
—*NK*, p. 512.

15. *śabdasyāpyanumānaviṣayatvena avinābhāvo pajivakatvenavā anumānatvam* —*SP*, p. 115.

the evidence of perception. It is called *laukika* or secular testimony when the words come from an ordinary reliable person of the world. It is called *śāstraja* or scriptual testimony when it proceeds from a liberated person of extraordinary powers and knowledge and relates to supersensible realities. The Mīmāṁsakas and Vedāntins give the status of this *pramāṇa* primarily to the Vedas. Hence, in these schools *śabda*pramāṇa or verbal testimony is known as *śāstra*, *śruti* and *āgama* also.[16]

MĪMĀṀSĀ VIEW OF VERBAL TESTIMONY

According to the Mīmāṁsakas *śabda* as a *pramāṇa* consists in the true knowledge of objects, derived from the understanding of the meaning of a sentence. It is called *pauruṣeya* or personal when constituted by the words of trustworthy persons, and *apauruṣeya* or impersonal when constituted by the words of the Vedas. The Prābhākara School of the Mīmāṁsā, however, takes *śabda* to mean only *vaidika* or scriptural testimony about the existence of supersensuous realities.

VEDĀNTA VIEW OF VERBAL TESTIMONY

According to the Vedāntists, *śabda* or *āgama* as a source of valid knowledge consists in sentences or propositions which assert a certain relation between things that is not contradicted in any way. In the Sāṁkhya-Yoga system too, we find a recognition of *śabda* or verbal testimony as a valid method of knowledge. Yet with some of the Sāṁkhyas, we directly find *śabdapramāṇa* being named as *āptavacana*.[17]

The Mīmāṁsakas, Naiyāyikas and Vaiyākaraṇas have a discord among themselves regarding the nature of *śabda*.

---

16. *pratyakṣamanumāno tathā śāstram* — *PP*, p. 44
arthāgamo nirupyate — *VP*, p. 80.

17. *dṛṣṭamanumanāptavacanam ca* — *SK*, 4.

Kumārila Bhaṭṭa recognizes *śabda* as eternal and all-pervading substance (*dravya*).[18] Prabhākara Miśra also accepts eternality of *śabda*. According to him, all sounds heard are in the shape of some letters. In the view of the Prābhākaras, it is the letter that is the direct cause of verbal comprehension, and neither perception nor inference can give any idea of the *śabda* as apart from its constituent letters. The grammarians explain the eternality of *śabda* in a different way. According to them, "word" is successive sounds of a series called letters. A series of such letter sounds manifests one inarticulate sound essence called *sphoṭa*. This *sphoṭa* is an eternal essence that exists corresponding to every word. The Naiyāyikas do not accept the eternality of *śabda*. Both the Mīmāṁsakas and the Naiyāyikas oppose the theory of *sphoṭa* of the grammarians.

NYĀYA VIEW OF VERBAL TESTIMONY

Gautama in his Nyāya philosophy defines verbal testimony as the statement of a reliable person. The reliability of a person making a statement is a condition ensuring the validity of the knowledge derived in this way. Gautama defines *śabdapramāṇa* as *āptapodeśa*.[19] This *āptapodeśa* means a communication from or assertion of a trustworthy person. Manu understands *upadeśa* only in the sense of an instructive statement or assertion.[20] From the *bhāṣya* of Vātsyāyana it is understood that only the Prācīna Naiyāyikas understood this *upadeśa* in the sense of an instructive assertion. But if Gautama's *upadeśa* is understood in the sense of an instruction, all non-instructive statements or assertions uttered by the trusted person (*āptas*) will not

18. *śrotramatrendriyagrāhyaḥ śabdaḥ śabdatva-jātimān dravyam sarvagato nitya kumārila mate matuḥ* — *MM*, p. 218.

19. *āptapodeśa śabdaḥ* — *NS* 1.1.7.

20. *upadeśa anuśāsanam* — *Manu*, 12.206.

obtain the status of the *śabdapramāṇa*. It will limit the scope of *śabda* very much. Probably on this account, some Navya-Naiyāyikas used the word *vākya* in place of the word *upadeśa* in the context of defining *śabda*.[21] They did it only to widen the scope of *śabdapramāṇa*. So from this definition, it is clear that the basic character of *śabdapramāṇa* is a sentence instructive or non-instructive, uttered or used by an *āptapuruṣa* (trustworthy person). The Mīmāṁsakas, however, do not accept it for the following reason: The Nyāya definition presupposes that all verbal statements are made by persons. But according to them, Vedic statements are not made by any person. According to Nyāya, Vedic statements are statements of God who is a supernatural person. But according to the Mīmāṁsakas, there is no God and hence Vedic statements are impersonal and thus hold the Nyāya definition too narrow. According to Śabara, verbal testimony is the knowledge of an object which is not perceived by a sense-organ, but is the result of knowledge of words.[22] Kumārila Bhaṭṭa defines verbal testimony as a statement which produces in the mind of the hearer, who knows the meaning of words, a knowledge of facts that lie beyond the range of his perception. The Prābhākaras following Śabara call *śabdapramāṇa* as *śāstrapramāṇa* (scriptural word). Prabhākara while commenting on the *Śābarabhāṣya* holds that the term *śāstra* applies to the Vedic injunctive sentences (*vidhi*) only which alone bear upon verbal testimony.[23] Thus, according to the Prābhākaras it is only the Vedic sentence that can be called *śabdapramāṇa*.[24] This *śāstra* or

---

21. *āptavākyam śabdaḥ* — *TS*, p. 65.
22. *śāstram śabdavijñānād asannikṛṣṭe arthe vijñānam*
— *SB* under *MS*, 1.1.5.
23. *gurustvāha vaidikameva śabdamasti* — *MM*, p. 103.
24. *śāstram śabdavijñānādasannikṛṣṭe arthe vijñānam*
— *SB* under *MS*, 1.1.6.

śabdapramaṇa is, in the view of the Prābhākaras, the knowledge acquired regarding objects that are outside the scope of perception by way of knowing the words that constitute the sentence concerned.[25]

SĀṀKHYA-YOGA VIEW OF VERBAL TESTIMONY

It may be stated that in Sāṁkhya philosophy, *Sāṁkhyakārikā* is the earliest work to define verbal testimony. Its definition is precise but meaningful. The *Sāṁkhyakārikā* defines verbal testimony as the statement (*śruti*) of the reliable (*āpta*).[26] The author of the *Sāṁkhyakārikā* tries to satisfy both the sections of the Sāṁkhyists namely atheists and theists, by the very definition of verbal testimony. From the atheist standpoint it may be explained as words which convey that uncontradicted knowledge is authentic. The compound word *āptaśruti* may mean the words derived from reliable persons are trustworthy. Īśvarkṛṣṇa does not explain the word *āptaśruti* himself, but later on it was interpreted by his successor.

Among the commentators on the *Śāṁkhyakārikā*, Gauḍapāda is the earliest one. He explains the *kārikā* in a different manner. According to Gauḍapāda, *āpta*s are the speakers, but figuratively it stands for the words written by them, and *śruti* means the Vedas. The words of the trustworthy persons like the creator of the world — Brahmā and sages of his status are reliable. He has not discussed whether the Vedas are the works of God or eternal. He simply accepts *śruti* as the authoritative source of knowledge.

Māṭhara does not expound the compound word *āptaśruti*. But his manner of explanation indicates that the expounding

---

25. *tacca śabdam dvividham pauruṣeyam apauruṣeyaṁ ca,* — *MM*, p. 103.

26. *āptaśrutirāptavacanantu* — *SK*, K. 5.

sentence should be like this: *āptaḥ-āptebhyaḥ āgatāni śāstrāni śrutiśca*. He states the qualification of an *āpta*. The persons who are free and never go against the views of the Vedas are *āptas*. According to him, the Vedas are the main source of true knowledge. The works of the followers of the Vedas as qualified by positive and negative virtues mentioned before are also the source of true knowledge. Thus, he follows Gauḍapāda to a great extent.[27] The concept of an *āpta* is very essential to the concept of *śabdapramāṇa* or verbal testimony. Gautama in his Nyāya philosophy does not explain the term *āpta*. But the *bhāṣyakāra* explains the term. According to him, an *āpta* is one who has directly perceived the true nature of things and who is prompted to communicate the properly experienced ideas. Perception of objects may be termed *āpti*. As he is prompted to communicate by that very *āpti* he is called an *āpta*. Thus, this definition of the term *āpta* holds good equally with seers, Aryas and even Mlecchas.[28] Sometimes, even thieves and decoits may speak the truth. According to Viśvanātha, *āpta* is one who possesses a perfect knowledge in respect of the meaning of the sentence of the context.[29] Annambhaṭṭa explains the term *āpta* as a truthful speaker, i.e. who speaks about the things as they really are.[30] Nāgeśa in his

---

27. *āptaśrutirāptavacanaṁtu, tṛtiyam pramāṇam, āpta brahmāndayaḥ ācāryyāḥ śrutirvedastadetadubhayam āptavacanam, āptiḥ sākṣādarthaprāptiryathārthopalambhava, tayā varttato ityāptaḥ sākṣātkṛtadharma yathārthāptyā, śrutārthagrāhī taduktamāpta vacanam...... āgamo hyāptavacanamāptam doṣakṣayādviduḥ, kṣīṇadoṣo 'nṛtaḥ vākyam na vrūyāddhetvasambhavāt, svakarmanyabhiyukto yorāgadveṣa vivarjitaḥ, pujitastadvidhoirnityamāpto jñeyaḥ sa tādṛśaḥ* ॥ — *MV* on *SK*.K. 5.

28. *āptaḥ khalu . . . vyavahāraḥ pravarttanta iti* — *VB* under *NS*, 1.1.7.

29. *prakṛtavākyārthayathārthajñānavān* — *NSV*, under *NS*, 1.1.7.

30. *āptastu yathārthavaktā* — *TS*, p. 65.

Paramalaghumañjūṣā refers to Patañjali, the author of the *Carakasaṁhitā*, according to whom *āpta* is one who comes to be fully aware of something through experience and who does not make false or distorted version of own experience even out of any passion.[31] According to Jayanta Bhaṭṭa, an *āpta* should be able to communicate adequately. He explains the point of this criterion, by saying that a dumb person cannot be an *āpta* even though he possesses the relevent knowledge, for he lacks in the ability for adequate communication. He can of course communicate through gestures but it can hardly be counted as adequate communication. However, this is too general a requirement, for one may be very good at communication and yet be a villain, i.e. be far from an *āpta*.

Now the question arises as to how do we know the person who is *āpta*. To this question, the answer is that a person who possesses expert and relevant knowledge in the given area can be known mostly by past experience about the given person.

The *Yuktidīpikā* states that the word *āptavacana* of the *Sāṁkhyakārikā* may mean reliable statement. The statements may be of two kinds: (i) occurring in the Vedas, and (ii) uttered by some worldly authority. The *Yuktidīpikā* states that the definition applies to both the kinds of statements. To derive the sense denoting both the above kinds from a single statement of the *Sāṁkhyakārikā*, the *Yuktidīpikā* holds that it is a case of *ekaśeṣa* compound, i.e. one component factor which is similar to the next one is dropped according to the rule of grammar.[32] The first denotes the Vedas which are not a creation of human

31. *anubhavena vastutattvasya kārtsnyena niścayavān rāgādivasādapi nānyathāvādi yaḥ sa āptaḥ iti carake patañjaliḥ* — *PU*, p. 7.

32. *āptaśrutiścāptaśrutiścāpta śrutiḥ sarūpanāmityekaśesaḥ* — *YD* on *SK*, K. 5.

beings. The term *āptaśruti* occurring second time refers to the statements of the Smṛtis, the argumentation, historical records, Vedāṅgas, Purāṇas and those proficient in many arts but free from attachment, aversion, etc. According to Vācaspati Miśra, the term *āpta* is used in the definition to exclude the source books of the Bauddhas, the Jainas and the Cārvākas which are not actually sacred literature from the domain of the Śruti literature. Vācaspati Miśra further states that *āptaśruti* as a *pramāṇa* does not refer to the wording but the knowledge arising out of it.

The *Yogasūtra* uses a new term namely *āgama* instead of *śruti*. Vyāsadeva the commentator of the *Yogasūtra* brings out clearly the significance of the term *āgama*.[33] The authoritative person communicates his knowledge to others by words.[34] These words constitute an authentic work. According to Vyāsadeva, all the trustworthy persons cannot directly know all matters related to their works. All matters cannot be perceived. Some matters are perceived but other transcendental matters or substances are only inferred. All the commentators of *Sāṁkhyakārikā* agree on this point. According to Vācaspati Miśra and Vijñānabhikṣu, Veda is the absolute authority and God is the author of the Vedas. In the view of Vācaspati, a reliable person is one who is endowed with the realization of object, piety and efficiency of organs. The Smṛtis of Manu, etc. are reliable because the original speaker there is God.[35] According to Vijñānabhikṣu a reliable person is one

---

33. *āptena dṛṣṭo 'numito vā arthaḥ paratra svabodha saṁkrāntaye śabdenopadis 'yate śabdāt tadarthaviṣaya vṛttiḥ śroturāgamaḥ*
— *YB* on *YS* 1.7.

34. *tattvadarśana kāruṇya karaṇapātavābhisaṁbandha āptiḥ tayā varttata ityāptastena dṛṣṭonumito vārthaḥ* — *TV* on *YS*, 1.7.

35. *ya kaścitkasyacitdharmaḥ manunā parikīrtitaḥ sa sarva abhihite vede sarvajñānamayo hi saḥ* — *TV* on *YS*, 1.7.

who is devoid of defects like confusion, negligence, desire for selfish gain and inefficiency of organs.[36] According to Vācaspati Miśra verbal testimony is restricted to the Vedas only. According to him, statements of wordly authority are not included in verbal testimony. The statements of the Purāṇas and Smṛtis are authoritative not because of their authors but because they are based upon the Vedas. The founder of Sāṁkhya philosophy is Kapila, and Hiraṇyagarbha is the founder of Yoga philosophy, who are human beings only. Now the question naturally arises as to how can these systems be taken as authoritative and their founders as *āpta* or reliable. On this point Vācaspati Miśra replies that Sāṁkhya philosophy is an interpretation of the Vedas. This philosophy is not an imagination of Kapila but it is the result of Śruti texts which Kapila had memorized in the earlier cycle of creation. He had remembrance of the Śruti read in earlier birth just as a person has the memory of knowledge of earlier day after getting up from deep slumber the next day. He quotes the authority of Jaigiṣavya in the *Mahābhārata* who narrates in his discussion with Ātavya the memory of his past ten births. In this way Sāṁkhya is rooted in the Vedas and is, therefore, authoritative.[37] According to Vācaspati Mīśra the statements of the Vedas are valid because these are not composed by any wordly authority, and therefore faultless.

The *Sāṁkhyasūtra* discusses elaborately about the non-eternality of the Vedas. The Vedas are not eternal because

---

36. *bhramapramādavipralipsākaraṇā pātavā didoṣa-rahitena*

— *YV* on *YS*, 1.7.

37. *ādividuṣaśca kapilasya kalpādau kalpāntarādhita śrutismaraṇa samvabaḥ suptapravudhasyeva pūrvedyuravagatānāmarthānām paredyuḥ*

— *STK* on *SK*, K. 5.

they themselves speak of their production.[38] The Vedas are composed by human beings and as these are composed by human beings these are non-eternal, because all created objects are non-eternal. Neither the liberated nor the unliberated person is the author of the Vedas. The unliberated man is not omniscient and hence cannot be the author of the Vedas. Again a liberated man also cannot be the author of the Vedas because he is indifferent to everything by his very nature. The Īśvara cannot be the author of the Vedas because the existence of Īśvara is not established.[39] The *Sāṁkhyasūtra* further states that the Vedas being free from human agency does not mean its eternality. The case may be like that of sprout, etc. which are not created by any human being, but are non-eternal in nature.

The Mīmāṁsakas deny the existence of God as the creator of the universe since every creator must be corporeal. They do not agree on this point that God is the author of the Vedas. In their opinion the Vedas are eternal. On the other hand the *Sāṁkhyasūtra* states that the Vedas came out of the self-born spontaneously without any effort or without giving thought to create them. The Cārvākas, the Buddhists and the Jainas challenge the trustworthiness of the Vedas. Jayanta Bhaṭṭa and Udayana, the stalwarts of the Naiyāyikas, establish the authority of the Vedas. According to the Naiyāyikas, the authority of the Vedas can only be established if they are the works of God.

The Nature of Word

The word named *pada*, as grammarians state, technically means an inflected word or the stem of a noun in the middle cases

---

38. *na nityatvam vedānām kāryatvaśruteḥ* — *SS*, 5.45.

39. *īśvarapratisedhāditi śeṣah* — *SPB*, 5.46.

and before some *taddhitas*.[40] But the Naiyāyikas and the Mīmāṁsakas opine that sound having capability to express the meaning of the object is termed as word or *pada*.[41] The function of such a word is associated with its meaning as well. A statement, as we are concerned, is a cluster of words or *padas* arranged in a certain way. A word, again, is a group of letters arranged in a settled order to express meaning. Sometimes a mere word is loosely regarded as *pada*. Therefore, the definition of 'word' covers three aspects: sound, letters and meaning conveyed. In the first aspect, letters and meaning are not involved, sound is a physical phenomenon. It is the attribute of an intangible and all-pervading substance called *ākāśa* or the ether. Sound is a product of the conjunction of two bodies or of the disjunction of the parts of one composite body. It is, therefore, non-eternal or subject to origin and cessation in time. The Mīmāṁsakas, however, hold that sound is eternal since it is not produced, but only manifested by the contact of two bodies. Regarding the eternality of the word, the Mīmāṁsakas and the Naiyāyikas differ from one another. The Mīmāṁsakas uphold the theory of the eternality of the word and the Naiyāyikas regard the word as non-eternal. The Mīmāṁsakas maintain that words are manifested in the form of sounds by human effort; they are not created by any one. The Naiyāyikas on the other hand are of the view that words do not exist before their production by human effort, nor there exists any veil which covers them.[42]

Sound is of two kinds, namely *dhvani* and *varṇa*. A *dhvani* is an inarticulate sound, e.g. the sound of a bell or a drum. It has no

---

40. *suptinantam padam, kṛttaddhita samāsāśca* — *Pa Su*, i.4.14-15.

41. *saṁnatyastham abhidadhati vākyam ekārthaḥ, padasamuho vākyam iti vākya-vidaḥ* — *NM* (1), p. 366.

42. *prajatanāntaraṁ upalabdheḥ kāryaḥ śabdaḥ* — *NS*, 22.18.

fixed nature of its own, nor any fixed relation to other like-sounds. On the other hand, *varṇa* is a sound produced by the action of the vocal organ of human beings, e.g. the alphabet. *Varṇa* is a letter which has a fixed character and a definite place in the alphabet of any language.

In the second aspect of the definition of word, it can be said that a word is a group of *varṇa*s or letters arranged in a certain fixed order. The essential nature of a word lies in its meaning. The meaning of a word is known only when its relation with its meaning is known. The relation between word and its meaning is that of expresser and expressed.[43] There is power of expression in word and that of being expressed in meaning.[44] Aniruddha in his *Sāṁkhyasūtravṛtti* states that acceptance of such a relation implies rejection of the relation of identity between word and its meaning. Otherwise the seeing of an object would imply the seeing of word, and mouth would have been burnt by uttering the word *'fire.'*[45] Vācaspati Miśra, alike the followers of Prābhākara School of Pūrva-Mīmāṁsā, holds that such a relation is known through inferring it by observing that a person is prompted to a particular activity after hearing particular words. The observer infers from such a relation between word and the object involved in the activity performed. This process is popularly known as *vṛddhavyavahāra*. The *Sāṁkhyasūtra* states that the relation between a word and its meaning is determined by three means.[46] These according to its commentators are: information from the reliable person (*āptapodeśa*), the usage of the old men

43. *vācyavācaka sambandhaḥ śabdārthayoḥ* — *SS*, 5.37.

44. *arthe vācyatākhyā śaktiḥ śabde vācakatākhyā śaktirasti* — *SPB*, 3.37.

45. *tādātmypakṣe ghaṭo 'pi śrotragrāhyaḥ syāt, śabdo'pi cāksuso bhavet, agnyādyuccāraṇe, mukhadahādiprasaṁga* — *SSV*, 5.37.

46. *trivi saṁbandhasiddheḥ* — *SS*, 5.38.

(*vṛddhavyavahāra*) and association with the word already known (*prasiddhapadasamānādhikaraṇa*).

According to the Naiyāyikas, there are three kinds of meaning of a word, namely, *abhidhā, paribhāṣā* and *lakṣaṇā*. By *abhidhā* is meant the primary meaning of a word. It is also called *śakyārtha, vācyārtha* and *mukhyārtha*. The meaning called up by the *śakti* or inherent potency of a word is its *abhidhā* or *śakyārtha,* i.e. primary meaning. The word which possesses such a meaning is called *śakta* or *vācaka* word. When *saṅketa* or the direct relation between a word and its meaning is non-eternal or changeable, it is called *paribhāṣā*. By *lakṣaṇā* is meant the secondary meaning of a word. It is the indirect or implied meaning in which a word with its direct or primary meaning does not consist with other words. When it is said that the house is on the Ganges, the word 'Ganges' is taken not in its primary meaning of the current of the river but in the secondary meaning of "the bank of the Ganges." The rhetoricians recognize another kind of meaning of words, namely, *vyañjanā*. This stands for such meanings of words as are neither directly nor indirectly related to them, but only suggested by them. Thus, the sentence "the house is on the Ganges" means that the house is cool and sacred. This is the suggested meaning. Words are divided into four kinds namely, *yaugika, rūḍha, yoga-rūḍha* and *yaugika-rūḍha*.

Now it could be discussed what does a word signify or refer to. According to the Sāṁkhyas a word refers to the particular (*vyakti*). By an individual is meant a composite material body possessing specific properties. It is a substance which has a limited dimension and may have such qualities as smell, taste, colour, touch, etc. It is manifested and open to sense perception, e.g. in the expression "that cow stands" mean the individual called cow. According to the Jainas a word denotes the particular form (*ākṛti*). The form (*ākṛti*) of a thing consists in the particular arrangement of its component parts and the constituent particles of those parts. In the opinion of the Mīmāṁsakas and the Advaitins a word signifies universality (*jāti*). The universality or *jāti* is the basis of similar cognitions with regard to different individuals. According to the old Naiyāyikas, a word refers to all the three — *vyakti*, *ākṛti* and *jāti*. For the later Naiyāyikas the referent is the particular characterized by the universal, whereas the grammarians hold both the particular and the universal as the referent. It may be said that the Sāṁkhyas, like the Mīmāṁsakas, hold that the relation between the word and the object denoted is learnt from elders and is natural, e.g. the child knows the denotative relation with reference to the object which is in operation, and the activity and desisting from activity are possible in case of an individual object only. So, according to Sāṁkhya, a word denotes a *vyakti*. However, in the system of Yoga, a word denotes generality to which particularity lies as subordinate in forming the nature of an object and it is exemplified by stating that the referent of a word is known to the child by considering the entire sentence.

The way of conveying the meaning of a particular word can be discussed based upon the Sāṁkhya-Yoga view. According to Sāṁkhya-Yoga the meaning of a word is understood by the *buddhi*'s act of taking the form of an object. The form is not presented by the organ of sense. The organ of sense involved is ear which has sound as its object, but does not reveal the object denoted. Speaker's organ of speech also produces sound only and cannot form the image of the object denoted in listener's *buddhi*. The *Yogabhāṣya* offers a solution on conveyance of meaning of word in the light of the theory of *sphoṭa*, without mentioning it by name: the meaning is conveyed through a word. The word is not the sound itself. It is revealed by sounds and is the meaning-bearing unit. One apprehends a word after listening to the phonemes separately when collected together in succession. Though the letters uttered earlier to the completing one help in revealing that word, the form of the word is not completed without last letter. For example, after hearing each letter like "go" and "au" one gets the idea of their being a single unit, and comprehends them as a single word.

Logical Structure of a Sentence

Authority, as we have seen, gives knowledge about certain things through the understanding of the meaning of a sentence, either spoken or written by some authoritative person. The knowledge deduced from the Vedic statement is also authoritative but it is not connected with human being on Supreme Bliss. But any single word of a sentence cannot imply the complete sense. A sentence is a combination of words having a certain meaning. Any combination of words, however, does not make a significant sentence. The construction of an intelligible sentence must conform to four conditions. These are: *ākāṅkṣā*, *yogyatā*, *sannidhi* and *tātparya*. Words mutually having the link of expectation, semantical suitability, contiguity and purport express their meaning. It is said that expectancy, compatibility and contiguity have been regarded as accessory causes in verbal understanding.[47] Some later logicians add the fourth one named purport to make a sentence.

47. *atrākāṅkṣā ca yogyatvaṁ sannidhiś ceti tattrayaṁ* ।
vākyārthāvāgame sarvaiḥ kāraṇatvena kalpyate ॥ — *Mm*, p. 100.

EXPECTANCY

The words must be such that the expectancy set up by each is satisfied by the others. By expectancy is meant those words of a sentence by which they expect or imply one another.[48] Generally speaking, a word like "cow," "horse," "man," "elephant" cannot by itself convey a complete meaning. It has to be brought into relation with other words to express a full judgement.[49] When one hears the word *bring* he at once asks "what"? The verb "bring" requires some other words denoting some object or objects, e.g. "the cow." So expectancy is the mutual need that the words of a statement have for one another in order to express a complete sense.[50] This need or requirement is called *ākāṅkṣā* or mutual expectancy.

COMPATIBILITY

The second condition of the combination of words in a statement is their mutual fitness and in short, compatibility. It is also called suitability. A string of words may be syntactically well-formed but may not constitute a meaningful statement. It requires compatibility. It consists in the absence of contradiction in the relation of objects denoted by a statement.[51] In other words, the relation of one meaning with the meaning of another word or words is called compatibility.[52] So when the meaning of a statement is contradicted, there is no

---

48. *yat padena vinā yasyānanubhāvakatā bhavet* ।
    ākāṅkṣā . . . *Kā*, p. 421.
49. *gauraśvaḥ puruṣohastityākāṅkṣā rahiteṣviha* ।
    anvayādarśanāt tāvad ākāṅksā parigṛhyate ॥ — *MM*, p.101.
50. *tatra padārthānām paraspara jijñāsā viṣayatva yogyatvam ākāṅkṣā*
    — *VP*, p. 80.
51. *yogyatā ca tātparya viṣayībhūta saṁsargābādhaḥ* — *VP*, pp. 84-86.
52. *eka padārthe para padārtha sambandha yogyatetyarthaḥ*
    — *NMV*, p. 420, cf. *SPR*, p. 209.

compatibility between its constituent words. The statement "moisten with fire" is faulty of unfitness, since there is a contradiction between "fire" and "moistening" and so in this case there is no verbal understanding.[53]

CONTIGUITY

Contiguity is the third condition of verbal knowledge. It consists in the juxtaposition or proximity between the different words of statement[54] and it merely requires that there is no long gap between the uttering or writing together of the words making up the statement. Spoken words when separated by long interval of time cannot make a statement. Similarly written words cannot form a statement when they are separated by long intervals of space. Thus, absence of contiguity is of two kinds, not being near and not being signified by words. The words "bring a cow" will not construct a statement when the utterance spreads over several days or writing takes several pages, even though they have the first two requirements, expectancy and compatibility.[55] Hence, it can be concluded that contiguity is understanding the meaning created by words without interruption.

PURPORT

Some later logicians add a fourth requirement, that a string of words must be uttered with intent to communicate a

---

53. *vahninā siñcatītyādau seke vahnikaraṇakatvā bhāvarūpayogyatā niścayena pratibandhān na śabda-bodhaḥ* — NMV, p. 420. *Ibid.*

54. *śabdhaiḥ sannihitatvena bodhitatvam hi padārthānām sannidhir ityucyate* — MM, p. 101.

55. *evam ekaikiśaḥ prahare sahoccāritāni gām anayetyādi-padāni na vākyam satyam api parasparākaṅkṣāyām satyam api parasparānvaya yogyatāyām paraspara sānnidhyabhāvāt* — TB, p. 48.

proposition and that it is the nature of this intention or purport which unequivocally identifies the meanings of the constituent words. Purport as a condition of verbal knowledge stands for the meaning intended to be conveyed by a sentence. A word may mean different things in different cases. Whether it means this or that thing in a particular case depends on the intention of the person who uses the word. Thus, when a man is asked to bring *saindhava*, he is at a loss to understand whether he is told to bring salt or a horse, for the word means both. This can be ascertained only if one knows the intention of the speaker. Hence, the understanding of a sentence depends on the understanding of its purport or intended meaning. In the case of ordinary sentences used by common people one may ascertain their purport from the context in which they are employed. In case of understanding the hymns of the Vedas one takes the assistance of the logical rules of interpretation systematized by the Mīmāṁsakas.[56]

With regard to the importance of purport as a condition of verbal knowledge there is much difference of opinion among Indian philosophers. Some hold that a definite knowledge of the purport or the intended meaning is an essential condition of verbal knowledge. Others think that purport is necessary only in the case of equivocal terms and ambiguous expressions having two or more possible meanings. Others again think that purport is not to be admitted as a separate condition of verbal knowledge, but should be included within the first condition of *ākāṅkṣā* or syntactic expectation.

According to the Sāṁkhyas a statement is a sentence composed of words arranged in a certain way. A word is a sign which denotes something (*vācaka*) and its meaning is the

56. *tat ca tātparyam vede mīmāṁsā pariśodhitanyāyād evāvadhāryate, loke tu prarakaraṇādinā* — *VP*, p. 100.

thing denoted by it (*vācya*). To understand a sentence the knowledge of the meaning of the words which comprise it is essential. The knowledge of the meanings of the words can be had in eight different ways:[57] (a) Knowledge of verbs, indeclinables, suffixes, compounds, etc. can be had from grammar, i.e. *vyākaraṇa*. Thus, the *śakti* (meaning) of the root *bhu* is "to exist," the meaning of the root *gam* is "to go." The indeclinable *ca* is used in the sense of "and." The suffixes *su, au, jas,* etc. are used to denote a word in their respective ways. (b) Knowledge of similarity can be obtained through comparison, i.e. *upamāna,* e.g. a *gavaya* is similar to that of a cow. (c) Knowledge of synonymous terms, etc. can be gathered by consulting a dictionary, i.e. a *kośa.* Thus Viṣṇu, Nārāyaṇa, Kṛṣṇa, Rādhākānta, etc. are all the different names of the Lord Viṣṇu. (d) The example of knowledge derived from *āptavākya* is, when a reliable person utters that *pika* means "a cuckoo," the listener gathers the knowledge of cuckoo from the word *pika.* (e) The example of the knowledge of *vyākaraṇa* is that it is laid down in the *śāstra* — *yavamayaḥ caruḥ bhavati.* Now what is the meaning of the word *yava*? Different people give different definitions. Naturally doubt arises among the common people as to the clear conception of the word *yava.* To remove the doubt one has to depend on *śāstra* then. It is laid down in the *śāstra* that when all the corns are decayed *yava* remains fresh. (f) To express the meaning of a word by another word is called *vivaraṇa.* Thus, *pacati* means *pākam karoti.* So we can convert the English word *cook* to Sanskrit *pacati* and *pākam karoti.* Both are correct. (g) *siddhapada sānnidhya* means the knowledge of a word which is very near to a famous word, i.e. a *siddhapada.* Thus, for example, when somebody says "*iha*

57. *śaktigraham vyākaraṇopamānamkoṣāptavākyād vyavahārāśca* ।
vākyasya śeṣāt vivṛtervadanti sānnidhyataḥ siddhapadasya vṛddhāḥ ॥
— *BP*, p. 71.

sahakāra tarau madhuram rauti pikaḥ" *Sahakāra* means "a mango tree." So by the word *pikaḥ*, it is to be understood as cuckoo because there is natural relation of cuckoo with that of a mango tree. (h) *Vṛddhavyavahāra* means usage of an elderly people, some knowledge which one can derive from the usage of superiors.

Classification of Verbal Testimony

There are two kinds of verbal testimony, human and transhuman. This division is made by the Mīmāṁsakas and the Naiyāyikas. According to Vātsyāyana, verbal knowledge is of two kinds, namely *dṛṣṭārtha* or that relating to perceptible objects and *adṛṣṭārtha* or that relating to imperceptible objects.[58] The first is limited to the ordinary sensible objects of this world, while the second is related to the supersensible objects of this world which cannot be known by perception. Under the first head we are to include the trustworthy assertions of ordinary persons, the saints and the scriptures. Thus, the evidence given by witnesses in law courts, the scriptural injunctions about certain rites for rainfall, the knowledge of plants that we get from a reliable cultivator are illustrations of *dṛṣṭārtha śabda*. The second includes the trustworthy assertions of saints, prophets and the scriptures as they bear on supersensible realities. Thus, the scientist's assertions about atoms, ether, the scriptural texts on God, heaven, future life are the illustrations of *adṛṣṭārtha śabda*. Both these divisions are again sub-divided into two — namely, revealed and perspective. Authority may either give information as to the existence of objects or give direction for the performance of some action. The former indicates revealed and the latter denotes the perspective. The perspective again can be brought under two

58. *sa dvividho dṛṣṭādṛṣṭārthatvāt* — *NS*, 1.1.8.

heads, namely, instinctive and exemplary. The instruction runs like this, "Do this in this way." As for human example "Ravi is fed *śāli* rice with ghee and milk porridge." The transhuman example is, "Create paradise by the *darśapūrṇamāsa* sacrifices by obeying the process of the *prayāja, avaghāta*"[59] and the like. The exemplary is meant "Do this like this." As for human instance, "Sutapā is to be fed in the similar way as Ravi is." The transhuman instance is "Rouse divine splendour by the solar sacrifice as by Āgneya."

The Mīmāṁsakas are interested in the transhuman authority of the Vedas and that is because the Vedas give directions for performing the sacrificial rites. The Vedas are eternal, since the words of which they are composed are eternal. The relation of word and its meaning is natural and not produced by convention. In addition to the transhuman Vedic authority, the statement of a reliable man also is accepted by the Bhāṭṭas as a valid source of knowledge.

Again, according to the later Naiyāyikas there are two kinds of *śabda* or verbal testimony — namely, *vaidika* or the scriptural and *laukika* or the secular. The Vedas are created by God and are, therefore, valid on all points. *Vaidika* or scriptural testimony is thus perfect and infallible by its very nature. As distinguished from this, *laukika* or secular testimony is not all valid. It is the testimony of human beings and may, therefore, be true or false. Of *laukika* testimony, only that which proceeds from trustworthy persons is valid but not the rest.[60]

---

59. *Prayāja* is a principal ceremony or sacrifice and *avaghāta* means threshing corn by bruising it with a wooden pestle in a mortar of the same material — *PR*, pp. 74-75, cf. *SPR*.

60. *vākyam dvividham, vaidikam laukikañca* — *TS*, p. 73.

In conclusion, it can be said that verbal testimony as a source of knowledge is applied by all human beings in their day-to-day dealing. If one does not believe in the validity of the utterances of one's teachers and experienced persons, one will never be able to learn anything from elder's experiences. It is, of course, true that on many occasions what is learnt from a so-called reliable person turns out to be false, but this fact should not minimize the importance of verbal testimony as a source of learning in human life.

6

Conclusion

It has already been discussed in the preceding chapters that the expounders of Sāṁkhya-Yoga system of thought accept only perception, inference and verbal testimony as the means of valid knowledge.[1] But for this reason one should not firmly believe that there are only three *pramāṇa*s and nothing else. Besides the above mentioned three *pramāṇa*s, there are other sources of knowledge which find their place in different systems of philosophy. These are *upamāna* (comparison), *arthāpatti* (postulation), *abhāva* or *anupalabdhi* (non-apprehension), *sambhava* (probability), *aitihya* (tradition), *pratibhā* (intuition) and *ceṣṭā* (gesture). The Sāṁkhyaists, however, hold that number of means of knowledge is determined by nature of objects to be known. Since all the objects can be cognized through three means only, the Sāṁkhyaists do not feel the need for other means of knowledge. They maintain that if some process gives rise to valid knowledge, yet it can be included under any of the means of knowledge accepted by them.[2] According to them if, however, some process does not give rise to valid knowledge, it ceases to be means of knowledge. The Sāṁkhyaists affirm that additional means of knowledge postulated by other systems cannot be considered as independent means of

1. *dṛṣṭamanumānam āptavacanam ca* — *SK*. K. 4.
2. . . . *sarvapramāṇa siddhatvād trividham, pramāṇamiṣṭam,* — *SK*, K.4

knowledge. Since no reference regarding the inclusion of additional means of knowledge under the three means of knowledge is found in the authentic early texts of Yoga system, the discussion is based upon the Sāṁkhya texts. The other means of knowledge which are not accepted by the Sāṁkhya and Yoga Schools are as follows:

Upamāna (Comparison)

The word *upamāna* has been variously translated as comparison, analogy, identification, knowledge by similarity and knowledge by assimilation, etc. It is derived from the words *upa* meaning *sādṛśya* or similarity and *māna* meaning cognition (*upa* √*mā* + *lyuṭ*). Hence, *upamāna* derivatively means the knowledge of the similarity between two things. When we see a certain object and recall another, the knowledge that we have of the similarity of the recalled object to the seen one is said to be due to the comparison.[3] So knowledge of similarity is due to comparison. The Naiyāyikas, the Mīmāṁsakas and the Advaita Vedāntins accept comparison as an independent or additional source of knowledge. The Nyāya and the Mīmāṁsā systems hold that comparison consists in the perception of similarity by one who has heard an application (*atideśavākya*). But, according to the opponents, this view is wrong because in the stock example, the wild cow called *gayal* is known through perception and similarity is remembered. Thus, it is either a case of perception or a case of memory which is a form of invalid knowledge. It is not an additional source of knowledge. The Jainas reduce comparison to recognition (*pratyabhijñā*). According to them, recognition is a kind of synthetic judgement of perception and remembrance.

3. *upamānam ca mānāntram, anumānād eva tadarthāsiddheḥ* — *NL*, p. 531.

The Cārvākas contend that comparison is not a source of knowledge at all, since it cannot give us any true knowledge about the denotation of words as maintained by the Naiyāyikas or Mīmāṁsakas. Though the Buddhist logicians recognize it as a form of valid knowledge, they do not admit it to be an independent means of knowledge, but include it within perception or verbal authority.[4] The Sāṁkhyaists do not consider *upamāna* as a distinct source of true knowledge. According to them, the knowledge obtained through *upamāna* is verbal, inferential or perceptual as the case may be. Even the upholders of *upamāna* also differ over the details of *upamāna*. According to the Naiyāyikas, resultant knowledge through *upamāna* refers to denotative relation while according to the Mīmāṁsakas, it refers to the similarity which the remembered object bears to the directly perceived one. Moreover, the Naiyāyikas lay more stress on authoritative statement, while the Mīmāṁsakas do not consider it essential at all. Vācaspati Miśra discusses both the Nyāya and the Mīmāṁsā views of *upamāna* and criticizes them from the Sāṁkhya standpoint.

THE NYĀYA VIEW OF UPAMĀNA

The Naiyāyikas hold that when one finds out the meaning of an unfamiliar word by means of a statement which contains resemblance, it is the resultant consciousness of comparison (*upamiti*), and the sentence which contains resemblance is the instrumental cause (*upamāna*). According to the Naiyāyikas comparison is the relation between the denoter (*saṁjñā*) and the denoted (*saṁjñī*). Comparison is the source of knowledge

---

4. *bhuyas tu sārūpyam gavā gavayasya ityevam pratipadyate tasmānnopamānam pratyakṣāgamābhyām bhidyata iti gavā gavaya sādṛśyam pratipadyate gavayasattām vetti, aho pramāṇabhijñātā bhadartasya*
— *NV*, pp. 172-73 (1.1.6).

of relation either between a name (*saṁjñī*) and a thing (*saṁjñā*) or between a word and its denotation.[5] The Naiyāyikas illustrate their argument thus: A citizen hears the word *gavaya* when he intends to go to a forest for the first time. Then he is instructed by an experienced inhabitant of the forest that a cow is similar to a *gavaya*. On seeing an unfamiliar deer resembling a cow he remembers the instruction of the forest dweller. He then ascertains the meaning of the word *gavaya* that the animal seen is denoted by the word *gavaya*. Gautama argues that *upamāna* is neither perception nor an inference. The reason for its not being perceptional is that its content includes a reference to linguistic usage of the word *gayal*, and usage cannot be perceived. It is not inference, he says, since inference gives us knowledge about things which can be verified through perception.[6]

THE MĪMĀṀSĀ VIEW OF UPAMĀNA

The Mīmāṁsakas consider *upamāna* as an independent source of valid knowledge. According to them, knowledge of similarity about an absent object is obtained by the means known as comparison. For example — one who has seen a cow previously in a town or other place, goes to a forest and finds a *gayal* and perceives its similarity to the cow which is not present there. He may then obtain by comparison the further knowledge that the cow in a town or elsewhere is like the *gayal*.[7] Such type of knowledge cannot be brought under

5. *yathā gaur evaṁ gavayaḥ ityupamāne prayukte gavā samāna dharmamārtham indriyārtha-sannikarṣād upalabhamānaḥ asya gavayaśabdhaḥ saṁjñā iti saṁjñā-saṁjñī sambandham pratipadyate* — *NBh*, pp. 169-70.
6. *nāpratyakṣe gavaye pramāṇārtham upamānasya paśyāmaḥ* — *NS*, 2.1.47.
7. *nagara-dṛṣṭa-gaḥ puruṣasya vana-sākṣāt-kṛta-gavaya-sādṛśya-syānena sadṛśī nagaragā gaur iti dhīḥ* — *PR*, p. 77, cf. *SPR*.

perception. From their argument it is clear that there are two similarities. From the knowledge of one similarity, one acquires knowledge of the other similarity. The other similarity being imperceptible must be known to another distinct source of true knowledge. It does not come under memory, since though the object was perceived in the past, its similarity to the present object was not then known. Therefore, this similarity cannot be said to be memory recalled. It is also not an inference. From a knowledge like "this *gayal* is like the cow in a town or elsewhere," we cannot infer the cow in a town or elsewhere is like this *gayal*, unless we have another premise like "all things are similar to other things which are similar to them." Such an invariable coherence between two terms is not really used in the above case where one arrives at the knowledge of absent cow's similarity to the present *gayal*, from the perception of the *gayal* as similar to the cow. Such knowledge cannot be brought under verbal testimony, since the man who hears that a *gayal* is like a cow is not given any further idea of the *gayal*'s attributes and so does not know that *gayal* denotes the animal until he sees it.[8] Śabara Svāmin thinks that *upamāna* in Indian philosophy is what is named in Western logic as analogy. For example, "just as one feels the existence of one's own self, similarly by analogy one can believe that others also feel the existence of their own selves." Śabara Svāmin defines *upamāna* as knowledge of an unperceived object as being similar to some known object.[9] According to Mīmāṁsakas, comparison may be brought under two heads, namely, comparison of similarity and comparison of dissimilarity. The example of

---

8. *sādṛśyasyānimittatvān nimittasyāpratītitaḥ samayo durgrahaḥ pūrvam śabdenānumayāpivā* I — *NK*, 3.11, p. 121.

9. *upamānam api sādṛśyam asannikṛṣṭerthe buddhim utpādayati* — *Mb*, p. 12.

comparison of similarity is already explained. The comparison of dissimilarity is as follows. "the camel is dissimilar to the horse."

The Mīmāṁsakas conclude that comparison is different from perception, inference, memory and verbal testimony. In this case, the knowledge of the similarity and dissimilarity found in the cow is the causal condition par excellence and the knowledge of similarity of the *gayal* to the cow and that of dissimilarity of the camel to the horse are the results of comparison.

ADVAITA VIEW OF UPAMĀNA

The Advaitins accept *upamāna* (comparison) as the source of valid knowledge. *Upamāna* is the means of the knowledge of similarity. A person, who has perceived a cow in a town, goes to a forest, and perceives a wild cow. He has an apprehension "this animal is similar to a cow" owing to the intercourse of his eyes with the animal. Then he has an apprehension, "my cow is similar to this animal." This knowledge of similarity of a cow with a wild cow is acquired by comparison. The knowledge of similarity cannot be acquired from perception, since the cow is not in presence of the eyes. It cannot be acquired from inference also for similarity existing in a wild cow cannot serve as a mark of inference. For example, my cow is similar to this wild cow, because she is the correlate of similarity existing in this wild cow. Whatever is the correlate of similarity with another thing is similar to it, as Caitra, the correlate of similarity existing in Maitra, is similar to Maitra. According to the Advaita Vedāntins, the reason "similarity existing in a wild cow with a cow" does not exist in the subject "my cow." Therefore, the knowledge of similarity existing in "my cow" with a wild cow cannot be acquired from inference. It is acquired from comparison. It is neither perception nor inference but an independent means of valid knowledge.[10]

THE SĀṀKHYA CRITICISM OF UPAMĀNA

The Sāṁkhyaists do not consider *upamāna* as a distinct source of valid knowledge. According to them, the knowledge obtained through *upamāna* is verbal, inferential or perceptual, as the case may be. Thus, *upamāna* has been illustrated by means of verbal testimony. It is said "*gavaya* is like the cow." This is purely verbal when it is uttered by an elderly experienced person (*vṛddhavyavahāra*) to cognize an inexperienced person about the unknown animal *gavaya*. In the opinion of Vācaspati Miśra, the instructive sentence that the cow is similar to a *gavaya* which is held to be a distinct source of knowledge is really verbal testimony.[11] The *Yuktidīpikā* is aware of the Nyāya view and includes *upamāna* under verbal testimony and states that mere similarity does not lead to knowledge of some objects, rather it is a valid statement which leads one to the knowledge obtained through *upamāna*.[12] Like verbal testimony *upamāna* also depends upon the fact whether the speaker has visualized the object, or not. Knowledge is justified only when the speaker is an authority. Further like verbal testimony or *śabda*, *upamāna* also depends upon particular words. The statement of similarity is only a mode of expression and is not a factor for making *upamāna* an independent means of knowledge. If this kind of mode is taken as a condition for an independent means of knowledge, the other modes of conveying the meaning like waving the

---

10. *VP*, ch. iii.

11. *tathāhi upamānam tāvadyathā gaustathā 'gavaya' iti vākyam tajjanitādhirāgama eva* — *STK* on *SK*, K 5.

12. *upama......., āptopodeśasiddheḥ yathā gaurevam gavaya iti cāptopodeśabalāt pratipattāpprasiddham gavayamupalabhate na sādharmyāt* — *YD* on *SK*, K4.

hand and closing the eye would also be independent means of knowledge. Gauḍapāda includes *upamāna* under verbal testimony.[13] According to Jayamaṅgalā, *upamāna* can be included under verbal testimony or inference. When a person comes to know from some authoritative person that the animal similar to cow is called *gavaya*, it is a case of verbal testimony.

Secondly, *upamāna* can be included in inference. The conclusion of Udyotkāra that the word *gavaya* denotes an animal which is similar to a cow is really inferential, according to Vācaspati. Māṭhara[14] and Vijñānabhikṣu[15] include *upamāna* under inference.

Thirdly, *upamāna* may be included in perception. It is purely perceptual when the knowledge arises in this way — "the animal before our eyes is similar to the cow." Thus, when the cow is remembered and its remembrance is seen in the *gavaya*, it is perception. When some portions of the component parts of the body of one animal is found to be almost the same as that in the body of another, it is resemblance or similarity. These points of similarity must be one and equal so that the direct perception of one can indirectly denote the perception of another (*gavaya*). The similarity is the collection of the components of cow and *gavaya* and is perceived directly on the sight of either of the two.[16]

Thus, it may be concluded that *upamāna* or comparison is not accepted as an independent *pramāṇa* by the Sāṁkhyaists.

---

13. *upamānaścāptavacane* — *GB* on *SK*, K. 4.

14. *upamānam yathā gaustathā gavaya ityānumānameva* — *MV* on *SK*. K. 4.

15. *upamānaitihyādinām cānumānaśabdoyoḥ praveśaḥ* — *SPB*, 1.88.

16. *yattu gavayasya cakṣuḥsannikṛṣṭasya gosādṛśya jñānam, tat pratyakṣameva* — *STK* on *SK*, K. 5.

The knowledge obtained through *upamāna* is verbal, inferential or perceptual. Therefore, *upamāna* is by no means the fourth *pramāṇa* according to the Sāṁkhya. The Yoga also does not accept *upamāna* as an independent means of valid knowledge on the same ground on which Sāṁkhya rejects it.

Arthāpatti (Postulation)

The Mīmāṁsakas and the Advaita School of Vedānta advocate the hypothesis of *arthāpatti* (postulation) as a distinct source of valid knowledge. *Arthāpatti* is the presumption of something for the explanation of a known fact. The word *arthāpatti* goes under various translations as presumption, postulation, supposition, implication and assumption. The definition of *arthāpatti* given by the Advaita School of Vedānta is as follows: *arthāpatti* is the presumption of the ground of explanation through the knowledge of what is to be explained.[17] When a given or perceived fact cannot be explained without some other fact we have to presuppose or postulate the existence of this other fact even though we do not perceive it. A phenomenon is presented to our experience and we find that there is a seeming contradiction involved in it. We try to get over this contradiction by supposing some other fact which explains away the contradiction. The given fact which is to be called *upapādya* and that which explains it is called the *upapādaka*. When a particular person named Caitra known to be alive is not found in his house, it is assumed that he must be somewhere outside. When one notices apparent contradiction in various forms of knowledge he presumes something to remove the apparent contradiction in it. What is presumed is said to be a distinct source of knowledge.

---

17. *tatropopādyajñānena upapādakakalpanamarthāpattiḥ* — *VP*, p. 214.

According to Śabara, *arthāpatti* is the presumption of an unperceived object on the ground of a fact already seen or heard that cannot be explained without that presumption, for instance, if it is found that Devadatta who is alive is not in the house, the presumption would be that he is somewhere outside as otherwise the fact of his being alive and not in the house could not be explained.[18] Kumārila and Prabhākara both regard *arthāpatti* as a means of knowledge, but they differ in the details regarding the nature of *arthāpatti*. According to Prābhākaras, there is an element of doubt in presumption while Kumārila denies its existence in it. There is doubt, according to Prabhākara, as to the truth of the two perceived facts which cannot be reconciled with each other. The assumption of another fact removes the doubt, and reconciles the apparently inconsistent facts.

The element of doubt, according to Prabhākaras, distinguishes presumption from inference. There is no element of doubt in inference. From the undoubted perception of smoke, we can infer the existence of fire. The sign is free from doubt. But the perceived absence of Devadatta from his house leads to the presumption of his living outside his house only when it has made the fact of his living doubtful. Thus, there is doubt in presumption, while there is no doubt in inference. Presumption retains doubt and cannot be regarded as inference.

But in the opinion of Kumārila there is no doubt in presumption. One perceives the absence of Devadatta from his house. He knows that he is alive. In order to reconcile these two well-known and undoubted facts he assumes that

---

18. *arthāpattirapi dṛṣṭaḥ śruto vā artho 'anyathānopapadyata ityarthakalpanā yathā jīvati devadatte gṛhābhāvadarśanena vahirbhāvasyādṛṣṭasya kalpanā* — *SB*, 1.1.5.

he has gone out of his house. If the knowledge of his living were doubtful, it could not be the sound basis of presumption.[19]

According to the Advaita Vedānta and the Mīmāṁsakas, *arthāpatti* is a separate source of knowledge, because it gives us a knowledge of facts which cannot be otherwise explained. It cannot be explained by perception, since the fact known through *arthāpatti* is not perceived by us. Presumption cannot be regarded as an inference. It cannot be reduced to *anvayī* inference, because there is no *anvaya* or agreement in presence between fatness and eating at night as between smoke and fire. Negative concomitance is not admitted by the Advaita Vedānta. The *kevalavyatirekī* inference based on negative concomitance is nothing but presumption.[20]

The Sāṁkhya Criticism of Arthāpatti

The Sāṁkhyaists do not consider *arthāpatti* as an independent means of knowledge. They hold that it is a case of inference. The *Yuktidīpikā* explains the opponent's position which states that *arthāpatti* is found in the case where two objects are observed to be invariably together, and after seeing or hearing one of them, there arises the knowledge of the other. Thus, *arthāpatti* is of two kinds: (i) when knowledge of one correlative arises through seeing the other correlative and (ii) when knowledge of one correlative arises through hearing of the other correlative, e.g. in the first case, after seeing a treacle one knows its sweetness. The second case is exemplified as after hearing the word *treacle* one comes to know its sweetness. According to *Yuktidīpikā* the above kinds are known as *dṛṣṭārthāpatti* and *śrutārthāpatti*. The *Yuktidīpikā* does not accept

19. *PP*, pp. 113-15.
20. *VP*, ch. V.

arthāpatti as an independent means of knowledge. It states that sometimes presumption refers to some object which is misunderstood to be invariably concomitant, e.g. when it is stated that the conjunct object is non-eternal, it connotes that the object which is non-conjunct is eternal. Such a conclusion is not applicable in case of objects like action which is non-conjunct but is still non-eternal. Again where the invariable concomitance is present in that case also *arthāpatti* should not be considered as an independent means of knowledge because in that case *arthāpatti* is reduced to a case of inference.

Vācaspati Miśra criticizes the validity of *arthāpatti* and holds that it is a case of inference. In his opinion, absence of an object at a place indicates its presence in some other place,[21] for instance, Caitra is absent in his house therefore the existence of Caitra somewhere outside the house can be inferred through his absence in the house. Hence, presumption can very well be a case of inference. Māṭhara[22], Jayamaṅgalā[23] and Gauḍapāda[24] include *arthāpatti* in inference. Jayanta Bhaṭṭa also in his *Nyāyamañjarī* does not accept presumption as a distinct source of knowledge. The Yoga system also does not accept *arthāpatti* as an independent means of valid knowledge on the same ground on which the Sāṁkhyaists reject it.

Anupalabdhi (Non-apprehension)

In Indian philosophy, *anupalabdhi* or *abhāva* (negation) has been discussed in two forms, viz. as ontological reality and as a

---

21. *gṛhābhāvadarśanena bahirbhāvasya adṛṣṭasya kalpanāmarthāpattirabhimatā* — *STK* on *SK*, K. 5.

22. *sā arthāpattiranumānameva* — *MV* on *SK*, K. 4.

23. JM on *SK*, K. 4.

24. *tatrānumāne tāvadarthāpattirantarbhūtā* — *GB* on *SK*, K. 4.

way of knowing. In the first form, it is mentioned by such words as *asat, alīka, nirupākhya, niḥsvabhāva,* etc. and in the second form, it is referred to as *anupalabdhi.* The Bhāṭṭa Mīmāṁsakas and the Advaita Vedāntins accept *anupalabdhi* as a distinct source of knowledge.

THE MĪMĀṀSĀ VIEW OF ANUPALABDHI

According to Kumārila Bhaṭṭa, *anupalabdhi* is an independent source of knowledge. The Bhāṭṭas hold that *abhāva* is the non-existence of an object in a specific locus and its ascertainment requires an independent means of knowledge called *anupalabdhi.* When one says "there is no jar in this place" one cognizes the absence of the jar. Absence or non-existence (*abhāva*) cannot be apprehended by perception,[25] which stands in need of sense-contact with present object which is not possible in this case. Non-existence of the jar is not inferred from its non-perception, because such an inference is possible if one knows that there is universal relation between non-apprehension and non-existence. The knowledge of the jar's non-existence is neither derived from comparison, nor from testimony, nor from postulation. Thus, *anupalabdhi* is considered as an independent source of valid knowledge. Again Kumārila states that without accepting *anupalabdhi* or non-apprehension as an independent source of knowledge we cannot solve the conflicts between the results of Vedic and non-Vedic performance. Again the relationship of its part and the whole also cannot be explained.[26]

---

25. *na ca tad aindriyakam, indriyavyāpārabhave 'pi tajjñānotpatti darśanāt . . . tasmān na pratyakṣo bhāvaḥ* — *SD*, pp. 243-44.

26. *karmāṇi sarvāṇi phalaiḥ samastaiḥ sarvair yathāvat ca yad aṅga-kāṇḍaiḥ* ।
na saṅgatānīha parasparam ca nāṅgam tad etat prabhavaṁ kratūnām ॥
— *SV*, p. 348.

But all cases of non-apprehension do not prove the non-existence of what is not perceived. A pot which exists in a room is not perceptible due to the darkness of the room. There are atoms, ether, virtues, etc. which are imperceptible. But we never say that they do not exist. If a thing should have been perceived under certain conditions, then only its non-apprehension under those conditions proves its non-existence. This non-apprehension is the source of the knowledge of non existence.

ADVAITA VIEW OF ANUPALABDHI

According to Advaita Vedāntins, the particular cause, i.e. the instrument of the cognition of non-existence which is not generated by any knowledge, is called *anupalabdhi*. The statement that "there is no pot on the floor as it is not cognized" is an example of *anupalabdhi* which is an independent means of knowledge through cognition of non-existence. The non-existence of a jar on the ground is known by non-apprehension when the jar is removed from the ground, we perceive the ground, the locus of the non-existence of the jar, but we do not perceive the non-existence itself. We know the non-existence by non-apprehension. Though the locus of non-existence is perceived, the non-existence itself is not perceived. Non-existence is known by non-apprehension. It can never be known by perception.

Some scholars deny negation as a means of valid knowledge. Others accept negation but not as an additional means of knowledge. The Prābhākara School does not admit the negation as a separate source of knowledge. When we perceive a jar on the ground, we perceive the ground as related to the existence of the jar. But when the jar is absent, we perceive the bare ground or more space. The non-existence of the jar is nothing but the existence of its bare locus, the ground.

The knowledge of the sustainer by itself (*tanmātradhi*) is erroneously called non-apprehension. However, source or means of knowledge is necessary only to establish the knowledge of a certain object. There is no distinctive category to be named as non-existence, so there requires no extra means of valid knowledge termed non-apprehension.[27] The Buddhists hold that non-existence, is directly perceived by the sense-organs and no separate source of knowledge is required to apprehend it. The ground and the absence of the pot on the ground is percieved through sense-organs. The Naiyāyikas and the Vaiśeṣikas hold that absence is perceptible. Hence, knowledge about absence can be included under the means of perception, inference or any other positive means of knowledge. So an independent means of knowledge called non-apprehension is not acceptable. The Saṁkhyaists also do not consider *abhāva* as a distinct source of knowledge. According to *Yuktidīpikā*, *abhāva* is the postulation of invariable association of objects of opposite nature, just as presence of fire is known through presence of smoke, absence of fire is through absence of smoke. The postulation of invariable association of objects of opposite nature, however, is a case of *arthāpatti*.[28] But in the case of heated iron ball invariable association of absence of fire and smoke is not applicable. Again the *Yuktidīpikā* explains *abhāva* in a different way. When it is said that Caitra is not in the house, it is deduced that he is somewhere outside the house. According to *Yuktidīpikā*, it is a case of *arthāpatti*. Since *arthāpatti* is a case of inference, *abhāva*

---

27. *pramāṇam khalu kasyāpi prameyasyāvabodhakam* । *tatrābhāvasya kim tāvat prameyam iti cintyatām* । *meyābhāve tato mānam abhāvākhyam kalham bhavet* । — *PP*, pp. 12-14.

28. *abhāvo nāmo tad yathā dhūmasya bhāvādagner bhāvaḥ pratīyate evam dhūmāvādagnyābhāva ityayam pratidvandvisāhacaryakalpanā yārthāpattirabhihittaḥ* — *YD* on *SK*, K. 4.

is also a case of inference.[29] Vācaspati, however, considers *abhāva* as a case of perception. According to him, non-apprehension or negation is not a distinct source of knowledge. In the example "absence of pot on the ground" is a particular type of change of ground in the form of bare ground. This bare ground can be cognized directly by perception and there is no need of assuming some additional *pramāṇa*.[30] Jayamaṅgalā[31] and Vijñānabhikṣu[32] also include *abhāva* under perception. Gauḍapāda includes it in verbal testimony. Māṭhara includes it under inference. According to Māṭhara, *abhāva* is of four kinds: anterior, posterior, mutual and absolute. All these are the cases of inference. For example, after observing dried up plants one infers absence of rains.[33] The Yoga also does not accept *anupalabdhi* as a distinct means of knowledge on the same ground on which the Sāṁkhya rejects it. The Sāṁkhyaists feel the necessity of admitting *anupalabdhi* in case of excessive distance, proximity, destruction, suppression, and intermixture with other like-objects.[34] The non-perception of these is due to its subtlety and others but not due to its non-existence, since it is actually apprehended through its effect.[35]

---

29. *arthāpattiścānumānam — Ibid.*
30. *pratyakṣānabaruddha viṣaya yatrabhāvāhvayam pramānāntaram-avyupeyeteti,* — *STK* on *SK*, K. 5.
31. JM on *SK*, K. 4.
32. *anupalabdhādīnām ca pratyakṣe praveśa iti — SPB*, 1.88.
33. *abhāvaśca pragitaretarapradhvaṁsātyantābhāva bhedāccaturdhā, yathā bṛhiśoṣaṇadarśanānna bṛṣṭodeva iti bṛṣṭerabhāvam sādhyati sopyanumānabhedaḥ* — *MV* on *SK*, K. 4.
34. *atidūrāt sāmipyāt indriyaghātānmano 'navasthānāt saukṣmyātyavadhānāt abhibhavāt samānābhihārācca — SK*, K. 7.
35. *saukṣmyāttadanupalabdchirnābhāvāt, kāryatastadupalavdheḥ* — *SK*, K. 8.

Sambhava (Probability)

The Paurāṇikas are the propounders of *sambhava* as an independent means of knowledge. They require *sambhava* to get the knowledge of a part from the knowledge of the whole. If somebody has the knowledge of a crowd of thousand people he will obviously have knowledge of hundred people within that crowd. Vallabha holds that an unperturbed knowledge of a segment from a plenteous association of aggregate is regarded as concurrence.[36] None of the other major systems share the Paurāṇika view. The Buddhists like Śāntarakṣita and Kamalaśīla state that the knowledge of a hundred from that of a thousand is inferred in the form of deduction because element of combination lies in the formation of an aggregate.[37] The Sāṁkhyaists also do not consider *sambhava* as an independent means of knowledge. In the opinion of Vācaspati, *sambhava* is included in inference.[38] The *Yuktidīpikā* also includes it in inference through its inclusion under postulation. Another example of probability is that when words like *droṇa* or *prasthāna* are uttered, one comes to know the presence of half *droṇa* or some less weight, etc. As there is presumption of invariable association of less weight in *droṇa* it is clearly a case of *arthāpatti*. Since *arthāpatti* is included in inference, probability is also included in inference. Māṭhara[39] and Jayamaṅgalā[40] include *sambhava* in inference. Gauḍapāda[41] includes *sambhava*

---

36. *prācura-sāhacarya sambhedanāt buddhir abādhitā sambhavaḥ yathā sambhavati meghejalaṁ iti* — *NL*, p. 542.

37. *samudāya vyavasthāyā hetavaḥ samudāyinaḥ śatādi sambhava jñānam sahasrāt kārya liṅgajam* — *Ts*, p. 590.

38. *sā cānumānameva* — *STK* on *SK*, K. 5.

39. *sāpyanumānameva* — *MV* on *SK*, K. 4.

40. JM *on SK*, K. 4.

41. *sambhava .... āptavacane* — *GB* on *SK*, K. 4.

in verbal testimony. The Yoga also does not accept *sambhava* as a distinct means of knowledge on the same ground on which the Sāṁkhyaists reject it.

Aitihya (Tradition)

The Paurāṇikas are the propounders of *aitihya* as an independent means of valid knowledge. It is a mere continuity of a vague assertion of which the original source cannot be traced. It has no particular speaker but has come from tradition. It is a belief transmitted from generation to generation. "There is a ghost in this tree," is an example provided to explain the nature of *aitihya*. None of the other major systems share the Paurāṇika view. Mere report is not a source of valid knowledge, since there is no determination at all.[42] If its validity is proved, it can be included in verbal testimony.[43] The Sāṁkhyaists also do not consider *aitihya* as a distinct source of knowledge. According to them, it is included in verbal testimony. In the *Yuktidīpikā* also it is stated that *aitihya* is a case of verbal testimony.[44] Vācaspati Miśra includes *aitihya* in verbal testimony.[45] Vācaspati states that *aitihya* is a mere continuity of a vague statement, the speaker of which is not known. The word *aitihya* conveys two contrary meanings: (i) the authentic statement and (ii) the popular sayings based on belief only. In the example "there is a ghost in this tree" everybody will say that they have no direct knowledge about the sayings. If one tries to find out the authenticity of the saying everybody will say that people say so. As its original

42. *aitihyam apyapratīyamānamūla-bhūta pramāṇāntaram puruṣa paramparā vacana mātram na pramāṇatām pratipadyate* — *PP*, pp. 292-93.

43. *prāmāṇye 'pi vāgame 'ntargatatvān na pramāṇāntaram* — *SD*, p. 246.

44. *aitihyāvacanamāptopadeśāt siddheriti* — *YD* on *SK*, K. 4.

45. *āptavaktṛkatvaniścayetvāgama eva* — *STK* on *SK*, K.5.

source being undetermined, it can never be regarded as a distinct means of cognition. If the source of this knowledge is traced out and the source is known to be reliable then it is included in the verbal testimony. The authors of Jayamaṅgalā,[46] and the *Sāṁkhya-candrikā*[47] as well as Gauḍapāda[48] and Vijñānabhikṣu[49] also include *aitihya* under verbal testimony. Māṭhara[50] includes it under inference. The Yoga School also does not consider *aitihya* as an independent means of knowledge on the same ground on which the Sāṁkhya rejects it.

Ceṣṭā (Gesture)

Some Tāntrikas consider *ceṣṭā* as one of the means of valid knowledge. Gesture is explained as the operation of the limbs of the body.[51] When one puts his hand on the belly which is slightly hollowed, it indicates some intention. That conveys hunger and the like which are not otherwise known, and hence is said to be a means of knowledge. But it is a case of inference. If the performance of bodily operation, which is associated with the desire for meals, etc. gives rise to the knowledge of its associates, it cannot be said to be different from inference. Annambhaṭṭa refutes it by saying that as it can be proved by testimony, so there is no need of admiting it separately.[52]

46. JM on *SK*, K.4.
47. *SC* on *SK*, K. 4.
48. *aitihya . . . āptavacane* — *GB* on *SK*, K. 4.
49. *aitihyādinām cānumānaśabdayoḥ praveśaḥ* — *SPB*, 1. 88.
50. *aitihyam yathā asminvate yakṣiṇī prativasatīti janā vadantītyukte sā vighnam karoti dhanādi yacchatitijñānam tadapyanumānameva* — *MV* on *SK*, K. 4.
51. *ceṣṭā nāma abhiprāyasūcaka* — *YD*, p. 145.
52. *ceṣṭāpi śabdānumānadvārā vyavahāra heturīti na pramāṇāntaram* — *TS*, p. 396.

Pratibhā (Intuition)

Some thinkers consider *pratibhā* as one of the valid means of knowledge. *Pratibhā* or intuition is the power of immediate understanding of something without conscious reasoning or study. It is conviction of certainty that comes quite suddenly and instantly. One is convinced that what comes to him is true. Vātsyāyana mentions a kind of direct or immediate knowledge in the form of apprehension or insight called *pratibhā*. In the Buddhist philosophy there is reference of the word *prajñā*. Intuition is to some extent equivalent to *prajñā*. When some near and dear one dies in a far away place and such conviction or assertion comes true, it is an example of intuition. Praśastapāda maintains that for ordinary people intuition occasionally becomes valid knowledge. But for the sages intuition is always valid knowledge. He gives intuition the status of *ārṣajñāna*.[53] Again some thinkers consider *pratibhā* as imagination. One who has repeatedly experienced the particular objects as giving rise to pleasure etc. the knowledge of that object arises merely through the utterance of the word denoting that object even without the presence of that object. This is imagination. For example, when it is stated that a tiger lives here, the actions as sweating and trembling of the body take place even without the external object merely through the earlier practice.

None of the major systems of philosophy have regognized *pratibhā* as an independent means of valid knowledge. The Mīmāṁsakas do not consider intuition as valid means of knowledge. They argue that through intuition ascertainment

---

53. *cātma-manasoḥ saṁyogād dharma viśeṣācca yat prātibham yathārtha-nivedamjñānam utpadyate tadārṣam ityācakṣate* — *PB*, p. 628.

or apprehension of valid knowledge cannot be achieved.[54] Jayanta Bhaṭṭa classifies intuition as a kind of perceptual knowledge and admits it as valid.[55] *Pratibhā* is not accepted as an independent *pramāṇa* by the Sāṁkhya philosophers. Because, if the knowledge caused by the impression of past experience is admitted to be imagination, it comes to be either perception, inference or verbal testimony. Jayamaṅgalā includes it under perception and inference when it is correct, otherwise it is not *pramāṇa*. Māṭhara includes it under inference and Gauḍapāda includes it under verbal testimony. Vācaspati and Candrikā do not mention about *pratibhā*. The archaic knowledge also cannot be caused by *pratibhā* because it is stated that the knowledge of the illustrious Supreme seer is of accomplished nature. The knowledge was already in him at the time of birth and hence he did not acquire it through means of knowledge. It cannot be the knowledge of the sages because it is not accepted (*anabhyupagamāt*). It cannot be worldly knowledge, because it is not ascertained (*aniścitatvāt*). Hence, it can be said that *pratibhā* should not be mentioned as a separate *pramāṇa*.

Reviewing all the hypotheses of the sources of valid knowledge it can be said that there are three *pramāṇas* or means of cognition, according to the Sāṁkhya system. All other *pramāṇas* which find their place in different systems of philosophy can be included under *pratyakṣa, anumāna* and *śabda*.[56] Manu in his *Saṁhitā* clearly mentions threefold division

---

54. *kāśyapīyāḥ punaḥ pratibhā jñānamṛṣīnāṁ dharme pravarttata ityāhuḥ tat tu liṅgādyā bhāsajatvāt pramāṇam na bhavati* — *SD*, p. 52.

55. *api cānāgatam jñānam asmadāder api kvacit pramāṇam pratibhaṁśvo me bhrātāgantetidṛśyate* — *NM*, p. 98.

56. *dṛṣṭamanumānamāptavacanañca, sarvapramāṇa siddhatvāt*
— *S.K*, K. 4.

of valid sources of knowledge.[57] The *Devībhāgavata* is also unanimous in this respect.[58] The hypothesis of the Sāṁkhya logic has been accepted by the great sages like Manu and others. It is justified that the unnecessary multiplication of the number of the valid sources of knowledge is of no use. Perception has not been disputed by any school of philosophy. Inference though disputed, is unavoidable for the transaction of worldly affairs. Therefore, inference has got its importance. Verbal testimony cannot be set aside because it is a source of knowledge to a great extent. Therefore, these three sources of knowledge, viz. perception, inference, and verbal testimony are indispensible for ascertaining valid knowledge.

Epistemology of the Sāṁkhya-Yoga School is a wide subject. In many works on the Sāṁkhya-Yoga system, the epistemology of the Sāṁkhya-Yoga School has not been thoroughly discussed. Only by a logical analysis of the other rival epistemologies the true character of the Sāṁkhya-Yoga epistemology can be ascertained. Again the extant texts of the Sāṁkhya-Yoga leave behind many epistemological problems unanswered. This is mainly due to the fact that systems of Sāṁkhya-Yoga basically aim at suggesting the means of attaining liberation and lay more stress on the explanation of metaphysical doctrines than their epistemology. But it does not mean that the Sāṁkhya-Yoga epistemology has no value. In fact, the contribution of the Sāṁkhya-Yoga theory of knowledge is not really inferior to that of any other theory of knowledge. Many of the epistemological contributions of these schools are of great value even in the modern age of excessive fondness for rationalization.

---

57. *pratyakṣamanumānam ca śāstram ca vividhāgamam trayam suviditam kārya dharmaśuddhimabhīpsatā* — *Manu*, XII.105.

58. *trīṇyeva hi pramāṇāni pathitāni supaṇḍitaih pratyakṣam cānumānañca śabdāncaivatṛtīyakam* — *DV*, 1.8.23.

Bibliography

Original Works

Amarakoṣa of Amarasiṁha, ed. by Pt. Haragovinda Śāstri, Varanasi: The Chowkhamba Sanskrit Series Office, 1970.

Arthaśāstra, Banaras: Chowkhamba Vidya Bhawan, 1962.

Aṣṭādhyāyī of Pāṇini (vol. II) ed. by S.C. Basu, Delhi: Motilal Banarsidass, 1962.

Aṣṭādhyāyī-Sūtrapāṭha, ed. by Brahmadattajijñāsu, Amritsar: Ramlal Kapur Trust Press, 1955.

Aṣṭasahasrī (the Ṭīkā on Aklaṅka's Aṣṭaśati), by Vidhyānandi, Bombay: Nirnaya Sagar Press, 1915.

Bhāgavata Purāṇa, ed. by Tarkaratna with Śridharasvāmin's comm., Calcutta: Vangavāsi Press, 1920.

Bhāṣāpariccheda (Kārikāvalī and Muktāvalī) of Viśvanātha Nyāyapañcānana with the comm. Muktāvalī-saṁgraha of Pañcānana Śāstri, Calcutta: Sanskrit Pustak Bhandar, 1374 (Baṅgābda).

Bhāṭṭacintāmaṇi of Gāgabhaṭṭa, ed. by Suryanarayana Sukla, Banaras: Chowkhamba Sanskrit Series, 1933.

Brahmasūtra with Śaṅkara's comm., ed. by M.M. A.K. Shastri, Bombay: Nirnayasagar Press, 1938.

Buddhacarita, in *Sanskrit Sāhitya Samvār*, vol. I, Calcutta: Nabapatraprakasan, 1979.

Chāndogya Upaniṣad, ed. by Umesh Mishra, Poona: BORI, 1942.

Devībhāgavata Purāṇa with an introduction by Dr. Pushpendra Kumar, Delhi: Nag Publishers, 1986.

Gauḍapādabhāṣya on Sāṁkhyakārikā of Īśvarakṛṣṇa, tr. by H.H. Wilson, Calcutta: The Bengal Theosophical Society, 1887.

Gītagovindam of Jayadeva, in *Saṁskṛta Sāhitya Samvār*, vol. VI, Calcutta: Nabapatra Prakasan, 1979.

Jayamaṅgalā (With Sāṁkhyakārikā and Māṭhravṛtti) ed. by Satkari Sarma, Varanasi: Chowkhamba Sanskrit Series, 1970.

Kārikāvalī, Viśvanātha Nyāyapañcānana, Banaras: Chowkhamba Sanskrit Series, 1982.

Kaṭha Upaniṣad, in *Upaniṣads* (vol. I and II), ed. by S.M. Bhaumik, Calcutta: Prabartak Publishers, 1950.

Kiraṇāvalī by Udayanācārya, Calcutta: Asiatic Society, 1911.

Kumārasambhavam, of Kālidāsa, ed. by Kumudranjan Ray, Calcutta.

Mahābhārata of Veda Vyāsa, Poona: Bhandarkar Oriental Research Institute, 1940.

Mahābhāṣya of Patañjali ed. by Cārudev Śāstri with Hindi Trans. Varanasi: Motilal Banarsidass, 2025 Samvat.

Maitrāyaṇī Upaniṣad, ed. by Shivananda Swami, Bombay: Nirnaya Sagar Press, 1948.

Mānameyodaya of Nārāyaṇa Bhaṭṭa, Madras: Theosophical Publishing House, 1933.

Manu-Smṛti of Manu with Bhāṣya of Medhātithi, tr. by Ganganath Jha, Calcutta: University of Calcutta, 1924.

Māṭharavṛtti (with Sāṁkhyakārikā and Jayamaṅgalā), ed. by Vishnu Prasad Sharma, Varanasi: Chowkhamba Sanskrit Series, 1970.

Matsya Purāṇa, ed. Gaurinath Shastri, Calcutta: Nabapatra Prakasan.

Mīmāṁsāsūtra (*with Śābarabhāṣya*), Poona: Ananda Ashrama, 1970.

Naiṣadhacarita in *Saṁskṛta Sāhitya Samvār*, vol. XIV, Calcutta: Nabapatra Prakasan, 1982.

Nyāyabhāṣya of Vātsyāyana, Benaras: Chowkhamba Sanskrit Series, 1924.

Nyāyabindu of Dharmakīrti, Banaras: Chowkhamba Sanskrit Series, 1954.

Nyāyabinduṭīkā with Nyāyabindu, Dharmottara and Dharmakīrti, Śrīnivāsa Śāstrī, Mewar, Sahitya Bhandar, 1975.

Nyāyadarśana, ed. by Ganganath Jha and Dhundhiraj Shastri, Benaras: Chowkhamba Sanskrit Series, 1925.

Nyāyakandalī of Śrīdharācārya, Varanasi: Medical Hall Press, 1917.

Nyāyakoṣa, ed. by M.M. Bhīmācārya Jhalkikar, Poona: BORI, 1928.

Nyāyakumudacandra (the commmentary on Laghīyastraya), Prabhācandra, Bombay: Manikya Chandra Digambar Jaina Granthamala, 1938.

Nyāyakusumāñjalī of Udayanācārya with the commentary of Prabhā, ed. by Narayana Misra, Benaras: BVP, 1968.

Nyāyalīlāvatī of Vallabhācārya, Dhundhiraj Shastri, Banaras, 1939.

Nyāyamañjarī of Jayanta Bhaṭṭa ed. by Pt. S.N. Shukla, Benaras: Chowkhamba Sanskrit Series, 1936.

Nyāyaratnamālā of Pārthasārathi Miśra, ed. by Pt. Gangadhar Shastri, Benaras: Chowkhamba Sanskrit Series, 1900.

Nyāyasāra, ed., S.C. Vidyābhuṣan, Calcutta: The Asiatic Society, 1910.

Nyāyasūtra of Gautama, tr. by Mahāmahopādhyāya Satish Chandra Vidyābhūṣaṇa, Allahabad: The Panini Office, Bhuvaneswari Asrama.

Nyāyavārttika of Uddyotakāra, com. on Vātsyāyana's bhāṣya on Nyāyasūtra ed. by Vindhyesvariprasad Dvivedi, Benaras: KSS, 1916.

Nyāyavārttikatātparyaṭīkā of Vācaspati Miśra, ed. by Pandit Sri Rajeswara Shastri Dravid, Benaras: CSS, 1985.

Paramalaghumañjūṣā of Nāgeśabhaṭṭa with the comm. Tattvaprakāśikā ed. by Alakhadeva Sharma, Benaras: CSS, 1974.

Pātañjalayogadarśanam of Kapila with Vyāsabhāṣya, Tattvavaiśāradī of Vācaspati Miśra and Yogavārttika of Vijñānabhikṣu, ed. by Narayana Misra, Varanasi: Bharatiya Vidhya Prakashan, 1981.

Prakaraṇa Pañcikā of Śālikanātha Miśra, ed. by A. Subramanya Sastri, Benaras: Banaras Hindu University, 1961.

Pramāṇanyāyatattvāloka of Vādidevasūri, Ujjain: Sri Vijayadharmasuri Granthamala, 1908.

Pramāṇaprakaraṇa of Madhva, Madras: Adyar Library, 1968.

Pramāṇasamuccaya of Diṅnāga, Mysore: Mysore University.

Prameyakamalamārtaṇḍa of Māṇikyanandi's Parikṣāmukha by Prabhacandra, Bombay: Nirnaya Sagar Press, 1941.

Praśastapādabhāṣya of Praśastadeva, ed. by Gopinatha Kaviraja and Dhundiraj Sastri, Benaras: CSS, 1924.

Praśna Upaniṣad, ed. by Sivananda Swami, Bombay: Nirnaya Sagar Press, 1948.

Pravacanasāra, Kundakunda, Agas: Srimad Rajachandra Ashrama, 1984.

Ṛgvedabhāṣya of Sāyaṇācārya, Poona: Vaidic Samshodhan Mandal, 1946.

Śābarabhāṣya of Śabaraswāmī with Hindi translation, Published by Yuddhiṣṭhira Mīmāṁsaka, Sonepat (Haryana): Vahalgad, 1977.

Śabdakalpadruma by Rājā Rādhākānta Deb, Calcutta: New Delhi Press, 1932.

Ṣaḍdarśanasamuccaya of Haribhadra Sūri, Varanasi: Chaukhamba Sanskrit Series, 1957.

Saṁkhyacandrikā, ed. by Dhundiraja Sastri with Hindi translation, Varanasi, 1953.

Sāṁkhyakārikā of Mahāmuni Śrī Īśvarakṛṣṇa with the comm. Sārobodhinī of Pt. Śivanārāyan Śāstrī with Sāṁkhyatattvakaumudī of Vācaspati Miśra, Bombay: Nirnaya Sagar Press, 1940.

Sāṁkhyapravacanabhāṣya of Vijñānabhikṣu on Sāṁkhyasūtra by R. Garbe, HOS, vol. 2, Cambridge: Harvard University Press, 1943.

Sāṁkhyasūtra of Kapila with Aniruddha's commentary ed. by R.S. Bhattacharjee, Varanasi: Pracya Bharati Prakasan, 1964.

Sāṁkhyasūtravṛtti of Aniruddha, Vide *Sāṁkhyasūtra*.

Sāṁkhyatattvakaumudī of Vācaspati Miśra, Vide *Sāṁkhyakārikā*.

Saptapadārthī of Śivāditya, ed. by Amarendra Mohan Tarkatīrtha and Narendra Chandra Vedāntatīrtha, Calcutta: Metropolitan Printing and Publishing House, 1934.

Sārobodhinīṭīkā of Pt. Śivanārāyana Śāstrī, vide *Sāṁkhyakārikā*.

Sarvadarśanasaṁgraha of Mādhavācārya, Poona: Bhandarkar Oriental Research Institute, 1924.

Śāstradīpikā of Pārthasārathi Miśra, ed. with English translation by Venkatramiah, Baroda: Gaekwad Oriental Series (GOS), 1940.

Siddhāntakaumudī of Bhaṭṭojidīkṣita with the commentary, Bālamanoramā, Banaras: Chowkhamba Sanskrit Series.

Ślokavārttikā of Kumārila Bhaṭṭa with Sucarita Miśra's Kāśikā, Trivandrum: Trivandram Sanskrit Series, 1943.

Śrīmadbhagavad-Gītā, ed. by J.C. Ghosh, 14th edn., Calcutta: Baṅgāvda, 1382.

Śvetāśvatara Upaniṣad, ed. by A. Sen, S. Tattvabhusan, M. Ghosh, Calcutta: Haraf Prakasani, 1989.

Syādvāda Mañjarī, Mallisensa, Agas: Srimad Rajachandra Ashrama, 1979.

Tantravārttika of Kumārila Bhaṭṭa, ed. by V.G. Apte, Poona: CASS 1929.

Tarkabhāṣā, Keśava Miśra, Poona: Bhandarkar Oriental Reaserch Institute, 1937.

Tarkapāda ed. by Suryanarayana Sukla, Benaras: Chowkhamba Sanskrit Series, 1933.

Tarkasaṁgraha of Annambhaṭṭa with the commentary Nīlakaṇṭhaprakāśikā and Nyāyabodhinī, ed. by Sri Satkari Sarma Vangiya, Benaras: CSS, 1969.

Tārkikarakṣā, Varadarāja, Benaras: Vindhyesvari Prasada, 1903.

Tattvacintāmaṇi of Gaṅgeśopadhyāya, ed. by M.M. Kāmākhyanātha Tarkavāgīśa, Calcutta: Asiatic Society of Bengal, 1822 (Śakābda).

Tattvakaumudī of Vācaspati Miśra, 3rd edn., with English translation, ed. by Ganganath Jha and Har Dutta Sharma, Poona: OBA, 1965.

Tattvārthādhigamasūtra, Umāsvāti, Agas: Srimad Rajachandra Ashrama, 1932.

Tattvasaṁgraha with Pañcikā, Śāntarakṣita, Kamalaśīla, Swāmī Dwārikādās Śāstrī, Varanasi: Bauddha Bharati, 1981.

Tattvavaiśāradī of Vācaspati Miśra vide *Pātañjala Yoga Darśanam*.

Vaiśeṣikabhāṣya on Vaiśeṣikasūtra, ed. by Dhundhirāj Śāstrī, Kashi: Sanskrit Granthamālā, 1966.

Vaiśeṣikasūtra (with Praśastapādabhāṣya and Hindu trans.) ed. by Dhundirāj Śāstrī, Kashi: Kashi Sanskrit Granthamālā, 1966.

Vātsyāyana Bhāṣya vide *Nyāyabhāṣya*.

Vedāntaparibhāṣā by Dharmarājadhvarīndra, Calcutta: Sanskrit Pustak Bhandar, 1970.

Vidvattoṣiniṭippaṇī of Balarāma Udāsīna on Sāṁkhyakārikā and Sāṁkhyatattvakaumudī, Gaya: Ramamudrana Press, 1930.

Yatindramatadīpikā of Śrīnivāsācārya, Mumbai: Anandasrama Sanskrit Series.

Yogabhāṣya of Vyāsa on Yogasūtra, Vide *Pātañjalayogadarśanam*.

Yogasūtra of Patañjali, vide *Pātañjalayogadarśanam*.

Yogavārttika of Vijñānabhikṣu on Yogasūtra, vide *Pātañjala Yogasūtra*.

Yuktidīpikā commentary on Sāṁkhyakārikā, ed. Ram. Chandra Pandeya, Delhi: Motilal Banarsidass, 1967.

Modern works

Apte, Verma Shivram: *The Students Sanskrit-English Dictionary*, 2nd reprint, Delhi: MLBD, 1988.

Apte, Vidyadhar Vaman: *A Concise English Sanskrit Dictonary*, 1st reprint, Delhi: GPH, 1986.

Bahadur, K.P.: *The Wisdom of Yoga*, Reprint, New Delhi: Sterling Publishers Pvt. Ltd., 1988.

Bahadur, K.P.: *The Wisdom of Sāṁkhya*, reprint, New Delhi: Sterling Publishers Pvt. Ltd. 1988.

Banarjee, S.C.: *A Companion to Sanskrit Literature*, Delhi: Motilal Banarsidass, 1971.

Bangali Babu: *The Yogasūtra of Patañjali*, Delhi: MLBD, Reprint, 1979.

Barthakuria, A.C.: *A Critical Study of the Lokāyata Philosophy*, Calcutta: Sanskrit Pustak Bhandar, 1976 Reprint, 1977.

Barua Girish: *Bhāratiya Darśanat Ebhūmuki* (Assamese) 1st edn. Guwahati, 1976.

Bhatta, Govardhana P.: *Epistemology of the Bhaṭṭa School of Pūrva-Mīmāṁsā*, 1st edn., Varanasi: CSSO, 1962.

Bhātta, Govardhana P. : *The Basic Ways of Knowing*, 2nd edn., Delhi: MLBD, 1989.

Bhattacharjee, Haridas: *The Cultural Heritage of India*, vol. III, 2nd edn., Calcutta: The Ramkrishna Mission Institute of Culture, 1975.

Bijalwan, C.D.: *Indian Theory of knowledge based upon Jayanta's Nyāyamañjarī*, New Delhi: Heritage Publisher, 1977.

Bothra, P.: *The Jaina Theory of Perception*, Delhi: Motilal Banarsidass, 1976.

Chakrabarti, Pulinbihari: *Origin and Development of the Sāṁkhya System of Thought*, Calcutta: Metropolitan Printing and Publishing House, 1897.

Chatterjee, S.C.: *The Nyāya Theory of Knowledge*, Calcutta: University of Calcutta, 1939.

Chatterjee, S.C. and Datta, D.M.: *An Introduction to Indian Philosophy*, Calcutta: University, 7th edn., 1968.

Chattopadhyay, Narayan Kumar: *Indian Philosophy — Its exposition in the light of Vijñānabhikṣu's Bhāṣya and Yogavārttika: A modern approach*, Calcutta: Sanskrit Pustak Bhandar, 1979.

Colebrooke, H.T. and Wilson, H.H.: *Sāṁkhyakārikā* (with the Bhāṣya of Gauḍapāda) Text and Translation, Bombay: Tookram Tatya, 1887.

Dasgupta, S.N.: *Yoga Philosophy in Relation to Other Systems of Indian Thought*, Calcutta: University of Calcutta, 1930.

———, *A History of Indian Philosophy* (vol. 1) Cambridge: Cambridge University Press, 1951.

Desa, S.A. : *A Study of the Indian Philosophy*, Mumbai: Thacker and Co., 1906.

Garbe, Richard: *Sāṁkhya Sūtravṛtti*, Calcutta: Asiatic Society of Bengal, 1888.

Goswami, Ashok Kumar: *A Critique on Śabda (*Based on Viśvanātha's Bhāṣāpariccheda), Delhi: Sri Satguru Publications, 1991.

Goswami, Narayana Chandra: *Sāṁkhyatattvakaumudī with Kārikā of Īśvarakṛṣṇa*, Calcutta: Sanskrit Pustak Bhandar, 1982.

Hiriyanna, M.: *Outlines of Indian Philosophy*, 2nd impression, London: George Allen and Unwin Ltd., 1951.

Hiriyanna, M.: *Indian Philosophical Studies*, Mysore: Kavyalaya Publishers, 1957.

Ingalalli, R.I.: *Śabdapramāṇa, an Epistemological Analysis*, Delhi: Sri Satguru Publications, 1988.

Jha, Ganganath: *The Sāṁkhyakārikā of Īśvarakṛṣṇa* (*with Tattvakaumudī of Vācaspati Miśra*), Text and Translation, Bombay: Tattvavivecana Press, 1896.

Johnston, E.H.: *Early Sāṁkhya*, Delhi: *RASPPE 15*, 1937, Reprinted, 1974.

Kar, Vijayananda: *Indian Theories of Error* (An analytical study), Delhi: Ajanta Books International, 1990.

Larson, Gerald James.: *Classical Sāṁkhya*, 2nd edn., Delhi: MLBD, 1979.

Manikar, T.G.: *Sāṁkhya-kārikā of Īśvarakṛṣṇa* with Gauḍapādabhāṣya, Poona: Oriental Book Agency, 1964.

Prasad, Jwala: *History of Indian Epistemology*, Delhi: Munshiram Manoharlal 1958.

Radhakrishnan, S.: *Philosophy* (vol. II) New Delhi: Oxford University Press, 1989.

Saha, Biswarup: *Studies in the Pramāṇa-Ratna*, Calcutta: Sanskrit Pustak Bhandar, 1991.

Sarma, R.N.: *The Mīmāṁsā Theory of Meaning*, 1st edn., Delhi: Sri Satguru Publications, 1988.

Sastri, Suryanarayana, S.S.: *the Sāṁkhya-kārikā of Īśvarakṛṣṇa*, Text and Translation, Chennai: University of Madras, 1935.

Sengupta, A: *Classical Sāṁkhya — A Critical Study*, Patna: The United Press Ltd. 1969.

Sharma, C.D.: *A Critical Survey of Indian Phiolosophy*, Delhi: Motilal Banarsidass, 1964.

Shiv Kumar: *Upamāna in Indian Philosophy*, Delhi: Eastern Book Linkers, 1980.

Shiv Kumar: *Sāṁkhya Yoga Epistemology*, Delhi: Eastern Book Linkers, 1984.

Sinha, Jadunath: *Outlines of Indian Philosophy*, 2nd edn., New Central Book Agency, 1985.

Sinha, Jadunath: *A History of Indian Philosophy* (vol. 1 and II), Calcutta: Sinha Publishing House, 1956.

Sinha, K.P.: *Reflexions on Indian Philosophy*, Varanasi: Chaukhamba Orientalia, 1984.

Sinha, K.P.: *The Philosophy of Jainism*, Calcutta: Punthi Pustak, 1990.

Sovani, V.V.: *Critical study of Sāṁkhya System*, Poona, 1935.

Journals and Papers

Epistemology of the Prabhākara Mīmāṁsā, by Dr. R.N. Sarma, Mumbai: Bharatiya Vidhya Bhawan, 1987.

Sāṁkhya-Yoga Definition of Pramāṇa by Shivkumar, Poona: CASS Studies, No. 5, 1987.

The Nature of Perception by Brahmananda Gupta in 'Our Heritage', Bulletin of the Department of Post Graduate Tranining and Research, Calcutta: Calcutta Sanskrit College, vol. II, part II, 1964.

The Order of Naming the Pramāṇa in Indian Philosophy by Dr. A.K. Goswami, Krishna Kanta Handique Felicitation Volume, ed. by Dr. M.M. Sarma, J.B. College Golden Jubilee Celebration Committee, Guwahati, 1983.

The Theory of Triple Perception by Dr. R.N. Sarma, Lokaprajñā, Pt. Srinivasa Shastri Felicitation Volume, ed. by S.D. Joshi, Puri, 1987

Index